THE PROMISE AND PERIL OF
INTERNATIONAL TRADE

THE PROMISE AND PERIL OF INTERNATIONAL TRADE

::

JEFF COLGAN

broadview press

LIBRARY AND ARCHIVES CANADA CATALOGUING IN PUBLICATION

Colgan, Jeff, 1975-
    The promise and peril of international trade / Jeff Colgan.

Includes bibliographical references and index.
ISBN 1-55111-680-4

    1. International trade—Social aspects. 2. Canada—Commercial policy.
I. Title.

HF1766.C628 2004   382   C2004-905782-0

BROADVIEW PRESS, LTD. is an independent, international publishing house, incorporated in 1985. Broadview believes in shared ownership, both with its employees and with the general public; since the year 2000 Broadview shares have traded publicly on the Toronto Venture Exchange under the symbol BDP.

We welcome comments and suggestions regarding any aspect of our publications—please feel free to contact us at the addresses below or at broadview@broad-viewpress.com / www.broadviewpress.com.

North America
Post Office Box 1243,
Peterborough, Ontario, Canada K9J 7H5

3576 California Road,
Orchard Park, New York, USA 14127
TEL: (705) 743-8990; FAX: (705) 743-8353

customerservice@broadviewpress.com

UK, Ireland and continental Europe
Plymbridge Distributors Ltd.
Estover Road, Plymouth PL6 7PY, UK
TEL: 44 (0) 1752 202301;
FAX ORDER LINE: 44 (0) 1752 202333;
ORDERS: orders@nbnplymbridge.com
CUST. SERV.: cservs@nbnplymbridge.com

Australia and New Zealand
UNIREPS University of New South Wales
Sydney, NSW 2052 Australia
TEL: 61 2 96640999; FAX: 61 2 96645420
infopress@unsw.edu.au

Broadview Press gratefully acknowledges the support of the Ministry of Canadian Heritage through the Book Publishing Industry Development Program.

Cover design by Black Eye Design.
Interior by Liz Broes, Black Eye Design.

This book is printed on 100% post-consumer recycled, ancient forest friendly paper.

Printed in Canada

10 9 8 7 6 5 4 3 2 1

To my Dad,
for his intellect and his courage

and my Mom,
for her wisdom and her strength

To both of them,
for their love

CONTENTS

ACKNOWLEDGEMENTS

This book would never have been published were it not for the suggestions, advice and support of my friends and family. Thank you.

Three life-long friends—André Bernier, Nic Thorne, and Amod Lele—were the earliest editors of this book. They were joined soon after by Ben Atwater, Christine Cheng, Marcia Sweet, and both my parents. Together, these eight provided the main intellectual proving ground for my ideas. Marcia was also the first to give me practical guidance on how to get my work published. Each of them has reviewed multiple versions of the text, pushed me on both style and content, and provided encouragement when I needed it. I owe them all a great debt of gratitude. One of them (Marcia) has already called upon me to review her own book; I stand ready to return the favour for the rest.

I also owe thanks to dozens of others friends, colleagues, and teachers who have helped me along this journey. Among them, thanks to Andrew Colgan, Terry and Donna Colgan (for their computer), Tim Lewis, Susan London (for her interest where she had no interest), Neil Macker, Shirley Dunn, Virgil Duff, Michael Harrison, and Johanna Bristow. Special thanks go to my professors and fellow graduate students at the Goldman School of Public Policy at the University of California, Berkeley. The themes of this book crystallized while I was at Berkeley; the first draft was written in its libraries; virtually every page borrows from its ideas.

Finally, two women served as inspiration for this work. The first is Helen Hope Salmond, my maternal grandmother. A woman of fierce independence and incredible ability, Nana was the first female president of the

Canadian Institute of International Affairs. Actress, teacher, and Canadian tennis champion, she is a woman of talent and grace. She continues to inspire her many grandchildren.

My favourite muse is January Abigail Angeles. Her ideas, smiles, and encouragement were all part of making this book possible. She was the first to share in the joy of its completion. Indeed, she is doubly glad to see it finished: proud for me, and relieved that I shall stop rambling about my latest idea for the next chapter. For her love—and her patience—I owe her no end of thanks.

PREFACE

This book is about international trade and trade-related social issues. It is intended to shed light on how the trade system affects the critical elements of a national society, such as the environment, the economy, and the arts. The book's aim is to be accessible to the general reader, but deep enough to serve as an introductory text at the undergraduate or graduate level.

This is a Canadian book. It is written by a Canadian, primarily for Canadians. Much of the book focuses on Canada, but not exclusively. It also addresses the impact of international trade on developing countries with small economies. In part, this is because Canada is—by global standards—a small economy, and shares some similarities with developing countries. At other times, developing countries are discussed to illustrate the responsibilities developed nations have toward the rest of the world. In this sense, Canada is more like the US or Britain, and has the characteristics and responsibilities of a rich, industrialized nation. For both these reasons, an account of Canada's role within the international trade system would be incomplete without a discussion of small, developing economies.

In scope, this book focuses mainly on the impact of the World Trade Organization (WTO) and the North American Free Trade Agreement (NAFTA) on Canada and other countries. Other international institutions, like the World Bank and the International Monetary Fund, are dealt with only insofar as they relate to international trade. Likewise, international finance and global capital markets are largely addressed only tangentially. Without these restrictions, this book would easily fill thousands of pages over several volumes.

Recognizing the increasing influence of international trade and globalization, some observers have concluded that nothing short of a world government is required to manage today's complex economic and social forces. This book does not share that point of view. While it is true that there is an increasing need for international cooperation on global issues such as climate change or biological diversity, a world government is not the only vehicle for addressing that need. Moreover, any attempt to design a world government would need to address the significant problems of representation, legitimacy, taxation, and feasibility.

Instead, there may be a need for greater national sovereignty, rather than less. The challenge for policy makers is to design and operate international institutions that exercise an appropriate level of authority at a global level while minimizing the loss of national sovereignty on issues that can and should be addressed at a national level. For instance, the WTO is not equipped to address the political tradeoffs necessary to govern issues like genetically modified food, where social consensus does not exist within a country or across countries. National governments will continue to be the appropriate place to govern such issues.

How should a country like Canada interact with the WTO? How should trade deals like NAFTA be structured to do the most good, both for Canada and its trading partners? How well are we managing trade today? This book is designed to help answer these questions.

Jeff Colgan

chapter ONE

INTRODUCTION

With over 40 million victims worldwide, AIDS is now the worst plague since the Middle Ages; in time, it will probably be the worst ever.[1] It seems particularly harsh that over 70 per cent of its victims live in Sub-Saharan Africa, a region of the world already struck by poverty, disease, and hardship. Nearly 19 million people have died from AIDS; nearly 4 million were children under the age of 15.[2] Of the 14 million children orphaned by AIDS, 92 per cent of them live in Africa.[3] It would be astonishing if the governments of Africa—at least the ones that care about the lives of ordinary citizens—did not make an effort to stave off this human tragedy.

The tragedy is made worse by the shocking expense of the drugs necessary to prolong the lives and ease the pain of AIDS victims. Until recently, the average cost of a year's drugs for an AIDS patient in Africa was $12,000 (US).[4] Imagine how this cost must look to Africans, most of whom have a yearly income of less than $1,000. The cost is prohibitive in the region where 85 per cent of the world's AIDS deaths occurred.[5] What makes this so tragic, however, is that this prohibitive cost to Africans is utterly artificial.

Giant pharmaceutical companies, such as Merck and GlaxoSmithKline, hold the patents to most of the drugs required for AIDS treatment. These patents drive up the cost of the drugs, nominally to reward companies for doing the research and development necessary for delivering the drug to market. Most of the research for modern AIDS medicines, however, was done at public institutions in industrialized nations, funded by taxpayers' money.[6] While the pharmaceutical corporations do invest millions of dol-

lars in the drugs' development, this is typically to satisfy regulatory requirements in the rich nations of North America and Europe. The fact that the
drugs can then also be sold to AIDS victims in poor nations around the world
is, from the corporate perspective, just a small financial bonus.

Unfortunately, the financial profits reaped by the pharmaceutical giants
are paltry compared to the human cost of the international patent rights
on AIDS drugs. Patent rights in the industrialized countries are already
designed to give corporations adequate financial reward for the development of new medicines. Thus a reasonable price for the AIDS drugs in impov-
erished African nations would be based on the actual physical cost of
producing the drugs. Some pharmaceutical companies, like the Indian
firm Cipla, have demonstrated that identical copies of the drugs could be
made for a tiny fraction of the price that the major corporations were
demanding.[7] Still, the multinational pharmaceuticals insisted on enforcing their patent rights. In doing so, they kept the price of AIDS drugs
high, even as millions of people were dying.

In the late 1990s, South Africa made a bold effort to do something about
this. Under mounting grass-roots pressure from the public, the government
declared AIDS a national health emergency. United Nations experts estimate that 20 per cent of the South African adult population is infected with
this fatal disease;[8] under these circumstances, the motivation for this law
is unimpeachable. South African leaders noted that the AIDS drugs could
be imported from India in generic "no-name" form. The new emergency
laws broke the multinational corporate patents and gave licenses to the manufacturers of the inexpensive version of the AIDS drugs, so that the medicine could be available to South Africa's people.

Pitilessly, the rich countries tried to bully South Africa into retracting this
law. The US, under pressure from its pharmaceuticals lobby, threatened trade
sanctions against South Africa unless it fully enforced the patent rights of
the multinational corporations. The intellectual property rules of the World
Trade Organization (WTO), the US said, prohibited South Africa from
breaking the corporate copyrights. In the hands of big business, the WTO's
trade rules were becoming a weapon against a small country.

Over time, civic-minded citizens worldwide would not stand for it.
Social activists spread the word about the pharmaceuticals' activities, and
then the media got hold of the story. As public pressure mounted, the companies had a harder time defending their position. The US government pulled
back, and eventually switched sides altogether, pressuring the pharma-

ceuticals to drop their case. The consequences of the WTO's agreement on patents were all too clear to see. Trade scholars, even defenders of the WTO, began to wonder aloud why any nation would "deliberately enter into a legal agreement condemning itself to early death?"[9]

In spite of the tide of public opinion, the pharmaceutical companies failed to take the hint. As South Africa moved to implement its law, a group of companies represented by the Pharmaceutical Manufacturers' Association challenged the emergency law in South African courts. South Africa's copyright laws, with text taken straight from the WTO's own regulations, were now going to decide whether the emergency health measure was constitutionally legal. The pharmaceuticals' lawyers did their best to drag out the court case, repeatedly requesting long delays. This came at a dreadful cost to society: the South African government reported that AIDS killed a thousand more people *each day* the lawsuit dragged on.[10] Indeed, the pharmaceuticals might have pursued this indefinitely, were their actions not so clearly deplorable.

Fortunately, in the spring of 2001, the pharmaceutical companies finally gave up. In the face of mounting public outcry and bad press, the companies were understandably worried about their public image. Moreover, it was clear that they were going to lose in court. Scrambling to minimize the damage, the lawyers made several attempts at an out-of-court settlement, which the South African government wisely declined. In April 2001, the corporations dropped their case altogether.[11]

THE PROMISE AND PERIL OF INTERNATIONAL TRADE

The struggle for affordable AIDS medicine highlights the tremendous promise of globalization, as well as a potent warning of its dangers. On the one hand, globalization enthusiasts will point out that it is only because of international trade that South Africa could even think of importing inexpensive drugs made in India. Declining transportation costs have made global distribution of economic goods like pharmaceuticals extremely cheap. In turn, this encourages companies all over the world, like the Indian pharmaceutical manufacturer, to consider export sales a major component of their business strategy. Moreover, defenders of the WTO can point to the fact that South Africa *did* eventually win the case. This is evidence, they say, that the WTO's trade regime is working.

On the other hand, opponents of globalization will point out the horrible implications of the struggle for affordable AIDS medicine. True, South Africa won—but at a huge cost of taxpayers' money in legal fees, years of delay in the delivery of the drugs, and a tragic toll in human life while trade bureaucrats were bickering over the paperwork. In retrospect, it took considerable courage for South Africa to stand up to the international community and multinational corporations by enacting this special health law in the first place. It did so at the risk of facing economic sanctions from the United States and in the face of the substantial uncertainty of the legal battle. Indeed, South Africa's leaders would likely have caved in to international pressure were it not for the enormous life-and-death needs of its people. How many other, less obvious injustices slip through the cracks of international trade law?

This book is written for those who want a deeper understanding of the debate surrounding globalization and its social, political, and economic consequences. Scores of books have been written on globalization. But the very fact that so many people–social activists, institutions, businesses, academics, journalists–feel the urge to speak authoritatively about globalization only increases the need to keep the debate informed by the facts. Some of those who are the most vocal and the most passionate about globalization seem to be the least informed. On one hand, anti-globalization protesters occasionally appear to enjoy the act of protesting more than they ever think of constructive solutions to social problems. Moreover, they often fail to see how the very policies they oppose could be used to achieve their own noble goals.

The opposite end of the spectrum can be no less foolhardy. Some of the international economic elite has stopped listening to the real horror stories of how globalization can affect people's daily lives. Market fundamentalists like to believe that if only governments worldwide stood aside, free markets and free trade could offer a nearly endless array of possibilities and material wealth. To be fair, few academic economists would make such a sweeping (and erroneous) statement, but nonetheless the idea persists as an implicit—or even explicit—ideology. The notion that unbridled free trade can bring us vast economic growth needs to be balanced by the realities of how trade actually affects our country and our world.

A CANADIAN PERSPECTIVE

The World Trade Organization proudly claims to be in the vanguard of those who wish to bring the Rule of Law to international affairs. Believers in the WTO feel that without it, small countries would suffer from the political clout and manoeuvring of the great global powers. Indeed, this claim is justified, up to a point. The WTO is perhaps the only international institution that is willing to render harsh judgment upon powerful actors such as the United States and Europe; as such, it can claim an objectivity that few other institutions possess. Nonetheless, the WTO also represents a great danger to small countries. Sometimes international trade rules have brought justice; other times, they have offered the large countries and their multinational corporations new weapons with which to bully the smaller ones.

In global terms, Canada is a small country. We are, of course, a huge country geographically, and medium-sized economically. However, Canada has a relatively small role to play among the world's powers. We do not have a permanent seat at the United Nations Security Council; our economy makes up just 2 per cent of the world's output; our people comprise less than 0.5 per cent of all humanity.[12] Despite our heavy dependence on the US, our trade with them constitutes less than 3 per cent of the American Gross Domestic Product (GDP).[13] Thus Canada is small in terms of our country's position in the international context of political economy.

Because we are a small country, our situation does not always fit well within the economic framework of our American and European friends. In some ways, Canada is more like a small country in Asia or Africa than it is like the US or France. In other circumstances, Canada must be understood as a global trade player—with corresponding responsibilities to less developed nations. As such, this book will occasionally play counterpoint to the "standard" economic view of the world. This book accepts standard economics only as the first step to understanding how globalization and international trade affect a country like Canada.

As remote as it may feel to many Canadians, the legal battle for AIDS drugs in South Africa represents the dramatic influence of the WTO's regime on the everyday lives on Main Street, Canada. If the WTO's rules can shape health care in South Africa, it should come as no surprise that it touches the lives of Canadians, too. In just the first eight years of its existence, the WTO passed judgement on our ability to protect our culture;

THE PROMISE AND PERIL OF INTERNATIONAL TRADE

on the way we regulate pharmaceutical drugs; and on the production of our food.

Canada is like the proverbial canary in the mineshaft: if something goes wrong in the international trade regime, Canada is usually among the first to feel it. Because of our proximity to the world's economic giant, and because our economy is based heavily on export products, international trade relations is an issue that pervades Canadian life. The Canada-US Free Trade Agreement dominated the federal election in 1988, as did the North American Free Trade Agreement (NAFTA) in 1993. Again in 1995, Canada was among the founding members of the WTO. Forty per cent of our nation's economy is directly involved with international trade; virtually all of the rest of it is indirectly affected.[14] It is essential that anyone interested in Canadian public affairs have an understanding of how globalization and trade policy affect our country.

Still, a globalization book cannot and should not be limited to Canada. Our position in the international community is loaded with lessons for America, Europe, and others. For example, Canada's relationship with poor countries is typical of the integral connection between developed and developing nations within the international trade regime. Those who live in rich nations must understand how governments and corporations that operate in our name affect the lives of people halfway across the globe. Only with that understanding can we possibly hope to quell the anger and violence toward the West that exists in pockets throughout the developing world. In the long term, a global regime built on fairness provides the best hope of creating a peaceful and just world.

A JOURNEY THROUGH GLOBALIZATION...

"Globalization" is becoming a globalized word; different people have defined it in different ways. Virtually everyone agrees that it indicates the increasing interconnectedness of the world: as a result of globalization, we are able to exchange ideas, information, and physical property with people halfway around the globe, almost instantaneously. Because the core of this exchange is economic, this book will use "globalization" to refer to international trade and trade-related social issues. This is not to suggest that globalization is not present in other areas, such as health. Canadians are now sufficiently familiar with SARS and mad cow disease to know that health conditions are no longer just local issues. Still, the economics of trade is the backbone of the larger concept of "globalization."

If the very word "economics" conjures up images of college blackboards choking with chalk, an endless array of meaningless graphs, and the headaches of grappling with an impossibly difficult subject, do not worry. Economics is not all like that, and this book (I hope) is not like that at all. In this book, economics is merely the skeleton; the political, legal and even ethical battles that mark the globalization debate are the flesh and blood of an eminently human story. As such, this book will delve into a vast array of everyday issues that are influenced by international pressures: the food we eat, the movies we watch, the environment we live in, and the immigrants who live in our neighbourhoods.

The Promise and Peril of International Trade takes a balanced view of trade. If managed well, trade drives economic growth and can provide everyone with an opportunity to improve their standard of living—including the global poor, who need that opportunity the most. But if it is managed poorly—or not managed at all, as market fundamentalists would like—international trade will create social injustice, economic hardship, and environmental disaster.

Trade policy is an ever-evolving process. With the Doha round of negotiations well underway at the WTO and persistent interest in the Free Trade Area of the Americas, trade policy is very much a live issue. If a small country could ever afford to be isolationist, it can no longer.

The question that remains is how globalization can be channelled to protect the prosperity, freedom and culture of our nation. To answer that question, we will need to take a look at the costs and risks of international trade. These are the very real aspects of globalization that most protestors sense intuitively but cannot always articulate. We will see how it causes increasing inequality between the rich and poor of our world, and how it can drive the brightest talent from small economies to migrate to large ones. We will look at how free trade stifles local culture in small countries. We'll look at the power of the World Trade Organization and the threat it poses to the sovereignty of nations, especially small ones. And while even this weighty list of dangers should not lead you to reject free trade, it ought to convince you to keep a wary eye on its future.

We cannot afford to simply curse the problems of our current system without trying to identify how the system might be made better. Accordingly, each chapter of this book comes with a recommendation on how international trade could be managed more constructively, both for Canada and the rest of the world. Better to light a candle than to curse the darkness.

The struggle for affordable AIDS medicine in South Africa vividly demonstrates how important it is that we, the public, participate in globalization through our democracy. Public pressure played a vital role in the AIDS case: first, in getting the US government to back down; and second, in eventually forcing the pharmaceutical companies to reconsider their relentless pursuit of financial profit. If there is a lesson to be found here, surely it is the importance of allowing your heart to be touched by the emotions of global hardship and injustice. But your heart is not enough; you also need your head to reason through the issue and articulate your vision. This book is designed to help you do that.

NOTES

1 UNAIDS, "Report on the Global HIV/AIDS Epidemic 2002" (Barcelona, Spain: 2002), p. 8.

2 J. Christensen "AIDS in Africa: Dying by the numbers," Cable News Network <www.cnn.com/SPECIALS/2000/aids/stories/overview/> Visited 14 Oct. 2002.

3 "14 million orphans": UNAIDS, p. 8. "92 percent live in Africa": Christensen, CNN.

4 1998 figures. UNAIDS, p. 146.

5 1999 figures. Christensen, CNN.

6 J. James, "Hundred Million Dollar Program for Public-Private AIDS Research and Outreach in Africa," AIDS Treatment News Issue #319, 21 May 1999. <http://www.aids. org/atn/a-319-04.html> Dr. F. Abbott, special legal counsel to the South African government for the AIDS medicine case, echoes this view. Personal communication, April 2001.

7 R. Zimmerman and J. Pesta, "Drug Industry, AIDS Community Is Jolted by Cipla AIDS-Drug Offer," The Wall Street Journal, 8 Feb. 2001.

8 Secure The Future Website, <www.securethefuture.com/aidsin/data/aidsin.htm> Visited 13 Aug. 2002.

9 See F. Abbott, "The TRIPS-Legality of Measures Taken to Address Public Health Crises: Responding to USTR-State-Industry Positions that Undermine the WTO," prepared for a Conference and Book in Honour of Robert Hudec, September 2000. Dr. Abbott was special legal counsel to the South African government for the AIDS medicine case.

10 F. Abbott, personal communication, April 2001.

11 "AIDS drug case adjourned," Cable News Network, 18 April 2001. <http://www.cnn.com /2001/WORLD/africa/04/18/safrica.drugs.02/>

12 United Nations Charter; Statistical Annex Tables of the OECD Economic Outlook; UN Population figures.

13 According to The Economist, Canada-US trade was approximately $280 billion in 2000. At the same time, US GDP topped $9 trillion.

14 According to The Economist. <www.economist.com/countries/Canada/profile.cfm?folder =Profile-Economic%20Structure> Visited 1 Aug. 2002.

PART ONE
THE ECONOMICS OF FREE TRADE

Free Trade and the Promise of Prosperity

Canada is a classic example of a trading nation. In the year 2000, Canada exported products worth over $280 billion (US), making it a whopping 40 per cent of our national output (known in economics as GDP—Gross Domestic Product).[1] In the four years starting in 1990, just after the Canada-US Free Trade Agreement was signed, Canadian trade with the US rose by almost 40 per cent (even adjusting for inflation). Compare this with the rest of the economy: Canada's GDP grew just 5.4 per cent over the same period.[2] No wonder trade policy is so important. Virtually every aspect of our national community is touched, directly or indirectly, by international trade.

Canadians know this. A study for the Department of Foreign Affairs and International Trade found that, "in the opinion of the majority of Canadians, international trade has made a significant contribution, over the past ten years, to the growth of the Canadian economy, to job creation in the provinces, and to the emergence of new Canadian technology and innovations."[3] More than 8 out of 10 Canadians agreed that international trade was an essential part of our economy.

Despite this recognition, thousands of Canadians hold a deeply rooted mistrust of globalization and international trade. Remarkably, it is an issue that can evoke anger so fierce that it literally drives people to riot in the streets. Anyone interested in being an active member of civil society—in politics, in business or in our national culture—needs to know what all the fuss is about. Our first step in that direction is to understand trade's tremendous promise for economic prosperity.

This chapter is unlike any of the others in this book. Most chapters deal with the social and economic implications of free trade for Canada and the world. This chapter, however, has the inglorious task of laying the economic foundations for the rest of the discussion.

WHAT EXACTLY IS FREE TRADE?

So to begin: What is free trade? By itself, international trade is a fairly simple concept: an exchange of products and services between countries. Trade is "free" when countries agree not to place any taxes on the products as they cross international borders. At one time, these taxes on trade (which economists call *tariffs*) formed a major portion of the government's revenue for almost every country in the world. Today, tariffs are low for most products in most developed countries. Still, no country really has absolute free trade, in the strictest sense of the word, because all governments keep at least some tariffs. Free trade is a relative concept, and some countries are closer to absolute free trade than others.

International trade can be divided into three general types: *restricted trade*, *managed free trade*, and *unbridled free trade*. Restricted trade occurs when tariffs are high. Usually this is because the country is being "protectionist," which is to say that it is actively discouraging international trade, so as to protect its own industry.[4] In contrast, both of the other two types of policy aim to keep tariffs as low as possible. The difference between them is that a policy of managed free trade (or simply, managed trade) does not rule out the use of other economic tools to influence the market economy, such as government subsidies to local industries or regulations on environmental impact. Unbridled free trade, on the other hand, occurs when national governments agree to use a minimum of tariffs, subsidies, regulations or any other interference in the activities of private businesses as they conduct international trade. These three types of international trade are central for an understanding of the debate around globalization.

Some clarification of the terms "managed" and "unbridled" free trade is in order. This book will use the term "managed trade" to mean managed free trade, which is different than it has sometimes been used elsewhere.[5] Also, it should be understood that "unbridled" free trade is a conceptual term. In its most extreme form, unbridled free trade would eliminate *all* government intervention in the economy. No country or institution has actually adopted this extreme. However, some advocates (referred to as *market fundamentalists*) are interested in moving government policy and international institutions as far toward that extreme as possible.

To put the three trade terms in perspective, consider Canada's history. From 1867 to World War II, Canada generally pursued a policy of restricted trade. Sir John A. Macdonald's National Policy in the nineteenth century, for instance, imposed high tariffs on virtually all international trade. (Today, one might point to North Korea as an example of highly restricted trade.) From about the 1950s onward, however, Canada has pursued free trade aggressively. Indeed, the restrictions on national policy for investment, energy resources, and labour requirements in the Canada-US Free Trade Agreement are characteristic of relatively unbridled free trade; these restrictions are even stronger in NAFTA. Canada's membership in the World Trade Organization's system of trade and investment treaties, discussed later in this chapter, is a mix between managed and unbridled free trade.

When people speak of being "for" or "against" free trade, what exactly do they mean? Being "against" free trade is relatively simple. Many protestors, including most labour unions, are in favour of restricted trade, and are opposed to "free trade" in general, managed or unbridled. (A small subset are even in favour of *no* international trade, but these are a small minority.) Not surprisingly, these activists are opposed to the WTO and NAFTA.

On the other hand, being "for" free trade is much less clear. Most of those who call themselves "free trade advocates" support unbridled free trade.[6] Daniel Schwanen, for instance, is a prominent Canadian free-trade advocate who argues that trade rules "fostering the openness of markets must encompass foreign investment issues since, in today's globally integrated economies, there really is no free trade without free FDI [Foreign Direct Investment]."[7] This desire to extend free-trade policies far beyond direct tariffs is the defining characteristic of unbridled free-trade advocates. For many reasons, this book will distinguish a middle path: managed free trade. To see why, we must first understand why the economics of free trade make it desirable.

Foundations: Absolute Advantage and International Trade

Free trade rests upon the economic theory of comparative advantage, which is usually attributed to David Ricardo in the early nineteenth century.[8] Analyzed for almost two hundred years, its acceptance by economists grew slowly and fitfully right up to the present day.[9] Today, the vast majority of economists view the theory of comparative advantage as fundamentally correct.[10] Indeed, the economic historian Douglas Irwin argues that free trade is "as sound as any proposition in economic theory which purports to have implications for economic policy is ever likely to be."[11]

The theory of comparative advantage boils down to a simple idea: two countries can both be better off by trading with each other than if they lived in isolation. To see this, consider a hypothetical case in two countries, Japan and Honduras. In each of these countries, local people have their own expertise: for the Japanese, it is making videotapes; for Hondurans, it is carpet weaving. Imagine for a moment that Japan and Honduras are the only two countries in the world, and carpets and videotapes are the only two products in the world. The two countries need resources to make carpets and videotapes: raw materials, equipment (capital) with which to work, and human labour to drive the process. Economists call this capital and labour the *input resources*. Suppose that in Japan it costs $100 in input resources to create 10 videotapes. Alternatively, for the same amount of money (input resources), they could make carpets. Of course, carpets take a long time to weave, and labour is expensive in Japan, so Japan could make only 5 carpets with $100. In Honduras, however, the situation is just the opposite. Labour in Honduras is quite cheap, so 10 carpets can be made with $100. On the other hand, Hondurans don't have a lot of the technological infrastructure to make videotapes, so $100 can make only 5 videotapes.

Japan and Honduras each start with $200, and each produce some carpets and videotapes. Their output is shown in Table 1a.

TABLE 1a. :: Absolute Advantage (before Trade)

	INPUT	VIDEOTAPES	CARPETS	TOTAL UNITS
Japan	200	10	5	15
Honduras	200	5	10	15
TOTAL	400	15	15	30

Now Japan and Honduras sign a free trade pact, and agree to specialize in what they are best at producing. Since this is *free trade*, each country knows that the other will not tax (or place a tariff) upon the things that it is making. So Japan concentrates on making videotapes, and Honduras focuses on carpets. This allows Japan and Honduras to produce more for the same amount of input, as shown in Table 1b.

TABLE 1b. :: Absolute Advantage (production specialization)

	INPUT	VIDEOTAPES	CARPETS	TOTAL UNITS
Japan	200	20	0	20
Honduras	200	0	20	20
TOTAL	400	20	20	40

Japan is better at making videotapes than Honduras, which economists call an *absolute advantage*. Conversely, Honduras has an absolute advantage in carpet making. Thus, both countries are now working on a product where they are very efficient. Once they have specialized, Japan and Honduras collectively have more goods (40) between them than they did before they specialized (30). They are now able to trade in such a way that benefits them both. Honduras offers Japan offers 6 of its carpets in exchange for 6 Japanese videotapes. The exchange is shown in Table 1c.

TABLE 1c. :: Absolute Advantage (after Trade)

	INPUT	VIDEOTAPES	CARPETS	TOTAL UNITS
Japan	200	14	6	20
Honduras	200	6	14	20
TOTAL	400	20	20	40

Look carefully at the numbers. Before these two countries began to trade, Japan had 10 videotapes and 5 carpets; but through the magic of trade, Japan now has 14 videotapes and 6 carpets—more of both products. This new wealth is generated even though the Japanese are working at the same pace as always. The same is true for the Hondurans—they have more than they started with now, too. With everyone concentrating on the work that they are good at, we have the storybook happy ending: everyone wins. Such is the magic of specialization and trade.

Comparative Advantage

All right, very impressive. But in the real world, some countries seem more productive at virtually everything than other countries. We in North America, for instance, are blessed with so much capital, such advanced technology, and such a diverse workforce, that it might seem unlikely that a poor country could have any absolute advantage compared to us. What happens when one country is so good at everything that the other country doesn't have an "absolute advantage" in the production of either videotapes or carpets? Does this mean that the countries shouldn't trade? Of course they should, says the economist. For no matter who has an absolute advantage in production, each country always has a *comparative advantage* relative to another. To see this in action, let us consider the case of the production of cars and wheat in two countries, say the United States and Thailand.

In the United States, industry is very effective. With $10,000 input resources, 10 cars can be made, or 50 tons of wheat. In Thailand, sadly, the workforce is not as effective and industry is inefficient. With the same $10,000 input, only 2 cars can be made, or 25 tons of wheat. Just as in the case of Japan and Honduras, each country starts by producing both cars and wheat. Table 2a shows what can be produced when each country starts with $20,000.

TABLE 2a :: Comparative Advantage (before Trade)

	INPUT	CARS	WHEAT	TOTAL UNITS
USA	20,000	10	50	60
Thailand	20,000	2	25	27
TOTAL	40,000	12	75	87

From the table, we can see that 10 cars can be made in the United States, whereas only 2 can be made in Thailand for the same resources. Because 10/2 = 5, we say that the United States is 5 times as efficient as Thailand in the production of cars. However, if we look at wheat, we can see that the United States is only twice (50/25 = 2) as efficient as Thailand in wheat. Because Thailand is relatively more efficient when producing wheat, economists say that Thailand has a "comparative advantage" in wheat production, *even though* the US has an absolute advantage in both wheat and car production. Likewise, the US has a comparative advantage in car production.

With this in mind, economists convince the Prime Minister of Thailand to sign a free trade agreement with the US, and the two countries begin to specialize. Since the United States is relatively much more efficient in car production, the US will make cars with most of their resources: the US will make 15 cars at a price of $15,000. The rest of their input resources ($5,000) will be devoted to wheat farming. And since both countries still want wheat, Thailand will devote all of its effort to farming.

TABLE 2b :: Comparative Advantage (production specialization)

	INPUT	CARS	WHEAT	TOTAL UNITS
USA	20,000	15	25	40
Thailand	20,000	0	50	50
TOTAL	**40,000**	**15**	**75**	**90**

Once again, as Table 2b shows, the total number of units has increased through trade (90 vs. 87). Certainly, it's not as impressive as the gains made by Japan and Honduras, when each country held an absolute advantage. Still, thanks to specialization, there are more cars in the world than there would have been otherwise (15 to 12), with no loss in the wheat harvest. Even this relatively small gain turns out to be enormously important. And, since the countries both have more to offer, they are eager to engage in trade. Thailand trades 25 tons of its wheat in exchange for 3 American cars. After trade (in Table 2c), each country has more than it did before trade.

TABLE 2c :: Comparative Advantage (after Trade)

	INPUT	CARS	WHEAT	TOTAL UNITS
USA	20,000	12	50	62
Thailand	20,000	3	25	28
TOTAL	**40,000**	**15**	**75**	**90**

Comparative advantage is the foundation of modern international trade. As we just saw, trade specialization between two countries allows each to benefit, even if one country is a more efficient producer of every possible good. In this case, trade specialization created three more cars than would have been produced without trade; the US got two of them, and Thailand got one. Of course, it could have been different: Thailand could have gotten two of the extra cars, or the US could have gotten all three. The laws of economics don't say anything about how the gains from trade ought to be distributed, which will be discussed more in Chapter 6. For now, we can simply note that trade makes greater wealth possible, and no country has to lose.

Applying This to the Real World

In the real world, there are more than two countries, and there are more than two products to make. The picture becomes more complicated when considering the many countries of the world: Japan might have a comparative advantage in creating videotape relative to Honduras, but not in comparison to the US or Thailand. The basic story, however, never changes; free trade allows each product to be produced wherever it can be created most efficiently (which, in economics, is the same thing as saying "most cheaply"). Each country concentrates its effort on the things it is good at, and trades for those things for which it is not.

Of course, there is a cost to shipping all these videotapes and carpets around the world, and that needs to be addressed. In the real world, transportation costs sometimes outweigh the benefits from free trade. Remarkably, however, the twentieth century proved how cheaply we can ship all kinds of things—everything from machinery to fresh fruit—across the oceans to facilitate international trade. For instance, the average cost of a ton of sea freight today is less than a third of what it cost in 1920.[12] Suffice to say that the principles of comparative advantage and economic efficiency still apply even when transportation costs are taken into account.[13]

Even so, there are other problems: different languages, different national laws and regulations, and so on. These obstacles need to be overcome. Still, the benefits of trade often make it worth it, especially when there are big differences in what countries are naturally good at creating. For instance, Kenya's climate allows it to grow coffee and sugar far more easily than anyone could in Canada; in turn, Canada's educated population makes hi-tech companies like Nortel and Ballard Power possible, whereas they would be almost impossible in Kenya. The huge differences across countries very often make the gains of trade worth pursuing.

In fact, we don't need to think about this in an international context at all. In Canada, there is a great deal of economic specialization and trade *within* the country. For instance, Ontario farmers have more luck growing tomatoes than anyone in Edmonton, and oil producers have considerably more success near Edmonton than in most places in Ontario. Each region specializes according to its own endowments of natural resources and human talent. Accordingly, the provinces in Canada trade a great deal with each other; in 1999, inter-provincial trade accounted for $189 billion.[14]

The principle of specialization and trade can be applied at virtually any level. Two people working within the same law firm, for instance, are not likely to have exactly the same skill set. One person might be a legal researcher, the other a courtroom litigator; each will concentrate on his or her special work tasks, and "trade" services to generate total revenue for the firm. Comparative advantage and trade are powerful concepts, and they drive a great deal of the economic activity in the modern world.

History suggests that countries that engage in more international trade have, on average, greater economic growth.[15] Economic growth creates new jobs and provides more income. As a result, economists in the last fifty years came to a growing consensus that specialization and trade held the potential for the generation of enormous wealth for all countries. Due to this growing consensus that the World Trade Organization was born in 1995.

The Role of the World Trade Organization

The World Trade Organization is an international organization based in Geneva, Switzerland. Its primary function is to promote international trade between countries. It does this by enforcing the rules of trade that are agreed upon by the WTO's 146 member nations.[16] It came into being in 1995 after over 50 years of international trade initiatives.

In July 1944, at the close of World War II, world leaders met in the little town of Bretton Woods, New Hampshire, to discuss how to shape the postwar world. In particular, their goal was to establish three important international organizations: the World Bank, the International Monetary Fund (IMF), and the International Trade Organization. The World Bank— known officially as the International Bank for Reconstruction and

Development—was initially set up to provide loans to help re-build war-torn Europe.[17] Only much later (in the 1970s) did the Bank take on its current controversial role in helping poor nations develop economically.

The International Monetary Fund also plays a powerful role in international economics. The purpose of the IMF is to facilitate international currency exchange between countries.[18] This was especially important immediately after World War II, since the major Western nations agreed to keep fixed exchange rates. (A "fixed" exchange rate between Canada and the US, for instance, would mean that the Canadian dollar would always be worth a certain amount in US dollars.) The IMF's job was to help stabilize the fixed exchange system. Unfortunately, the system didn't work very well, and the fixed exchange system collapsed in the early 1970s. Although its original purpose is now gone, the IMF continues to exist and, along with its sister institution the World Bank, plays a prominent role in international finances.

Thus two of the major institutions from the Bretton Woods meeting are still quite important today. The third, however, never even got off the ground: diplomats failed to create a workable structure for the International Trade Organization. When the US government announced its refusal to ratify its membership in 1950, the ITO was effectively dead. All that was left was something called the General Agreement on Tariffs and Trade (GATT), which was signed in 1947 and went into effect in 1948. Originally, this was an obscure treaty, intended to be a small part of the International Trade Organization. Instead, GATT shaped the course of history in international trade for nearly 50 years, and continues to be the backbone of the World Trade Organization.[19]

All of the signing countries, including Canada, agreed that tariffs should be held as low as possible in order to encourage international trade. The GATT was designed to ensure that each country gave the status of "most favoured nation" to every other country in the GATT. This meant that if Canada reduced any of its tariffs on, say, American goods, the same tariff reductions also had to be applied to the goods of every other GATT nation. This agreement was meant to bring down the overall level of tariffs as quickly as possible.

In the Cold War years, the Western democracies were eager to encourage international trade between the member nations to bolster their economic efficiency. As a result, the GATT was steadily revised through several rounds of negotiations. Each time it was revised, it grew economically more lucrative and more countries wanted to join. Partly as a result of this, it took longer and longer for each successive round of negotiations to be finished; for example, the Uruguay Round, the last one completed, took eight years. Indeed, the GATT system grew so large that it became unwieldy. The Uruguay Round involved over 100 nations, and without some central organization, the negotiations became exhausting. Other problems, especially in dispute resolution and the enforcement of the treaty, were starting to creep up. Negotiators decided that it was time to have another try at creating a permanent institution to regulate international trade.

So on January 1, 1995, the World Trade Organization was born. One of its main purposes is to hear disputes between countries. Importantly, it has the power to make binding rulings on the merits of a case, much as a judge does in a Canadian courtroom. If the WTO decides that a country is violating its agreement to the other WTO members, the country must change its trade laws accordingly. If it refuses, the WTO can authorize other nations to impose a punishment, in the form of higher tariffs on products from the offending country. In one case, for instance, the WTO authorized the European Union to impose $7.2 billion in retaliatory sanctions against the US.[20] Given the huge size of these punishments, the WTO is in a powerful position to influence the structure of the international economy.

The World Trade Organization is also designed to encourage future rounds of trade talks. In 2002, the current round of negotiations was launched in Doha, the capital of Qatar. Some believe that the "Doha Round" could be the most sweeping set of negotiations yet. The huge power of the WTO, combined with its ever-expanding role in the affairs of its member nations, led to some controversy. Throughout the 1990s, social activists had a myriad of objections to the WTO. Most notably, protestors in Seattle managed to essentially shut down the WTO meeting in 1999.

Much of this book will investigate the role the WTO has played in public affairs, particularly in Canada. For now, the important thing to know is that the WTO acts partly as referee and partly as cheerleader in the game of international trade. The WTO plays a large role in making trade "free"—meaning that the WTO tries to clear unnecessary obstacles in the path of international trade. To the extent that the WTO does this effectively and unobtrusively, it provides a great service to the world.

The Role of the North American Free Trade Agreement

Canada's trade policy extends beyond the WTO. While the WTO acts as the global framework, Canada holds a number of separate trade deals with individual countries, called *bilateral agreements*. The most important, of course, is our bilateral relationship with the US.

Starting in the 1960s with the Canada-US Auto Pact, Canada has engaged in increasingly free trade with the US. The landmark Auto Pact paved the way for the enormous growth of the automotive industry in Ontario and other parts of the country. By the 1980s, pressure was building for a broader, more inclusive free trade agreement. In 1988, despite significant controversy over the implications of the deal, Canada signed the Canada-US Free Trade Agreement. In turn, this led to the 1993 North American Free Trade Agreement (NAFTA).

For Canada, NAFTA itself was not a particularly important deal. We already had a free trade agreement with the US, which is by far our largest trading partner. Adding Mexico made little difference, since it constitutes less than 5 per cent of our annual trade. Collectively, however, the 1988 and 1993 agreements made a huge impact on our economy. Indeed, some of the provisions of the two deals are far reaching. For instance, one provision of NAFTA obligates Canada to sell energy resources to the US in times of American need. This was a critical negotiating point for the US, which was mindful of national security concerns and its heavy energy dependence. Still, it continues to be a sore point for Canadians. After all, there is no reciprocal clause: how will the US help Canada if we fall into hard times? We will return to this issue, and others, in chapter 11.

NAFTA is a cornerstone of Canada's intense relationship with the US. Almost 85 per cent of Canadian trade is with Americans, making it the most important bilateral trade relationship in the world. NAFTA is a critical guide and rulebook for that trade. However, in practice, most of the conceptual framework of NAFTA is borrowed from the WTO's legal structure. In fact, the WTO sits higher in the legal hierarchy, with NAFTA being created as a free trade area under the WTO's rules, GATT Article 24. Moreover, most of Canada's critical trade issues are addressed by the WTO. Some issues, like the softwood lumber dispute, are dealt with by both WTO and NAFTA tribunals. Other issues, like Canada's regulation of pharmaceutical patents, are addressed only at the WTO. Typically, the WTO sets the tone for global trade decisions.

Since the WTO is the dominant international trade body, this book will mainly focus on it. However, on issues where there is a significant difference between NAFTA and the WTO, we will have a look at both agreements. For instance, NAFTA is more aggressive than the WTO rules on investment, energy, and culture; chapters 7, 10, and 11, respectively, will look at the issues in greater depth.

Why should we Care about Free Trade?

How important is trade policy for our economy? Economic evidence suggests that it has added billions—probably trillions—of dollars of new wealth to the world economy since international trade negotiations began in earnest after World War II. Each of the eight rounds of GATT negotiations have resulted in a modest but important boost in the economic growth of the participating countries. For instance, economists found that the Tokyo Round of negotiations, completed in the early 1980s, boosted overall GDP growth by about 0.2 per cent.[21] One economic estimate suggests that the next set of talks, the Uruguay Round, added about $96 billion (US) to the world economy, or about 0.4 per cent of the world GDP.[22] The WTO's own estimate is quite a bit higher: it claims to have added $500 billion (US) to the world economy (a GDP rise of about 1.7 per cent) from the Uruguay Round.[23]

At first glance, these numbers might not look terribly impressive. Two pieces of context are important to put this into perspective. First, a fraction of one per cent of GDP may not sound like a lot, but it is worth *billions* of dollars to our economy. In fact, if we ranked government policy initiatives in terms of their economic impact, trade policy would be in the top tier, among the best things that a government can do to stimulate long-term economic growth. Few other federal government initiatives can boast such gains. Second, the estimates quoted above do not reflect the entire gains from trade, but only the additional benefit from the partial effort made in each round of negotiation. A complete elimination of global barriers to trade in goods and services would bring much larger gains. According to some economists, removing all such barriers would generate $1,857 billion (US) in gains for the world (or 6.2 per cent of world GDP).[24] This is in addition to the progress already made over the last 50 years.

Moreover, economists believe that the financial gains from comparative advantage represent only a portion of the true benefits from trade. Douglas

37

Irwin, for instance, argues that trade improves our economic performance in at least two additional ways: it makes our industries more productive, and it improves the variety of goods that are offered to consumers. Most Canadians remember the early 1990s as a tough time, when the country was fighting a recession. Irwin, however, argues that the short-term pain of the Canada-US Free Trade Agreement gave way to long-term gain for Canada's industrial productivity, as free trade shaped our economy. He writes, "Tariff reductions helped boost labour productivity [in Canadian manufacturing] by a compounded rate of 0.6 percent per year in manufacturing as a whole and by 2.1 percent per year in the most affected (i.e., high tariff) industries. These are astoundingly large effects. This amounts to a 17 percent increase in productivity in the post-FTA period in the highly affected sectors, and a 5 percent increase for manufacturing overall."[25] While economists do not agree on the overall effects of the Free Trade Agreement for Canada's economy, many believe that it did increase our labour productivity.

A second important consideration, according to Irwin, is the way in which international trade brings us products that would otherwise be unavailable. Especially in Canada, one does not have to go far to see that this is true—just check the fresh fruit in the local supermarket. An astonishing array of foods from around the world is available to us, made possible only by international trade. However, not every nation is so blessed. As Irwin writes, "consider consumers in East Germany and Poland who, after the collapse of Communism, found exotic and affordable fruits such as bananas and oranges in the marketplace for the first time in their lives. Or consider their newfound ability to purchase apples and cabbages without worms and rot. The effect of such changes on aggregate output [GDP] was minuscule, but the welfare gains from the availability of new and improved goods was not insignificant."[26] Even though economists have a hard time measuring it, variety and choice often improve our lives as much as abundance.

Therefore, it is not merely specialization and comparative advantage that make trade so attractive. International trade also broadens our horizons, adding new choices to what we buy and new techniques to improve our industry. Together, these benefits provide a powerful stimulus to Canada's economic progress.

Trade is also attractive for another reason. Nearly three billion people, or almost half of all humanity, earn less than $2 per day.[27] Poverty on this scale is almost overwhelming, and it is hard for even the most devoted people to know how to help. Stimulating international trade is one of the very few broad economic policies that we know *can* help. The UN Commission on Trade and Development reports that, "if rich nations opened their markets to developing countries, the increased export opportunities would generate an estimated $700 billion of additional trade for the developing world."[28] To put this in context, this $700 billion for developing countries would be five times as much as the total amount of foreign aid given by all countries.[29] For all of us who care about making the world a better place, international trade is a crucial element of a broader picture.

CONCLUSION: (MANAGED) FREE TRADE HAS ENORMOUS POTENTIAL FOR PUBLIC GOOD

International trade makes much of modern life possible. In Canada, we consume electronics from Japan, vegetables from California, and clothing made in China. These products are available to us at an incredibly low cost, something that would be impossible without globalization. Moreover, a *well-managed* international trade system can provide these benefits to Canadians even as it opens up new opportunities for the global poor. Recognizing the economic promise of free trade is not the end of our discussion on globalization; indeed, it is only the start. For instance, we have seen how comparative advantage can boost economic growth, but we have not yet looked at what economic growth really means for typical families. There is a lot buried within the concept of "growth" as economists define it. We return to that concept in the next chapter and ask whether growth in our Gross Domestic Product truly represents progress for our society. The answer is not as straightforward as one would like. Nonetheless, we can take the relationship between free trade and economic growth as a good starting point for an exploration of the consequences of globalization. From this point, we have many questions to address: Who benefits from economic expansion? How does the new wealth get distributed? What are the social consequences of generating wealth by international trade? Answering these questions will lead us into the heart of the controversy over globalization.

NOTES

1   According to *The Economist*, <www.economist.com/countries/Canada/profile.cfm? folder=Profile-Economic%20Structure> Visited 1 Aug. 2002.

2   W. Watson, *Globalization and the Meaning of Canadian Life* (Toronto: University of Toronto Press, 1998), p. 52.

3   Department of Foreign Affairs and International Trade, Government of Canada, "International Trade—The View of Canadians," 23 May 2002.

4   Not all restricted trade is protectionist, however. Tariffs could also be kept high by a government that wants to gain revenues from its trade. This often occurs in dictatorships, when the government can make more money in the short term from tariffs on international trade than it can from other kinds of taxes. This is almost always to the great detriment of the public good of that country's citizens, but dictators are rarely concerned about such things.

5   Some trade commentators, such as John Ruggie, have used the term "managed trade" to indicate trade policy that goes "well beyond cushioning the burden of [trade] adjustment. [Governments] negotiate or otherwise set market shares." J. Ruggie, "At home abroad, abroad at home: International Liberalization and Domestic Stability in the New World Economy," Jean Monnet Chair Papers (San Domenico di Fiesole, Italy: 1995), p. 22. Others see "managed trade" as policy that lowers tariffs for some but not all industrial sectors, in order to give preference and protection to some domestic industries. Both of these types of policy are actually quite protectionist, which is the term used in this book. See W. Orme, *Understanding NAFTA* (Austin: University of Texas, 1996), pp. 39–42. In this book, "managed trade" will be used according to the definition laid out above, i.e., a policy that prefers reduction of quotas and tariffs on *all* industrial sectors, but does not prefer the total elimination of domestic policies (subsidies, regulations, etc.) that support and shape market structure.

6   Naturally, there is a spectrum of belief on the extent to which trade liberalization should extend. Jagdish Bhagwati, for instance, is one of the most famous and influential free-trade advocates in the world, yet his position does not fully support unbridled free trade. See, for example, his position on free trade and films in Chapter 10.

7   P. Sauvé and D. Schwanen, *Investment and the Global Economy* (Toronto: C.D. Howe Institute, 1996), p. 4.

8   D. Ricardo, *On the Principles of Political Economy and Taxation*, first printed in 1817.

9   Besides Ricardo, major contributions to the theory of international trade include Adam Smith's *The Wealth of Nations*, 1776; the Heckscher-Ohlin-Samuelson model in P. Samuelson, "The Gains from International Trade Once Again," *Economic Journal* 72 (1962): 820–29; J. Bhagwati and V. Ramaswami, "Domestic Distortions, Tariffs, and the Theory of Optimal Subsidy," *Journal of Political Economy* 71 (1963): 44–50; J. Grandmont and D. McFadden, "A Technical Note on Classical Gains from Trade," *Journal of International Economics* 2 (1972): 109–125.

10 B. Frey *et al.* suggest that "95 percent of economists questions in the United States (and 88 percent of economists surveyed in the United States, Austria, France, Germany and Switzerland) support or support with qualification the proposition that "tariffs and import quotas reduce general economic welfare." Quoted in D. Irwin, *Against the Tide* (Princeton, NJ: Princeton University Press, 1996), p. 3.

11 Irwin, *Against the Tide*, p. 8

12 J. Frankel, "Integrating Transportation and Geography into Trade Analysis," in W. Coyle and N. Ballenger, eds., *Technological Changes in the Transportation Sector: Effects on US Food and Agricultural Trade* (Washington DC: Economic Research Service, USDA, 2000).

13 For a wonderful perspective on the issue of transportation costs, see M. Gehlhar, "Incorporating Transportation Costs into International Trade Models: Theory and Application," US Department of Agriculture, 2001.

14 Government of Canada, Transport Canada, "Transportation and Trade" <www.tc.gc.ca/pol/en/anre2000/tc0008be.htm> Visited 8 Dec. 2002.

15 For instance, see the World Bank study by D. Dollar and A. Kraay, "Trade, Growth and Poverty" (Washington, DC: World Bank, June 2001). While this article remains the most often quoted reference on the relationship between trade and economic growth, note that it has also come under severe criticism by other economists, notably D. Rodrik, "Comments on 'Trade, Growth and Poverty,' by D. Dollar and A. Kraay," Oct. 2001, Harvard University. These criticisms notwithstanding, most economists agree that free trade does support income gains and economic growth. See, for instance: J. Frankel and D. Romer, "Trade and Growth: An Empirical Investigation," NBER Working Papers 5476 (National Bureau of Economic Research, Inc., 1996); J. Bhagwati, "Trading for Development: Poor Countries *Caveat Emptor*," *The Economist* 20 June 2002, <http://www.columbia.edu/~jb38/paper2001/Economist%20June%2010%20Revised%20Final.pdf>; D. Irwin, *Free Trade Under Fire* (Princeton: Princeton University Press, 2002); J. Stiglitz, *Globalization and its Discontents* (New York: Norton, 2002).

16 See the WTO's web site, <www.wto.org>

17 See the World Bank's web site, <www.worldbank.org>

18 See the IMF's web site, <www.imf.org>

19 For further reading, see M. Hart, *Fifty Years of Canadian Tradecraft: Canada at the GATT 1947–1997* (Ottawa: Centre for Trade Policy and Law, 1998).

20 US dollars. ABC News, "EU calls for UN weapons inspectors to return to Iraq," 21 Sept. 2002. <http://abc.net.au/news/2002/08/item20020831082646_1.htm>

21 R. Jones and P. Kennan, eds., *Handbook of International Economics*, *Vol. 1* (Amsterdam: Elsevier Science Publishers, 1984), pp. 586–587.

22 G. Harrison *et al.*, "Trade Liberalization, Poverty and Efficient Equity," World Bank working paper (Washington, DC: 2001). Quoted in Irwin, *Free Trade Under Fire*, p. 31.

23 World Trade Organization web site, <www.wto.org/english/thewto_e/whatis_e/10ben_e/10b06_e.htm> Visited 17 Sept. 2002.

24 Irwin, *Free Trade Under Fire*, p. 31.

25 Irwin, *Free Trade Under Fire*, p. 38.

26 Irwin, *Free Trade Under Fire*, p. 34. He adds, in a footnote, "Economists are just beginning to estimate the gains from the introduction of new goods. Hausman (1997) estimated that the total consumer surplus generated by introducing Apple Cinnamon Cheerios was about $78 million per year, a substantial amount for a good for which many close substitutes already exist. Petrin (2001) finds that the total consumer welfare gain from the introduction of the minivan was $367 million in 1984, or $2.8 billion in consumer surplus over the 1984-88 period."

27 World Bank, *World Development Report 2001* (Washington, DC, 2001).

28 UNCTAD *Trade and Development Report*, 1999. Cited by the World Development Movement, October 2002.

29 Total development assistance transfers, 2000: $136 billion. OECD Development Assistance Committee, *International Development Statistics*, "Disbursements and Commitments of Official and Private Flows (Table 1)."

chapter
THREE

The Dangers of Market Fundamentalism

In Chapter 2, we saw the truly amazing potential of international trade to enrich us. As this potential became increasingly clear over the last half century, more and more countries opened their markets to trade. When the General Agreement on Tariffs and Trade was originally created in 1947, just nine countries signed on. By 1995, when the WTO was created, 128 countries joined, and the total continues to grow. With the addition of China and Taiwan in 2001, almost five billion people live in WTO-member countries—over 80 per cent of the world's population.[1]

This kind of popularity among policy makers does not come without reason. History suggests that countries that have succeeded in increasing international trade relative to the size of their economy have had stronger growth than those that have not.[2] As developing countries around the world watched the GATT members grow more prosperous, some decided that international trade was essential to their own success. The classic example of this is a small group of East Asian countries known as the "Asian Tigers."

THE RISE OF THE ASIAN TIGERS

Four countries are known as the "Asian Tigers": South Korea, Hong Kong,* Taiwan, and Singapore. After World War II, these countries made a conscious decision to promote domestic industries that would focus on

---

* Strictly speaking, Hong Kong was not a sovereign country in the twentieth century. Still, it operated primarily as an independent economy. For the sake of simplicity, it will be referred to as a country in this description.

exporting their products overseas. They did this with huge success; for several decades they achieved enormous economic growth, often increasing their GDP by 10 per cent or more each year. As a result, many free-trade advocates now point to the Asian Tigers as "proof" that free-market policies, especially unbridled free trade, generate huge economic rewards. Unfortunately for them, history does not support this claim.

The Asian Tigers did not dive into free trade head first, making the sweeping tariff reductions that free-trade advocates love.[3] Instead, they used subsidies, carefully planned incentives, and *targeted* tariff reductions to encourage trade. The Asian Tiger governments used subsidies (i.e., government funding) to import technology from overseas and keep corporate tax rates low. They also kept tariffs high in some industries, so that the Asian companies wouldn't have to face foreign competition. As a result, these industries flourished, and they were soon selling their products all around the world. As an economic policy, it was a huge success—but it was certainly *not* free trade. Free trade does not involve government subsidies or high tariffs to protect industries. People who point to the Asian Tigers as "proof" that unbridled free trade works often conveniently omit this part of the story.[4]

The main reason that the Asian economies did so well (at least until 1997, when many of them experienced a severe economic crisis) was that they were able to specialize in areas of their economy where they could become increasingly productive over time. Unfortunately, unbridled free trade does not always allow a country—especially a small country—to do this. In the next chapter, we will see how free trade could push a country toward specializing in industries that offer little hope for economic growth.

WHAT ARE FREE-MARKET POLICIES?

Most academic economists couch their support for free trade in terms of a broader set of economic policies, because they know that unbridled free trade is not a perfect policy. Nonetheless, there is an incredibly powerful section of the international economic elite that believes, explicitly or implicitly, that unbridled free trade is always a good idea. This belief almost invariably comes with its correlate: that economic markets work best when government stays out of the way. This ideology has come to be known as "market fundamentalism."[5]

Free-market advocates usually push a set of policies that involve as little government involvement in economic affairs as possible. This means that taxes of all sorts are to be kept low. This belief extends to tariffs on international trade, which naturally makes free-market advocates supporters of unbridled free trade as well. Since taxes are low, government spending on social programs must also be minimal: employment insurance, public education, and environmental regulations are all examples of programs that free-market advocates like to see kept to an absolute minimum. Canada's system of universal public health care lies in almost direct opposition to what market fundamentalists would propose.

Most democratic countries have members on the right wing of the political spectrum that urge these kinds of policies in a domestic context, with varying degrees of success. In the governance of international economic affairs, however, free market advocates have considerably more influence. Particularly in large international organizations like the World Bank and the World Trade Organization, market fundamentalists are in positions of great power.

Proponents of free market reforms were especially successful in the 1980s and early 1990s in pushing a fairly radical political agenda. Policy advisors at the World Bank and the IMF formed what is known as the "Washington Consensus" on how countries should conduct their internal affairs.[6] Because most developing countries owed the Bank and the IMF sizeable debts, these institutions had enormous influence over those countries' policies. The Bank and the IMF encouraged developing countries to dramatically reduce their spending on social programs and to sell off many of their national assets. The *privatization* of national energy and water companies often meant that the price of basic services skyrocketed, making them unaffordable to many citizens.[7] Needless to say, this made the World Bank rather unpopular in large parts of the developing world.

The Washington Consensus also encouraged developing nations to move toward unbridled free trade.[8] Countries were often compelled to lower their tariffs so dramatically that local industries that were previously protected from foreign competition soon found themselves on the verge of bankruptcy. Thousands of people found themselves without jobs. Joseph Stiglitz, a Nobel laureate and former chief economist at the World Bank, claims that the policies of the Washington Consensus caused widespread unemployment and social disruption.[9] The speed and manner in which free-trade policies were applied made them deeply destabilizing and harmful for the local population.

Market fundamentalists would like to believe that the countries that have grown economically have done it through unbridled free trade and, conversely, that unbridled free trade always causes economic growth. This is wrong on both counts. Regarding the first part of the myth, the Asian Tigers are perfect examples of countries that have transformed their economies *without* using free trade. Canada, Britain, France, Japan, the US—none of these countries adopted free trade until after they had made significant strides into a developed economy. In fact, no country has *ever* made the transition from developing to industrialized using unbridled free trade as an engine of economic growth.

Free Market Policies Don't Always Work

Let us now turn to the second part of the myth: that free trade is always good for a country's economic growth. The problematic word in this assertion is "always." On the one hand, free trade *can* help economic growth; it might even do so most of the time. Nonetheless, free trade does have the potential to be very destructive. It is ironic, for instance, that Argentina, a country that is mired in economic stagnation and recurring debt crises is the developing country that probably has done the most to adopt the free-market ideology. A full picture of Argentina's troubles would occupy an entire book on its own, but a quick overview of the last two decades of the twentieth century will suffice. Canada, along with most developed countries, posted economic growth for virtually all of the 1980s and 1990s; Argentina was not so fortunate. Argentina's economy shrunk (i.e., had negative GDP growth) in no fewer than eight of the twenty years between 1979 and 1999. In 1979, Argentina's debt to the World Bank was $367 million, but by 1999 that debt had skyrocketed to $8.3 billion. Unemployment rose equally dramatically, from 2.3 per cent in 1980 to 16 per cent in 1996.[10]

In 1991, Argentines elected Carlos Menem as their president. Menem broke with his election promises and set out to implement free-market reforms: he raised taxes, cut government spending, clamped down on inflation, and "privatized almost everything the state owned."[11] Notably, Argentina moved toward unbridled free trade by cutting tariffs and import restrictions. Menem also restructured the country's debt, but instead of reducing Argentina's debt service, its payments actually tripled.[12] By 1999, Argentina was paying one in every ten dollars it earned to its creditors— mainly the wealthy nations and investors of the world.

While these free-market policies seemed to work for a little while, they failed completely in 2000, when economic growth plummeted and the Argentine peso lost half of its value overnight. Millions of people's savings were wiped out. Finally, in 2002, Argentina defaulted on its $155-billion public debt, the largest default by any country in history. Even *The Economist*, normally a proponent of free-market policies, admitted, "Argentina was one of Latin America's ... leading free-market reformers. [Now, however,] there are no good options. But the worst is to deny that current policies have failed."[13] Clearly, free-market policies—which promote unbridled free trade and reduce government spending—are not always appropriate.

Unfortunately, Argentina is not alone. Free-trade advocates pushed the Washington Consensus economic formula around the world in the 1990s, and many countries bought in, Zambia being one of them. Weary of the country's big-government approach, in 1991 Zambians elected Frederick Chiluba, who had campaigned on a platform of economic reform. Virtually overnight, Chiluba rushed toward unbridled free trade, eliminated subsidies to farmers, and began to charge user fees for public schools and clinics. Free-market policies devastated Zambia's manufacturing base, eliminating 325,000 manufacturing jobs, almost half of those available in 1990. Chiluba inherited an economy that included more than 140 textile firms when he took office; today, the industry has been whittled to fewer than eight.[14] GDP growth was feeble in the 1980s, averaging just 1.6 per cent per year; under Chiluba in the 1990s, it was even lower, just 1.2 per cent per year.[15] Free-market policies actually lowered the average income per person. The government is buried in more debt than it can repay. Free trade is gradually replacing Zambia's full-time workforce with a growing "informal" economy that offers low wages, no benefits, and no job security.

Zambia and Argentina are inconvenient facts in the story that free-trade ideologues like to tell. For instance, the Fraser Institute (Canada's right-wing policy group) published this statement in February 2001: "Now, poverty is decreasing and democracy increasing in all nations which have embraced market reforms."[16] This claim is absurd; even as the Fraser Institute published that sentence, the Argentine economy was in full meltdown. Unfortunately, quite a few nations that embraced market reforms have come to economic ruin and rapidly *increasing* poverty.

The truth is that unbridled free trade is not a good idea for all countries in all circumstances. Can trade liberalization promote economic efficiency? In principle, certainly. But as history demonstrates time and time again, trade liberalization does not necessarily lead to economic development. Often it is development that leads to expanded trade, not the other way around.

Correlation is not Causation

The Economist consistently provides high-quality economic and policy analysis, making it probably the most widely read policy journal in the world. It offers excellent coverage of domestic politics in dozens of countries and the international relations between them. However, it does have a significant bias: it is a strong advocate of free trade. To its credit, it is open about this attitude in its editorial policy. Nonetheless, it can lead to a skewed perspective on the world.

In its issue of December 8, 2001, *The Economist* published a rather misleading article. It is worth quoting the abstract in its entirety:

> Opponents of globalization claim that poor countries are losers from global integration. A new report from the World Bank demolishes that claim with one simple statistic. With globalization measured simply as a rise in the ratio of trade to national income, it is seen that more globalized poor countries have grown faster than rich countries, while less globalized countries have seen income per person fall.[17]

The article notes that increased economic growth accompanies (or is *correlated* with) increased trade. That observation leads it to conclude that trade must *cause* growth. In fact, this is a classic mistake: correlation is not causation. For instance, suppose a woman crosses the street to the corner where her friend is standing. There is a correlation between the spot where her friend is standing and the fact that she crossed the street at that point. Perhaps her friend *caused* her to come over at that point—by waving to her across the street. But this is not the only possible explanation: perhaps she was going to come over anyway, to buy something at the corner store. Or perhaps there was *reverse causation*: when her friend saw her crossing the street, the friend moved to meet her.

In much the same way, the World Bank's statistic gives an unbiased reader no reason to think that free trade is working: yes, trade *might* be causing growth, but not necessarily. Perhaps it is the other way around: economic growth could be causing the increased international trade. After all, trade is a natural by-product of a healthy economy. In fact, it would be surprising to find that countries that had significant growth over the last few decades did not increase their international trade. Another alternative is that some other factor (say, national peace and stability, or corruption-free government) could cause both the economic growth and the rise in trade. *The Economist* is jumping to conclusions.

More important, even if one thinks that international trade does help economic growth, there is still no reason to think that governments ought to adopt unbridled free-trade policies.[18] The Asian Tigers are perfect examples of countries that increased their international trade to spur economic growth *without* using free-trade policies. The Asian countries' path to industrialization is an excellent reminder of the economic importance of *social* policies, particularly public education.[19]

The Economist's article makes a mockery of the anti-globalist position. Most people who protest the WTO are not opposed to international trade; they are opposed to the manner in which that trade is being conducted. "*Fair* trade, not free trade" is a common slogan. This makes it explicit that most social activists are not opposed to some international trade or economic growth. Rather, they are typically interested in ensuring that trade policies are managed, such that we do not harm the environment, reinforce corporate political power, or unfairly disadvantage local industries. The World Bank's single statistic certainly does not "demolish" these arguments. The mistake in *The Economist*'s argument is admittedly subtle, which many casual readers would not even notice. For a magazine that purports to deliver objective and rational policy advice, however, it is an astonishing lapse in judgment. *The Economist* allowed its bias toward unbridled free trade to blind it to alternative perspectives in this case.

The Dangers of "Cookie-Cutter" Policy Making

A similar bias also appeared in *The Economist*'s coverage of issues such as Argentina's economic crisis. The magazine was slow to recognize

Argentina's danger, and slower still to admit that free-market policies might not have been appropriate. As Argentina adopted free-market policies in 1992, the magazine called the economy minister a "miracle man."[20] The same article argued that, in the short-term, "Argentina's new policies will cause some pain, but the longer-term gains could be huge." In 1998, as economic crisis loomed, *The Economist* wrote, "By rights, Argentina should be looking forward to a period of prosperity and political tranquility, the reward of almost a decade of radical free-market reforms and a broad consensus about maintaining them."[21]

As the crisis bloomed, *The Economist* asked, "In the 1990s, Argentina was Latin America's star. How did it become a basket case?"[22] Even as late as 2001, the magazine was reluctant to give up on free-market policies, in particular unbridled free trade. They argued that Argentina's major free trade agreement, MERCOSUR, was good for the region: "MERCOSUR may drift into irrelevance. ... That would be a shame. Increased trade and political co-operation between MERCOSUR's members have bolstered stability, democracy and economic reform in the region over the past ten years. All would benefit if the integration continued."[23] Still reeling from the failure of the free market reforms, *The Economist*'s editors seemed keen to pin the blame somewhere else.

In all fairness, the power of hindsight makes it tempting to be overly critical of *The Economist*'s coverage of Argentina. The truth is that few observers, if anyone, foresaw Argentina's economic demise. Nonetheless, the lesson is that free-market policies that work in rich countries rarely, if ever, translate easily onto developing countries. It took decades—perhaps even centuries—for countries like Canada, Britain, and the US to build up the culture and institutional support for well-developed market economies. One cannot simply graft free-market policies onto developing countries and expect them to work. Canadian political economists Daniel Drache and Sylvia Ostry frame the issue well. While "the model is clear—the vibrant, resilient economy of the United States of America—there is no real understanding of 'how to get there from here,' where the initial conditions of 'here' are often those of a destitute, failed or geographically isolated economy."[24] They add, in a footnote: "In this regard, it is apposite to note that the United States reached its current position with a historical institutional framework that only gradually evolved into its current form."

Drache and Ostry suggest that advocates of unbridled free trade cause damage because they lack any clear understanding of nation building.

However, some activists argue that the truth is much more malicious. Ralph Nader's group, Public Citizen, suggests that the current international trade regime is deliberately designed to prevent developing countries from achieving the same economic status as rich countries. "We are pulling up the ladder on policies the developed countries used to become rich," says Lori Wallach, the director of Public Citizen's Global Trade Watch.[25] One can only hope that if this dark view of globalization is correct, it can be changed before it is too late. .

In any case, the precise formula for building a peaceful, prosperous, cooperative national culture remains a mystery. One thing is certain: "cookie-cutter" policy making, which blindly transfers free-market policies from rich countries to poor ones, is a recipe for failure. It is an inherently dangerous business, and market fundamentalists who practise it should rethink their approach.

Big-Country vs. Small-Country Economics

Orthodox economic theories were created mainly for large, open economies, like those of the US and Europe. As we have seen, these theories often fail when applied to developing countries. Even rich but economically small countries like Canada do not always fit the standard theories. Canada's small size and its dependence on international trade make it far more vulnerable to the bumps and shocks of the international economic system than large countries. Canadian political scientist Marjorie Cohen writes, "The extroverted nature of the economy has made Canada extremely vulnerable to external forces. When things go wrong ... the impact on Canada can be extreme."[26]

Standard economic models assume that countries have sufficient size and diversity to smooth out external shocks in the international economic regime. However, as globalization amplifies the size of those shocks, few economies are sufficiently large to withstand the jolts. The Asian Tigers found this out the hard way when their economies suddenly spiralled into crisis in 1997. Other countries, like Argentina, Brazil, even once-mighty Russia, have had a hard time maintaining stability. In the new world of globalization, Canada is not so big economically that it can ignore the dangers of unbridled free trade. Indeed, as later chapters will show, the distinction between small- and large-country economics has profound implications for national culture, the environment, and immigration.

MOVING BEYOND THE NUMBERS

In many ways, standard economics does not provide us with enough information to make good decisions about our country. For instance, consider the ubiquitous economic indicator Gross Domestic Product. Widely quoted in the media as the barometer of the Canadian economy, no other number is so important for our national politics. If GDP is rising, we happily conclude that our country must be heading in roughly the right direction; if GDP is falling, we demand change. It has become the scoreboard for our nation. Seldom do we stop to think about what GDP really means, and whether it is measuring progress in a true sense.

If we step back, however, we start to see what we are missing. GDP is actually a very limited indicator: it measures market activity, or money changing hands. As such, it misses some of our most important activities: leisure time, volunteer work, family support, and home care. Consider the man who works fourteen-hour days to raise his income, but loses all of his free time in the process. His contribution to our national GDP is rising with his salary, but economists do not measure the loss of his leisure time. Indeed, when the stress drives him to psychological counselling, the GDP swells due to the cost of the therapy—and this counts as progress?

A small organization of economists called Redefining Progress is challenging this traditional view of GDP. They point out that simply measuring market activity is an inaccurate way of measuring true costs and benefits to our society: "The GDP not only masks the breakdown of the social structure and the natural habitat upon which the economy—and life itself—ultimately depend; worse, it actually portrays such breakdown as economic gain."[27] Take pollution, for instance. Not only does GDP fail to account for the cost of waste when it is produced, pollution actually *adds* to the GDP when we spend money to clean it up. If we view GDP growth as unambiguously good, we ignore the perversity of situations like these.

Those who truly understand the limitations of GDP have been deeply concerned about its use for a very long time. Simon Kuznets, the Nobel-Prize winning economist who invented the modern GDP, was among the first to express his reservations. When he introduced his notion of the GDP to the US Congress in 1934, he tried to warn them of its limitations. "The welfare of a nation," his report concluded, can "scarcely be inferred from a measurement of national income as defined above."[28] As time went on, Kuznets' concern about the GDP deepened. By 1962, he believed that the national accounting needed to be fundamentally rethought. "Distinctions must be kept in mind between quantity and quality of growth, between its costs and return, and between the short and the long run," he wrote. "Goals for 'more' growth should specify more growth of what and for what."[29]

Despite the obvious limitations of GDP, economists resist attempts to replace it. They argue that a measure of national progress must be scientific and value-free. In their view, a new indicator that measures how the economy actually affects people would involve too many assumptions and value judgments. It is better, they say, to stick with GDP, which for all its faults has acquired an aura of hard-headed empirical science. The economists at Redefining Progress have a compelling reply to this: "Aura notwithstanding, the current GDP is far from value-free. To leave social and environmental costs out of the economic reckoning does not avoid value judgments. On the contrary, it makes the enormous value judgment that such things as family breakdown and crime, the destruction of farmland and entire species, underemployment and the loss of free time, count for nothing in the economic balance. The fact is, the GDP already does put an arbitrary value on such factors—a big zero."[30]

Leading Canadian economists are beginning to recognize that traditional economic metrics are only one part of the social equation.[31] John Helliwell, an economist at UBC, argues that economic circumstances such as personal income are only one factor in our overall well-being—indeed, a relatively small factor. Moreover, by over-emphasizing economic considerations in public policy, governments risk damaging the well-being of the society they serve and represent. Helliwell writes, "It is important for governments, which have an essential role in the maintenance of so many aspects of the social fabric, to avoid needless or heedless damage to these institutions in pursuit of what is called international competitiveness, often sought for its presumed ability to deliver sustained growth in material standards of living. The evidence [suggests] that a balanced evaluation of policies requires a much wider and richer canvas—one that takes full account of the sources of well-being."[32] Helliwell's insight richly deserves the attention that it is getting from Canadian economists and scholars.

Canada needs policies that are driven by principle, not economic indicators. We should be looking at how free trade affects our laws, our democracy, and our well-being. We need a system of trade that preserves our sovereignty, protects our environment, and allows our culture to flourish. We should be building an economy that provides for our society, not the other way around.

CONCLUSION

Advocates of unbridled free trade are prone to making exaggerated claims about the benefits of globalization. Several of their favourite claims are incorrect. First, the idea that the Asian Tigers prove that free trade is the best path for development can be easily refuted: countries like Singapore, South Korea, and Taiwan all used astute government intervention in the market to help their own industrialization. To say that the Asian Tigers used free trade is to ignore the facts of history.

The second false claim is that free-market policies are almost always good for a country's economic growth. Argentina and Zambia are two members of a growing contingent of countries that have struggled to follow free-market policies, only to see disastrous results. The claim that international trade causes economic growth may indeed be correct in some cases, but it cannot be "proved" by a simplistic correlation between the two. This ignores the possibility that, sometimes, it can actually be the other way around: growth causes more trade. The countries that have had some success in implementing free-market policies have done so gradually and carefully, allowing themselves more time to build up institutional support for market forces.

Finally, we should always remember that the numbers game in economics —measuring our success by GDP or the other economic indicators—never tells the whole story. As Simon Kuznets and John Helliwell remind us, we should be more concerned with what our economy does for our well-being than with how much it grows.

NOTES

1   WTO web site, www.wto.org.

2   See the references on trade and economic growth in Chapter 2. Also see Harrison *et al.,* "Trade Liberalization, Poverty and Efficient Equity," World Bank working paper (Washington, DC: 2001).

3   The term "free-trade advocates" is used in this chapter to denote those who support *unbridled* free trade, as distinguished from managed free trade in Chapter 2.

4   Several books and articles have investigated the policies that have led to the economic boom in East Asia. Among them are World Bank, *The East Asian Miracle: Economic Growth and Public Policy* (New York: Oxford University Press, 1993); P. Krugman, "The Myth of Asia's Miracle: A Cautionary Fable," *Foreign Affairs*, Nov. 1994; and J. Stiglitz, "From Miracle to Crisis to Recovery: Lessons from Four Decades of East Asian Experience," in J. Stiglitz and S. Yusuf, eds., *Rethinking the East Asian Miracle* (Washington, DC, and New York: World Bank and Oxford University Press, 2001).

5   The term "market fundamentalism" has gained acceptance since it was used by George Soros in his book, *The Crisis of Global Capitalism: Open Society Endangered* (New York: Public Affairs, 1998).

6   Originally coined by J. Williamson in 1990. In his words, "I originally formulated what I termed the Washington Agenda, or the Washington Consensus, in the background paper for a conference held by the Institute for International Economics in November 1989 which was published as the opening chapter in the conference volume *The Progress of Policy Reform in Latin America* in 1990" (IIE web site). For an updated perspective on the term "Washington Consensus," see J. Williamson, "What Should the Bank Think about the Washington Consensus," Background Paper to the World Development Report 2000, July 1999.

7   For an activist's description of the World Bank's involvement in Bolivia, see <www.globalexchange.org/wbimf/Shultz.html>. For a more academic description (though still highly activist in character), see Stiglitz, *Globalization and its Discontents.*

8   The Washington Consensus had additional tenets, beyond privatization and unbridled free trade. These included promoting deregulation, fiscal austerity and a strong, stable currency (usually entailing high interest rates).

9   J. Stiglitz, *Globalization and its Discontents*, p. 20. Also see J. Stiglitz, "Democratizing the International Monetary Fund and the World Bank: Governance and Accountability," *Governance* 16.1(2003): 111–139.

10   *World Development Indicators, 2001.*

11   "A Decline without Parallel," *The Economist* 2 March 2002: 26–28.

12   In 1979, Argentina's debt service was 3.2 per cent of GDP; in 1999, it was 9.3 per cent. *World Development Indicators, 2001.*

13   *The Economist* 3 Nov. 2001: 11–12.

14   J. Jeter, "The Dumping Ground," *Washington Post* 22 April 2002. <http://www.globalpolicy.org/globaliz/econ/2002/0422ground.htm>

15 *World Development Indicators 2001.*

16 F. McMahon, "The Debate over Free Trade," *Saint John Telegraph-Journal* and *New Brunswick Telegraph-Journal* 15 Feb. 2001.

17 "Going Global; Globalisation and Prosperity," *The Economist* 8 Dec. 2001: 87.

18 To be fair, *The Economist* article did not explicitly argue that free-trade policies were leading to economic growth. The article did, however, claim that the data "demolished" the anti-globalists' arguments. Since anti-globalists typically oppose free-trade policies, the inference is reasonable. It is also consistent with other articles that *The Economist* has published.

19 A. Sen, "Beyond the Crisis: Development Strategies in Asia," Second Asia and Pacific Lecture, Singapore, 12 July 1999. See also the references on the East Asian miracle cited above, particularly World Bank, *The East Asian Miracle: Economic Growth and Public Policy* (New York: Oxford University Press, 1993).

20 "Argentina's Economy: Nearly Time to Tango," *The Economist* 18 April 1992: 17–19.

21 "Clouds over Argentina," *The Economist* 4 July 1998: 29–30.

22 "A Decline without Parallel."

23 "Another blow to Mercosur," *The Economist* 4 May 2001: 32–33.

24 D. Drache and S. Ostry, "From Doha to Kananaskis: The Future of the World Trading System and the Crisis of Governance," proceedings from a conference of the same name, University of Toronto, 1–3 March 2002.

25 T. Rosenberg, "The Free-Trade Fix," *New York Times* 18 Aug. 2002: 28–33, 50, 74–75.

26 M. Cohen, "Exports, Unemployment and Regional Inequality: Economic Policy and Trade Theory," Chapter 4 in D. Drache and M. Gertler, eds., *The New Era of Global Competition* (Montreal & Kingston: McGill-Queen's University Press, 1991), p. 85.

27 C. Cobb, *et al.*, "If the GDP is Up, Why is America Down?" *The Atlantic* Oct. 1995. <http://www.theatlantic.com/politics/ecbig/gdp.htm>

28 Cobb, *et al.*, "If the GDP is Up."

29 Cobb, *et al.*, "If the GDP is Up."

30 Cobb, *et al.*, "If the GDP is Up."

31 For further reading on this topic, see the work done by the Centre for the Study of Living Standards, especially L. Osberg and A. Sharpe, "Trends in Economic Well-Being in Canada in the 1990s," in K. Banting, *et al.*, *The Review of Economic Performance and Social Progress*, vol. 1, June 2001.

32 J. Helliwell, *Globalization and Well-Being* (Vancouver: UBC Press, 2002), p. 53.

FOUR

Learning and the Risks of Specialization

Managed free trade has enormous potential to benefit our national economy. The previous chapter, however, reminded us that free trade is not always as successful as it might look on paper. Unfortunately, countries that rush into unbridled free trade can do serious damage to their national economies, from which it takes generations to recover. This chapter will illustrate how comparative advantage can encourage a country to specialize in an industry that offers little hope for economic growth. Even though specialization might offer economic rewards in the short term, it can hurt long-term development.

COMPARATIVE ADVANTAGE, REVISITED

Recall from the example in Chapter 2 how Thailand and the US set up a free trade agreement to increase their total production of cars and wheat. Since the US has a comparative advantage in car manufacturing and Thailand has a comparative advantage in growing wheat, each country specializes in the production of the good over which it has an advantage. By specializing in this way and trading internationally, each country ends up with a greater amount of wealth than it would have on its own.

Instead of talking about the US and Thailand, let us consider a more personal example. Think of a law firm with just two people: the senior partner Susan, and her junior partner, Jake. They are trying to use the concept of comparative advantage to increase their total revenue.

Susan is a senior lawyer with talent and experience both in courtroom arguments as well as legal research. Jake, though a promising young lawyer himself, is not as productive as Susan either in the courtroom or in the research library. This gives Susan an absolute advantage over Jake in both courtroom skills and research. Nonetheless, Jake has a comparative advantage, just as we saw that Thailand could have a comparative advantage even though it had no absolute advantage. In relative terms, Jake is better at researching, and Susan is better in the courtroom.

Jake's law-school debts are weighing on his mind. He wants to start a family, but his salary is already stretched pretty thin. Susan suggests that they could use specialization to improve their revenue. Susan would specialize in attracting clients and making the main courtroom arguments; Jake would specialize in researching the cases and handling the legal business behind the scenes. By specializing, Jake could bring home a bigger paycheque right away.

Some numbers will help illustrate the point. In Table 4a ("Before Specializing"), Jake and Susan each spend half of their time researching and half of their time in the courtroom. The table shows the amount of money that each person earns for their firm during a day; so for instance, Jake makes $100 while researching for half of the day, and another $80 during his court appearances, for a total income of $180 per day.

In Table 4b, Susan and Jake agree to specialize. As expected, their total income goes up, from $600 to $640. This extra $40 is considered the *gains from trade*, which in this case are divided evenly between Jake and Susan. They each take home $20 more per day than they did before. This is just like free trade: because of the gains from trade, each person—or each country—has more money than before. (Of course, in the real world, the gains from trade are not always split equally. We'll come back to that in Chapter 6.)

TABLE 4a :: The Effects of Specialization Over time (before specializing)

	RESEARCH	COURT	TOTAL ($ PER DAY)
Jake	$100	$80	$180
Susan	$200	$220	$420
TOTAL INCOME	$600		
Jake's Share	30%		
Susan's Share	70%		

TABLE 4b :: The Effects of Specialization Over Time (Specialization in Year One)			
	RESEARCH	COURT	TOTAL ($ PER DAY)
Jake	$200	$0	$200
Susan	$0	$440	$440
TOTAL INCOME	**$640**		
Jake's Share	**31.25%**		
Susan's Share	**68.75%**		

Jake and Susan have a "free trade agreement"; each of them specializes in one legal service. After a while, Jake and Susan find that they each improve at their task. Jake is spending a lot more time in the legal library now, and he can find information faster than before. Susan, too, is improving: the time she spends in the courtroom helps her make more compelling arguments to the judge and jury. Additionally, she is often at the courthouse, and her high profile allows her to attract more clients. All of this means more money for Jake and Susan's law firm.

Unfortunately, this new affluence does not necessarily mean that Jake is better off than he would have been had he not specialized according to his comparative advantage. Jake is a young, promising lawyer, but by spending all of his time in the legal library, he never gets the chance to learn how to be a truly great lawyer. In fact, his skills in the courtroom are languishing due to lack of practice. As he looks back over time, he realizes that maybe the choice to specialize as a researcher for his law firm wasn't such a great idea after all. If Jake wants to really increase his income, he might be better off splitting his time between the library and the courtroom, and learn to improve his overall performance as a lawyer.

Consider Jake and Susan's law firm a year after they make their trade agreement (Table 4c). Jake learns to be a better researcher, so his productivity improves by 10 per cent. Susan, however, is really making a name for herself in the town, and her services are in such high demand that she can raise her legal fees by 50 per cent. (For a lawyer, the library just isn't where the money is.) With both Jake and Susan improving their skills, their business has never been better.

TABLE 4c :: The Effects of Specialization Over Time (Specialization in Year Two)			
	RESEARCH	COURT	TOTAL ($ PER DAY)
Jake	$220	$0	$220
Susan	$0	$660	$660
TOTAL INCOME	$880		
Jake's Share	25% or $220		
Susan's Share	75%		

Jake is unhappy. Even though his income is now $220 per day, better than the $200 per day he was making in the previous year, and far better than the $180 per day he was making before he and Susan decided to specialize, something is nagging him. He can't help feeling that while their law firm is getting better and better, his own share of the profits is getting worse. Is he wrong to feel this way?

TABLE 4d :: The Effects of Specialization Over Time (Year Two without specialization)			
	RESEARCH	COURT	TOTAL ($ PER DAY)
Jake	$110	$120	$230
Susan	$220	$330	$550
TOTAL INCOME	$780		
Jake's Share	29.5% or $230		
Susan's Share	70.5%		

Jake does a few calculations, shown in Table 4d. He tries to work out what he would have made if he had never agreed to trade services with Susan and specialize on legal research. As he looks over the numbers, he realizes that if he had worked on his courtroom skills, he could be on his way to being a big-name lawyer like Susan. Even though the total income for the firm would not be as high as it was with specialization (only $780 per day, as opposed to $880 per day), his own income would have been higher. While he specializes as a legal researcher, he makes only $220; but if he were spending part of his time working in the courtroom, and learning at the same rate that Susan was, his income would be $230 per day. In other words, *the agreement to specialize and trade has cost him money.*

Naturally, this is a troubling realization for Jake. Ten dollars a day is only a little lost income, but it adds up to $2,500 over a year. Moreover, it would only get worse if this kept up in the future. The separation between his actual income and what he could have made would grow: in just five years, he would have lost over $100,000 in potential income.

Taken separately, each step in their trade agreement seems reasonable and fair. Last year, when he and Susan were discussing how to make more money for their law firm, it was clear that they could do better by specializing. This year, both of them improved their skills. Not only did their business become more profitable, but both of them were able to bring home more income than they ever had before. On the surface, it all seems so reasonable. It is only in the last part of the analysis that Jake realizes that he had lost something: his *growth opportunity.*

Understanding how specialization and trade can rob a person—or a country—of this growth opportunity is essential in understanding how free trade can affect our world. Before we look at how this applies to international trade, we should make one clarification about learning under specialization. What if the learning that Jake and Susan do in Year 2 is only possible because of their trade agreement and consequent specialization? If the reason that Jake and Susan get better at their jobs is because they concentrate on their specialties, then Table 4d is a false analogy. It would not be appropriate to consider Jake's learning without specialization, if specialization was the reason he did the learning in the first place.

Everyday experience refutes this objection, however. We are capable of learning to play a sport better, even if we are not a professional player specializing in that sport. We can learn new skills to improve our home, even if we do not specialize in construction. In dozens of ways, we learn without specialization. The same applies to Jake the lawyer: if he had continued going to court, he might have learned as much as Susan, perhaps even more. Specialization is not essential for learning; indeed, it could simply focus our learning in the wrong area.

FREE TRADE AND THE DEVELOPMENT OF FUTURE POTENTIAL

Like Jake the lawyer, countries that are considering free trade should wonder whether they are giving up their own potential for future development. Just as people (usually) become more knowledgeable and productive over the course of their career, countries become more productive, too.

Productivity growth is a term economists use to indicate how businesses learn to make their products more efficiently.* Sometimes an increase in productivity has to do with a change in technology, as when computers were first introduced into the office place. Sometimes an increase in productivity comes from better management, as Henry Ford proved when he pioneered the process of mass production. The economist classifies all of this increased efficiency under the term "productivity growth."

The trouble that Jake faces is that productivity growth is not the same in all fields of human activity. Computer power, for instance, has experienced explosive productivity growth, whereas jobs like school teaching are relatively constant in their efficiency. A country that gave up a high-growth industry (like computers) to specialize in a low-growth industry would be doing serious damage to its long-term interests.

Productivity Growth vs. Short-Term Gains

This is a powerful concern for unbridled free trade. One might defend free trade by arguing that countries that choose to sacrifice long-term growth in favour of short-term gains at least do so of their own free will. In the lawyer example, for instance, Jake entered the specialization agreement because he wanted more money immediately so that he could start a family and pay off his debts. His choice was costly in the end, but perhaps the immediate benefits were worth it. To some extent, this is where the analogy between Jake and a national community breaks down. It might be reasonable to hold an individual accountable for his choice, but countries are different. Countries often face intense pressure to concentrate on short-term goals at the expense of future development. Concentrating on short-term benefits could give help one generation, but impose costs onto future generations.

---

* "Efficiently," in this case, means that more products are created for the same level of input resources.

In Canada, the decade following the Second World War was a period when the public mood favoured immediate economic growth. According to McCall and Clarkson, "continentalist economic views were the accepted Liberal wisdom [after WWII] ... if US companies wanted to come north to sink wells, dig mines, or cut timber, so much the better."[1] At the time, Canada had fresh confidence, and was in a hurry to take its place in the global order.

> Unlike their Swedish or Japanese counterparts—who were encouraging their nationally owned industries to develop sophisticated, competitive products to sell internationally—the Canadian [bureaucrats] felt the start-up costs required to foster a balanced national economy that could compete on its own in world markets were too great to contemplate. Blessed with proximity to the post-war world's most powerful capital market and only industrial giant, they were content to concentrate on the lesser goal of responding to forces driving the American economy by shipping off cheap resources in their unprocessed form.[2]

Whether Canada made the right decision after World War II is a question best left to economic historians. The point is simply that, at times, democracies indulge in activities that provide benefits to the present generation, but which sacrifice potential growth for future generations.

In non-democratic countries, the problem of short-sightedness is usually far worse. Dictators usually have very little interest in developing their country for tomorrow's generation; they want to profit immediately. Many African nations have experienced this: dictators get fabulously wealthy by stripping the country of its economic resources. To take just one example, consider General Sani Abacha of Nigeria. In his short reign from 1993-1998, he repeatedly flouted democratic principles even as he extorted an estimated $1 billion (US) from public funds.[3]

Small countries are particularly susceptible to the dangers of specialization. If a large country makes a mistake, it is well protected by the sheer size of its economy. A sector within a large economy that is not doing well will be balanced by another sector with superior performance. In a small country, however, this is not true. A small country that specializes in an industry is more liable to be putting all of its eggs in one basket. The fact that a country is free to make an unwise choice about its trade policy is an unfortunate fact of life. There is no practical remedy; we do not have a world parental figure to correct a nation when it makes a mistake, nor would we want one. Nonetheless, the lesson that economic specialization carries considerable risks is an important one. Economists often neglect it in the discussion about free trade. Canada must remember that even if free trade offers to make our economy more efficient in the short term, that will not necessarily help us in the long run. Knowing this, we should not rush to increase our economic specialization.

AFRICA: THE DARK SIDE OF SPECIALIZATION

So how serious is this concern? We have seen how a trade agreement that appears beneficial may actually be damaging in the long term. At present, it is too early to tell what the long-term effects of recent free trade agreements will be. The WTO and NAFTA were formed in the mid-1990s, and many of their key provisions are being phased in over a ten-year period. The world economy is still adjusting to the new terms of trade; however, there are already early warning signs.

Many developing countries took advice from free-trade advocates like the World Bank and the IMF in the 1990s. These "experts" on international economics thought that free trade could be rushed into developing countries, and that it would spur growth. And perhaps it has—but not for the developing world. The new international trade rules in the 1990s increased world income by over $500 billion (US), according to the World Trade Organization.[4] Unfortunately, virtually none of that has made its way to sub-Saharan Africa; the World Bank reports that per-capita income in this area has continued to fall over the same period.[5] Worse still, Africa's specialization in agriculture may be costly in terms of potential for future growth.

Like many developing regions, West Africa is increasingly dependent on agricultural exports to earn foreign currency. Sadly, little of this money benefits the lives of the local people; most of the foreign currency is used to pay the interest on Africa's enormous foreign debt. Consider the contrast between Africa and the industrialized world: just 2.8 per cent of GDP comes from agriculture in rich countries,[6] compared to 21.8 per cent in sub-Saharan Africa.[7] The number of agricultural workers in West Africa increased by over 20 per cent between 1985 and 1995.[8]

Unfortunately, agricultural work in Africa is hardly a growth industry. While half of the countries in West Africa posted productivity growth between 1970 and 1993, the other half of the countries posted no gains or even significant *losses*.[9] On average, the countries of West Africa saw essentially no per-capita productivity growth in agriculture over more than two decades. By comparison, worker productivity in Canada grew by an average of 1.1 per cent each year over the same period, adding up to 30 per cent over the two decades.[10] Even within Canada, however, farmers experienced average productivity growth below the industrial average. Canadian farmers were becoming more productive at just half the rate of the automotive industry in Ontario; in the US, farmers posted productivity gains that were just a third of those in industrial machinery.[11] Clearly, it matters which sector you work in. To make matters worse, the commodities that Africa exports are declining in value. The *New York Times* reports,

> The commodities that poor countries are left to export are even more of a dead end today than in the 1950's. Because of oversupply, prices for coffee, cocoa, rice, sugar and tin dropped by more than 60 percent between 1980 and 2000. Because of the price collapse of commodities and sub-Saharan Africa's failure to move beyond them, the region's share of world trade dropped by two-thirds during that time. If it had the same share of exports today that it had at the start of the 1980's, per capita income in sub-Saharan Africa would be almost twice as high.[12]

Agriculture is not necessarily a hopeless sector, doomed to lose its value. Africa's poor performance in the agricultural sector is only a symptom of much deeper problems, not the least of which are war, dictatorship, and the AIDS pandemic. Unbridled free trade and specialization in low-growth sectors have only deepened Africa's troubles.

Historically, the sectors that rely heavily upon technology and an educated workforce are ones that have the greatest opportunities for growth. Free trade agreements almost universally encourage high-skilled jobs in rich countries, and low-skilled jobs with low-growth potential (like agriculture, oil extraction, and mining) in the poorer/weaker countries. Regardless of the consequences for future growth potential, free-trade advocates urge the developing countries to specialize in their resource sectors. While free trade might bring success in the short term, it could mean that developing countries specialize in sectors that have weak prospects for long-term growth.

Nor is this situation isolated to West Africa. In the 1990s, Argentina was a "model free-market reformer," according to trade advocates like *The Economist*, but that did not save it from economic stagnation and multiple financial crises. At the same time, Argentina's unbridled free-trade policies eroded its former strength in the manufacturing sector—which, in most countries, is an economic sector with great productivity growth potential. In 1979, Argentina's manufacturing sector accounted for one third (32.7 per cent) of the country's growth, but by 1999, that number had fallen to less than one fifth (18 per cent).[13] Argentina's manufacturing industry is struggling as it faces increasing competition from foreign multinational corporations. As more and more manufacturing firms go out of business in Argentina, the local population has no choice but to try to find jobs in the areas of Argentina's "comparative advantage." Sadly, those industries will likely be ones with little opportunity for productivity growth in the future.

In theory, specialization could offer every country an opportunity to become more efficient. History shows, however, that unbridled free trade can push a country to specialize in an industry that offers little hope for economic growth. If that is the case, a country might be better off without free trade at all.

SPECIALIZATION: AN IRREVERSIBLE PHENOMENON

Some economists would like to argue that even with the potential dangers, free trade is still unambiguously the right decision. After all, if a country really has made the wrong decision about specialization, it can always switch back to being a generalist.

Unfortunately, countries do not have as easy a time "unspecializing" as people do. Economic specialization is similar to scrambling an egg: it is not an easily reversible process. Once foreign competition has eliminated a local industry, it is very hard to rebuild. For instance, the individuals who hold the needed production expertise have gone on to do other kinds of work, or have left the country altogether. Even if the expertise can be found, it is very difficult for an infant industry to break into the world market against the established giants. It could take years for a small country to achieve the same level of efficiency that comes with mass production for international markets. Finding the financial support for an industry in those costly early years would be difficult, no matter how bright the industry's prospects for the future.

A look at Argentina's neighbour, Chile, can teach us some hard facts about free trade. In the last two decades, Chile has become an active participant in the global market, and much of its development has come as a result of foreign investment in its industries. However, recently its leaders have begun to worry that Chile is over-specializing in low-growth potential industries, such as agriculture and resource extraction. Consequently, Chile has launched a well-publicized campaign to diversify its exports, including high-end products such as kiwi fruit and chardonnay wine. Even so, Chile still earns 87 cents of every export dollar from low-value-added products like copper, fish meal, and wood pulp.[14] Once free trade is established, it is very hard to break out of the pattern of producing in low-growth sectors. This leaves future generations with few options.

Countries like Chile, Argentina, and many African nations are in danger of becoming like Jake the lawyer: *trading away their growth opportunity in the future for short-term gains today*. This lesson is crucial for everyone, from business barons to grass-roots activists, who seeks to participate in the globalization debate. Free trade is *not* necessarily good for all—especially if some of those involved are exchanging their future growth potential for today's income.

WHAT CAN BE DONE?

Trade advocates sometimes try to claim that free trade is unconditionally beneficial to all. On the contrary, unbridled free trade can seduce a country with short-term gains, even as the country loses its opportunity for economic growth. Indeed, faced with the risk to future productivity growth, one might be tempted to resist free trade altogether. That would be a mistake: doing so would needlessly forsake the benefits that free trade has to offer. As one trade economist allows, "free trade *may* actually reduce the growth rate,"[15] but "the preponderant evidence on the issue (in the postwar period) suggests that freer trade tends to lead to greater growth after all."[16] So while free trade may not be a panacea for all countries, the evidence suggests that it is indeed helpful to most. Canadians need to consider free trade in light of the balance between the short-term benefits and long-term development. As long as reasonable care is taken to prevent the economy from over-specializing, the benefits of free trade likely outweigh the risks of over-specialization.

Indeed, the Canadian government should resist the temptation to forecast excessively on the growth prospects of particular industries. Some, like James Laxer, have suggested that our government should explicitly focus on industrial "winners" and "losers," and formulate industrial policies designed to boost the former and phase out the latter.[17] History suggests that this sort of policy is virtually always counter-productive. Governments around the world—democratic, communist, and dictatorships alike—have been notoriously bad at selecting "high-growth industries." Latin America is full of examples of countries whose leaders believed they could hand-pick the next big thing in the world of economics. Unfortunately, governments are no more likely to be successful at this than most people are at choosing the next "hot pick" on the stock market—hardly an ideal model of governance.

So the lesson we should take away from our look at the risks of specialization is not that we need to turn away from trade altogether. Instead, it should remind us not to get caught up with those who preach unbridled enthusiasm for economic specialization and trade liberalization. In this chapter, as in each of the following ones, we begin to see that a balanced approach is needed.

NOTES

1 C. McCall and S. Clarkson, *Trudeau and Our Times: The Heroic Delusion*, vol. 2 (Toronto: McClelland and Stewart, 1994), p. 54.

2 McCall and Clarkson, *Trudeau and Our Times*, p. 55.

3 United Nations, "Nigeria: Abacha's son freed, to return over $1 billion," *IRINNews*, 24 Sept. 2002.

4 World Trade Organization. <www.wto.org/english/thewto_e/whatis_e/10ben_e/10b06_ e.htm> Visited 17 Sept. 2002.

5 Jeter, "The Dumping Ground."

6 In this case, "rich countries" refers to the members of the Organization for Economic Cooperation and Development (OECD).

7 B. Barber, *Jihad vs. McWorld* (New York: Random House, 1995), p. 34.

8 United Nations Statistical Yearbook 1994.

9 Benin, Burkina Faso, Cap Verde, Cote d'Ivoire, Niger, Nigeria, and Senegal were the countries that grew. Gambia, Ghana, Guinea, Liberia, and Sierra Leone all posted losses. Guinea Bissau, Mali, Mauritania, and Togo showed no substantial gains. UN Statistical Yearbook 1994.

10 R. Salgado, "Productivity Growth in Canada and the United States," *Finance and Development* Dec. 1997.

11 W. Gu and M.S. Ho, "A Comparison of Industrial Productivity Growth in Canada and the United States" (Ottawa: Industry Canada, and Cambridge, MA: Harvard University Press: 2001), Table 2, p. 9.

12 Rosenberg, "The Free-Trade Fix."

13 *World Development Indicators 2001.*

14 J. Friedland, "Green Chile: Across Latin America, New Environmentalists Extend Their Reach," *Wall Street Journal* 26 March 1997: A1.

15 J. Bhagwati, *Free Trade Today* (Princeton, NJ: Princeton University Press, 2002), p. 41. Italics added.

16 Bhagwati, *Free Trade Today*, p. 42.

17 J. Laxer, *Leap of Faith,* (Edmonton: Hurtig Publishers, 1986), pp. 119–137.

FIVE

THE DANGERS OF PROTESTOR MENTALITY

"NAFTA Costs Us Jobs!"
"Down with the WTO!"
"Free Trade = Death to Medicare!"

When the general public hears about free trade in the media, it is usually because of an anti-globalization protest. For instance, when thousands of social activists shut down the WTO's 1999 meeting in Seattle, media cameras were there to sensationalize the event. Sometimes, public demonstrations have a good effect. They demonstrate that citizens are passionate about a form of globalization that includes social justice. Moreover, they help set the policy agenda for international trade talks. Protestors bring issues to the table, like trade and the environment, that trade bureaucrats simply cannot be trusted to address without a storm of controversy. The trouble with demonstrations, however, is that they can destroy the credibility of legitimate concerns about unbridled free trade. Despite their good intentions, the anti-globalists often make claims that the facts simply do not support. To be fair, a megaphone and a noisy mob makes it easy for anyone to get carried away by their own rhetoric. To gain a real understanding of the globalization debate, we must examine the protestors' rhetoric in light of economic reality.

The case for free trade—managed or otherwise—is based on the economic gains from trade. Chapter 2 showed how trade can lower prices, offer more consumer choice, and generate billions of dollars of economic growth. It is a powerful argument, as most people view higher income, more jobs, and a higher material standard of living as a good thing. Still, there are some who challenge this notion. In fact, probably all of us have wondered at some point whether gathering wealth is really such a good idea, or whether human lives really improved over the last century as our financial means grew. Maybe more wealth *isn't* such a good thing. So it is worth pausing for a moment to examine the usual assumption about wealth accumulation.

Poverty should not be seen through rose-coloured glasses. In the words of John Kenneth Galbraith, "Wealth is not without its advantages, and the case to the contrary, although it has often been made, has never proved widely persuasive."[1] Despite what some protestors say, higher income is a wonderful and enormously important thing for virtually everyone, most especially in the developing world. Some have the romantic vision that poverty is a simpler, easier life; but in reality it leads to horrors such as the death of 25 per cent of children before their first birthday.[2] Higher income leads to better nutrition, better health, greater literacy, and longer life. When so many people on our planet do not even have the basic material conditions from which to escape suffering, economic growth from trade should not be lightly dismissed.

Unfortunately, it is easy to miss how globalization can be used to achieve exactly the kind of aims the anti-globalists themselves desire. It is precisely because we are not mired in poverty that we are able to pursue public health care and education. It is only because we have wealth that we can afford universities, which in turn generate much of the knowledge we need for running water, healthy food, and opportunities beyond the imagination of our ancestors. And it is ironic that anti-globalization protests are made possible only by the quintessential fruits of globalization: the Internet and modern means of transportation.[3]

So let us proceed with the assumption that economic growth is desirable, and that virtually everyone shares this belief at heart. This chapter will look at three common complaints about globalization and free trade, and whether the evidence supports them:

1. Globalization threatens to destroy Canada's government social programs;
2. Free trade has been bad for Canadian labour; and
3. Free trade encourages corporate monopolies.

Having examined these issues, we will step back to examine the anti-globalist movement as a whole, and ask whether it is time for a new vision for the social movement.

DOES FREE TRADE AMERICANIZE OUR GOVERNMENT SOCIAL PROGRAMS?

Protestors frequently voice their fear that globalization will lead to the destruction of Canada's most precious social programs, such as universal health care. As free trade shrinks the importance of national borders, the theory goes, countries will become increasingly similar to one another. Mounting capital mobility and corporate power will mean that governments are unable to raise the tax revenues they need to afford the public programs we hold dear. For Canada, this fear takes a particularly poignant form: free trade will Americanize our country.

Journalists and social commentators from a wide cross-section of political views share this fear. Richard Gwyn of the *Toronto Star* puts it this way: "To make our way in the global world we have little choice but to become more like much of the rest of the world. To exaggerate, but not by that much: In order to compete successfully with a South Korea, say, our wages, social systems and taxation schedules cannot be too different from those of South Korea."[4] The Canadian Labour Congress claims free trade is causing "pressure to harmonize social policies."[5] Maude Barlow of the Council of Canadians writes, "As we predicted during the free-trade debate, it is not possible to harmonize the economic systems of the continent and allow our social and environmental infrastructures to remain intact. ... With cutbacks in social services, education and welfare, we are witnessing nothing short of the Americanization of our social programs."[6] Even *The Economist* agrees: "As the world becomes more integrated, and as capital and labour can move more freely from high-tax countries to low-tax ones, a nation's room to set tax rates higher than elsewhere is being constrained."[7]

William Watson, a leading Canadian economist, debunks these myths.[8] Watson points out that the industrialized countries have moved into progressively deeper integration and greater free trade throughout the post-World War II period. If globalization really has the effects that anti-globalists fear, government spending should be on the decline. In fact, just the oppo-

FIGURE 5a :: A New Framework for Trade
source: Ministry of Finance, Government of Canada

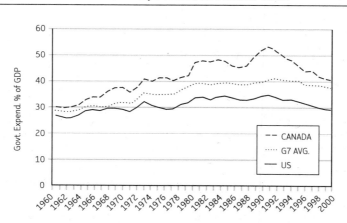

site is true. Government spending rose steadily from 30 per cent of Canada's GDP in 1961 to over 53 per cent in 1992. Watson's analysis uses data that stopped in 1993, just as public spending was at its peak. Since then, government expenditure has fallen to 40 per cent of GDP. Doubtless, this recent decline feels like evidence to anti-globalists: free trade is hurting Canadian social programs. Yet this ignores the broader view of history: the graph in Figure 5a is hardly compelling evidence for that view. Moreover, anti-globalists should not forget that government cutbacks had much to do with Canadian domestic politics, not globalization. In 1993, all of the major political parties were concentrating on how to reduce our rapidly mounting national debt. Much of the decrease in government spending since then has been a part of that effort.

In fact, a comparison between our debt and the American national debt provides more doubts about the anti-globalist position. If the protestors were right, Canada's government finances should be converging to look like American finances. Again, the evidence shows just the opposite. Figure 5b shows that, before 1975, our debt level was approximately the same as that of our neighbours to the south. Since 1975, as international trade intensified, the Canadian debt has risen rapidly, while the American debt level has increased only modestly.[9]

FIGURE 5b :: Total Public Debt

source: Ministry of Finance, Government of Canada

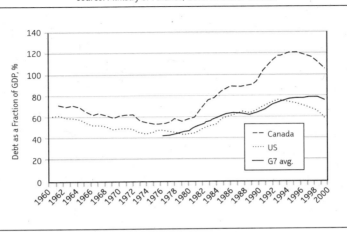

The trend in North America, showing significant government independence, follows the same trend in the Group of Seven (G7) countries.[10] Figure 5c shows the minimum, maximum, and average levels of government spending among the G7. Again, global integration over the last four decades has not led to any uniformity in the countries' approach to government. On the contrary, government spending appears to be diverging over time. Therefore, there is no evidence to support the claim that globalization is forcing our government to behave as a clone of other world governments. The divergence from the American government is particularly robust: despite our proximity, Canada maintains significantly higher levels of taxes and public spending.

Ironically, however, the anti-globalists could be weakening public support for the very social programs they wish to protect. The widespread *belief* that free trade compels our government to cut back on social spending could become a self-fulfilling prophecy. As social activists repeat this argument again and again, it comes to be accepted in the public mind. Conservatives are then able to use this mistaken belief to ratchet down government spending to suit their preferences. One example of this danger is an infamous letter written by Laurent Thibault, the head of the Canadian Manufacturers' Association, to the Minister of Finance in 1988:

FIGURE 5c :: Divergence in G7 Public Spending
source: Ministry of Finance, Government of Canada

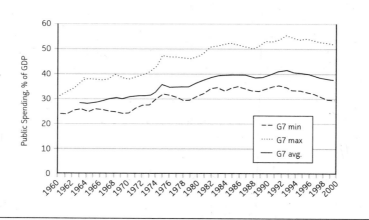

The Canada-US free-trade agreement that we fought hard for creates great opportunities but also makes it more urgent that we tackle the outstanding issues that affect our competitiveness. ... Since Canadian taxes are already high compared to our major competitors, the burden of reducing the deficit must fall largely on cutting expenditures.[11]

When leaked to the public, this letter created a public furor. For those worried about the effect of free trade on Canada's social programs, this letter confirmed their worst fears. Big business was demanding that the government cater to its wishes and Americanize our social programs.

The CMA's letter may have taught corporate lobbyists since then to be more careful with their words. Nonetheless, the belief that higher levels of social spending cannot be maintained in an era of globalization is taking root in the minds of the Canadian public. If social activists really want to protect Canada's most valuable social programs, this belief ought to be resisted, not accepted. Canada can and should maintain programs to educate the public, preserve the environment, and provide universal health care, even in a time of global integration and free trade.

DOES FREE TRADE CAUSE UNEMPLOYMENT?

Another frequent claim is that free trade means job loss for Canadians. The Canadian Labour Congress (CLC) was particularly vehement in its arguments against the North American Free Trade Agreement. The CLC argued that NAFTA has caused a host of social ills, including "skyrocketing unemployment,"[12] economic slowdown, and even child poverty. In March 1998, the CLC ran an article entitled "Canada, Inc.," arguing that free trade had sold Canada's economy down the river. The article was subtitled "US government on slow-track for economic expansion, Canada picks up free trade baton."[13] The CLC made this complaint at the height of the Internet boom and in the middle of the longest period of economic expansion in US history. Canada shared much of this economic success and saw a decade of consistent economic growth. If this is what the CLC considers a "slow-track for economic expansion," what exactly was it hoping for?

The CLC also complained of NAFTA's effect on Canadian unemployment. In 1998, the Congress admitted, "the unemployment rate dropped slightly at the end of 1997 from nine to 8.6 percent. But lest you believe that 'we've seen the worst' of the effects of globalization, corporate restructuring and deficit fighting on job loss in Canada, check out the following partial list of plant and mine closures."[14] The CLC goes on to give a long list of union woes.

Upon further reflection, however, this article is an excellent reminder of how misleading anecdotal evidence can be. Yes, there have been layoffs and plant closures in Canada in the years following NAFTA. But even in the healthiest of economies, there are always layoffs and plant closures. The life cycle of businesses, from birth to death, is in fact a sign of a robust economy. The real question is, what is happening to Canadian unemployment overall? Is free trade preventing Canadians from finding meaningful work?

In the five years since the CLC made its dire prediction, unemployment has hardly "skyrocketed." The CLC noted a dip from 9 per cent to 8.6 per cent unemployment in 1998; six years later, the unemployment rate sat at 7.5 per cent, comfortably continuing the downward trend since NAFTA was implemented.[15] At the tenth anniversary of NAFTA, we were yet to see the doomsday unemployment scenarios predicted by some among the anti-globalization forces. Canadian workers deserve better from union leaders.

If not job loss, then, what about wage loss? Many unions insist that cheap foreign labour is driving down wages here in North America. Economist and international trade expert Jagdish Bhagwati takes issue with unions' desire to portray free trade as the culprit behind declining wages for blue-collar workers. He argues, "instead of hurting real wages of workers, the effect of trade with poor countries is likely to have been even favourable, moderating the decline that would have occurred otherwise from unskilled-labour-saving technical change."[16] Labour unions often claim, for instance, that globalization is causing major corporations to pack up and move to other countries, particularly in the developing world where labour costs are low. Bhagwati argues that this claim "cannot withstand the fact that, during the 1980s, when the pressure on real wages was the most intense, there was also an almost equal *inflow* of DFI [direct foreign investment] into the United States. In fact, that DFI is a two-way street has been very much on the minds of international economists for nearly four decades; and there is no excuse really for having one's eyes trained only on the outflow."[17]

An example helps illustrate the point. *Wall Street Journal* reporters Bob Davis and David Wessel describe a stretch of Interstate 95 going through North Carolina now known as the Autobahn, where several top German multinationals have settled after the region lost textile factories to foreign locations. The low-paying jobs in textiles have vanished, it is true, but the workers have ended up getting paid far more at Siemens and other German firms. The workers are now rooting for globalization, for investment and trade in the global economy.[18] Moreover, economists have found that investing abroad has a positive impact on the wages that a company pays its employees in their own country. One group found that at "companies with global operations, average annual earnings are higher than comparable earnings at either larger or smaller plants without global operations." In fact, "wages for production workers were some 7 percent higher at large plants of companies with global operations, and 15 percent higher at small plants with global operations. ... And the evidence suggests that blue-collar workers actually gain relatively more, on average, from working at plants with global operations than do [white-collar] workers."[19]

Overall, the evidence strongly suggests that international trade is in fact good for national employment rates. Typically, Canadian workers and consumers reap the rewards of free trade without even knowing it. Too often, we hear complaints about trade; it is rare that we celebrate its success.

That is not to suggest, however, that there is no reason to be concerned about the impact of international trade on job quality or security. Even Bhagwati, well known for his advocacy of free trade, admits that the Global Age is "beginning to change the landscape in a way that contributes to job insecurity."[20] This rise in the rate of job turnover, or economic churn, is distinct from the overall employment rate. As the evidence on overall employment suggests, most workers are not permanently forced out of a job. However, the rise in job turnover does have some serious negative effects. Aside from the disruption of benefits like pensions and health coverage, the psychological toll of layoffs is often discounted or ignored by economists. Labour unions do have cause for complaint, after all.

To a significant degree, the erosion of job security stems from foreign competition. Bhagwati calls this competition *kaleidoscopic comparative advantage*, referring to the way in which comparative advantage shifts rapidly between firms and countries in the modern age. In other words, an increasingly integrated global market means that it is difficult for any one firm to hold a competitive edge for a sustained period: "Indeed, the continuing integration of the world's financial markets, and the increased transnationalization of production by multinationals, both important elements in the globalization process, have combined ... to make competition among firms across nations fairly fierce."[21] This fierce competition among economic players has the effect of making the job market increasingly unstable, as companies hire and fire according to their success in global markets.

This job insecurity is particularly acute for older workers, for whom job security was traditionally strong. Labour economists have documented how older, educated workers are experiencing a rising rate of displacement and unemployment.[22] The incentive to lay off these workers comes in part from technological change to which the older employees are not well suited. It is also partially caused by a desire among large companies to "exploit" younger workers by employing them at a stage in their career when their wage is low relative to their productivity. Bhagwati argues that globalization makes it increasingly attractive for large firms to hire young workers and lay them off as they gain seniority (and thus become more expensive).[23] The combination of these factors is making older workers significantly more susceptible to job insecurity and economic churn.

Thus while it is clear that international trade has significant effects on job markets, it is rare that labour unions focus directly on the issues with which they should be most concerned. Too often, labour unions' arguments are based, consciously or unconsciously, on the explicit desire for protection from foreign competition. Giving into anti-trade arguments would cause significant damage to the economy for the sake of a special-interest lobby. Instead, policy makers should focus on mitigating the real impact of globalization on the labour markets, such as its effects on job security.[24]

DOES FREE TRADE ENCOURAGE CORPORATE MONOPOLIES?

Protestors are fond of suggesting that free trade causes increased corporate control in the marketplace. This is particularly disturbing in the media industry, where massive corporate mergers mean that average citizens are getting a progressively narrower editorial perspective in our newspapers and TV broadcasts. The 1990s saw the creation of AOL-Time-Warner, the biggest media corporation in history, which ultimately would control huge swaths of the US market. Here in Canada, the Asper family's control of CanWest and Southam newspapers is equally disturbing.

These are legitimate concerns. As always, however, we need to consider the evidence before pointing the finger to blame free trade. There are good reasons to think that free trade can actually do a great deal to help *break up* corporate monopolies. Managed free trade can introduce foreign competition, resulting in cheaper and higher quality goods for consumers.

The economist Douglas Irwin addresses the question of monopolies and competition in the marketplace:

> There is much better, indeed overwhelming, evidence that free trade improves economic performance by increasing competition in the domestic market. This competition diminishes the [monopoly] market power of domestic firms and leads to a more efficient economic outcome. ... Firms with market power tend to restrict output and rise prices, thereby harming consumers while increasing their own profits. With international competition, firms cannot get away with such conduct and are forced to behave more competitively. After Turkey's trade liberalization in the mid-1980s, for example, price-cost margins fell for most industries, consistent with a more competitive outcome. Numerous studies confirm this finding in

other countries, providing powerful evidence that trade disciplines domestic firms with market power.[25]

As Irwin suggests, international trade can actually help foster competition, which is healthy for the marketplace and good for average citizens.

To see how this works, consider two countries, say Ecuador and Peru. Suppose that both countries initially had high tariffs to protect themselves from foreign competition. This allowed one major corporation in each country to build up a monopoly for a particular product, say bicycles. Perhaps without realizing it, the consumers in Peru and Ecuador are substantially over-paying for their bicycles, and the monopolists are reaping the profits. Now if Peru and Ecuador sign a free trade agreement, life gets tougher for the monopolies and better for consumers. Each company can see that there is money to be made in the other country, so they begin exporting bicycles, and selling them at a slightly lower price to undercut the competition. But because both companies are doing this, a price war ensues, and prices come down in both Peru and Ecuador.

Unfortunately, it may not be obvious to the people of either Peru or Ecuador that free trade has helped them to have cheaper bicycles. What will they hear in the media? Management in the bicycle companies will wail about the effect of foreign competition on their profits and will threaten to cut jobs. Union leaders will complain: their accustomed pay raises will be gone and they may even have to accept wage freezes or even cutbacks. The entire bicycle industry will be outraged by the "unfairness" of free trade.

Compared to this cacophony of complaints, free trade provides a small, unseen benefit to any individual consumer: a few dollars off on a bicycle. Only when one adds up the benefit provided to hundreds of individual consumers does one start to appreciate the economic efficiency of free trade. This is perhaps the single biggest political problem facing free trade: often, the benefits that it provides are very widespread and unseen, whereas the costs it imposes are focused on extremely vocal special interests.[26] Politically, this is usually a recipe for disaster: special interests are able to carry the day, and society as a whole loses as a result.

In sum, free trade does not necessarily lead to greater corporate control in the marketplace. Managed free trade can actually lead to greater competition, more efficiency, lower prices, and increased choice for consumers. Social activists who are wary of corporate power should think twice before condemning international trade.

NEW VISION FOR THE ANTI-GLOBALIST MOVEMENT

Canadian journalist Naomi Klein has become one of the leading voices in the anti-globalist movement. Her articles are syndicated in major newspapers around the world, including the *Guardian* in the UK and the *Globe and Mail* in Canada. The *London Times* described her as "probably the most influential person under the age of 35 in the world."[27] Yet the movement she leads is only a part of the force necessary to move the global trade system toward greater legitimacy and social justice.

In her best-selling book, *No Logo*, she writes that "This book is hinged on a simple hypothesis: that as more people discover the brand-name secrets of the global logo web, their outrage will fuel the next big political movement, a vast wave of opposition squarely targeting transnational corporations, particularly those with very high name-brand recognition."[28] Four years later, it is hard to find compelling evidence to support that hypothesis. Global sourcing of merchandise not only continues, it has become one of the fastest growing businesses strategies of recent years. And as the WTO finally addresses the issue of agricultural subsidies, many of Klein's supporters now wish that trade talks at the WTO would move faster, not more slowly.[29] The "wave of opposition" has not materialized.

Moreover, it is not clear that the protest movement that Klein symbolizes is the one that most Canadians are interested in joining. In 2002 more than 8 out of 10 Canadians agreed that international trade was an essential part of our economy.[30] Canadians *want* the range of products and choices that international trade provides; they *want* the jobs and economic benefits of a globally integrated economy. This suggests that where Canadians have concerns about free trade, they would prefer to see constructive, alternative approaches to our trade policy, rather than the complete reversal of it.

Opposition and protests do serve a purpose. They raise awareness about the importance of working towards justice and legitimacy as the foundations of our international economic system. They help shape a policy agenda that might otherwise be dominated only by corporations and others with narrow economic interests. Awareness and agenda setting, however, are only one half of the equation; they must be coupled with tangible policy proposals and constructive guidance for implementation. It is this latter portion of change that is most challenging, but ultimately the most rewarding.

Our collective challenge is to open up new channels for democratic accountability. For social activists, it is time to engage the public policy process more constructively. Creating new ideas and articulating a new vision for national policy will be far more effective than simply protesting again and again. To be fair, the responsibility lies on both sides of the barricades: policy makers should also consider it part of their job to engage social activists. The importance of forming bridges between those inside and outside the halls of power cannot be underestimated.

There are signs that this is already happening. Many Canadians, and particularly young Canadians, are finding new ways of engaging in the political arena. For instance, *Canada25* is a non-profit, non-partisan organization that is committed to revitalizing the roles of young Canadians in public policy debates.[31] The title of one of their *Globe and Mail* articles—"We're young and we're ready. So listen up"[32]—is characteristic of *Canada25*'s enthusiasm to generate discussion around policy innovation. The group disciplines itself to make its meetings and its publications constructive and action-oriented.

And the result? Policy-makers listen to *Canada25*. The top branch of Canada's civil service, the Privy Council Office, is not merely receptive and respectful of the group's ideas, it actively solicits *Canada25*'s position on future policy. Indeed, the Privy Council has paid *Canada25* to generate policy ideas to guide future policy agendas. Most anti-globalist activists could only dream of such access to policy makers. Yet *Canada25* has accomplished this goal by consistently taking a constructive approach to participatory democracy. Those with concerns about globalization could learn a lot from their example.

Canada25's example drives home another point: forward-thinking activists should take the issue beyond the WTO, the IMF, and the World Bank. These institutions are merely the rudder that guides the international economy. If we are going to be effective in our desire to change direction, it is time we talked to the ship's pilot. The national governments of North America and Europe are the ones that give the orders to the major international institutions.

There will always be a place for protests and demonstration. As long as there is injustice and bureaucratic ineptitude, there will be a need for creating a little havoc. The anti-globalist movement will be transformed, however, when it couples its ability to mobilize people with a credible, constructive vision for a better trade system.

CONCLUSION

Upon reflection, three of the most prominent claims about free trade appear less fearful than many anti-globalists would think. First, free trade has not destroyed Canada's social programs. Second, there is no evidence that free trade causes increased unemployment in Canada. And third, despite what many believe, international trade might actually be a positive force for breaking up corporate monopolies in the market place.

The fact that these arguments are misleading is noteworthy in its own right. However, the real danger of flawed arguments is that they detract from the credibility of much graver concerns about unbridled free trade. Part II of this book highlights some of the social impacts of trade. Trade has an amazing scope of influence: we will look at issues that range from the food we eat to the air we breathe. These are the issues where the Canadian government particularly needs to improve—public policy is perpetually trying to catch up to the complexity of an era of globalization. To manage these issues, we are best served to stay constructive and focus on solutions.

Before we move to the social consequences of free trade, however, we will have a look at economic inequality. This pivotal issue serves as an ideal bridge between the economics and the social aspects of free trade.

NOTES

1 J.K. Galbraith, *The Affluent Society* (Boston: Houghton Mifflin, 1998).

2 UNICEF, *Mortality of Children Under Five—World Estimates and projections 1950–2025* (New York: United Nations, 1988).

3 It is worth noting that this irony also applies to the opposing camp in the trade debate. Market fundamentalists would love to believe that the Internet is a product of free-market enterprise, a natural outgrowth of competitive forces. On the contrary, the Internet was largely developed out of the Pentagon—a government-funded, subsidized institution.

4 Quoted in W. Watson, *Globalization and the Meaning of Canadian Life* (Toronto: University of Toronto Press, 1998), p. 15.

5 "No Success Story," *Morning NAFTA* 12 (June 1998), <www.clc-ctc.ca/publications/morningnafta/june98/june98-1.html>

6 Quoted in Watson, *Globalization and the Meaning of Canadian Life*, p. 16.

7 Quoted in Watson, *Globalization and the Meaning of Canadian Life*, p. 17.

8 Watson, *Globalization and the Meaning of Canadian Life*.

9 Admittedly, during the time that this book was written (2002–2004), this trend was changing. Canadian debt-to-GDP was trending downwards while US debt-to-GDP was trending dramatically upwards, bringing them closer to convergence than had been previously seen. However, it is hard to believe that this convergence is a result of globalization forces. Rather, it has to do with the dramatic changes in tax policy and military expenditures introduced by the administration of George W. Bush.

10 The G7 countries are Canada, the US, the UK, France, Germany, Italy, and Japan. Data taken from the Department of Finance, Canada.

11 Quoted in Watson, *Globalization and the Meaning of Canadian Life*, p. 14.

12 "Nothing for Workers," *Morning NAFTA* (June 1998), <www.clc-ctc.ca/publications/morningnafta/june98/june98-3.html>

13 "Canada, Inc.," *Morning NAFTA* (March 1998), <www.clc-ctc.ca/publications/morningnafta/mar98/mornaftamar98-2.html>

14 "Jobs still going," *Morning NAFTA* (March 1998), <www.clc-ctc.ca/publications/morningnafta/mar98/mornaftamar98-10.html>

15 Statistics Canada, Nov. 2002.

16 Bhagwati, *Free Trade Today*, p. 85.

17 Bhagwati, *Free Trade Today*, p. 87.

18 Bhagwati, *Free Trade Today*, pp. 87–88.

19 T. Moran, *Beyond Sweatshops* (Washington, DC: Brookings Institution Press, 2002), p. 144.

20 J. Bhagwati, *The Feuds Over Free Trade* (Singapore: Institute of Southeast Asian Studies, 1997), p. 44.

21 Bhagwati, *The Feuds Over Free Trade*, p. 45.

22 See for instance, the work of H. Farber, or T. Idson and R. Valletta, as described in Bhagwati, *The Feuds Over Free Trade*, p. 47.

23 Bhagwati, *The Feuds Over Free Trade*, p. 48.

24 Note that rising job insecurity may not be the only effect of increased international trade on the labour market. For instance, there is an ongoing debate surrounding the "servicization" of Canadian jobs—that is, the substitution of high-quality, high-wage jobs in manufacturing for low-quality, low-wage jobs in the service sector. However, the economic evidence on this effect is unclear.

25 Irwin, *Free Trade Under Fire*, pp. 32–33.

26 This sentence is dedicated to John Ellwood, Professor of Public Policy, UC Berkeley.

27 Quoted in L. Rumack, "Naomi Klein," *Now* 26 Sept. 2002. See also <www.nowtoronto.com/issues/2002-09-26/cover_story.php> Visited 8 Feb. 2004.

28 N. Klein, *No Logo* (Toronto: Vintage Canada, 2000), p. xviii.

29 For example, see "World: Rich and Poor Clash Over Farm Aid," <www.corpwatch.org/news/PND.jsp?articleid=8450>, first reported by the BBC. Visited 8 Feb. 2004.

30 Department of Foreign Affairs and International Trade, Government of Canada, "International Trade—The View of Canadians," 23 May 2002.

31 <www.Canada25.com>

32 A. Medd, "We're young and we're ready. So listen up," *Globe and Mail* 27 June 2003: A17.

chapter

SIX

FREE TRADE AND THE RISE OF INEQUALITY

In Chapter 2 we saw how comparative advantage and specialization create economic gains from trade. However, we also saw that economic theory does not guide how the gains from trade will actually be distributed. In practice, most of the gains from trade have been captured by the rich nations of the world. In the last fifty years, as international trade has accelerated, global inequality has skyrocketed. Moreover, the process of trade liberalization is dramatically increasing *the rate* at which global inequality increases. In 1960, the income gap between the 20 per cent of the world's people living in the richest countries and the 20 per cent in the poorest countries was 30 to 1. Thirty years later, that number was 60 to 1.[1] Just eight years after that, in 1998, it was 82 to 1.[2]

Most Canadians can feel the world growing more polarized. A poll conducted for the federal government found that Canadians perceive large businesses as benefiting more from international trade than their own family. Twice as many people said that trade "greatly benefited" large corporations as the number who said it "greatly benefited " their own family.[3] Canadians also feel a sense of responsibility for the global poor: eight in ten believe that "Canada can do more to help the developing world by opening up our markets to imports from developing countries."[4]

Many free-trade advocates, especially market fundamentalists, view the distributional inequity caused by unbridled free trade rather callously. They argue that while inequality is unfortunate, it has nothing to do with trade policy. Instead, we should focus on creating the greatest possible economic growth, which will supposedly benefit rich and poor alike. For market fundamentalists, the free market is not only economically efficient; it is also the most fair and reasonable way to distribute economic wealth. At most, they would see the issue of income redistribution to the poor as a "secondary" matter, to be pursued on the fringes of economic policy. This chapter will address this contention within the context of the trade policy of the WTO.

THE FACE OF INEQUALITY

From the comfort of Canadian society, it is difficult to imagine that almost half of humanity lives in squalor, barely able to put a roof over their head and food on their tables.[5] The poor have no savings, no safety net in times of trouble. Over a billion people do not have access to clean drinking water, the building block of all life; often they must walk several miles to get what water they can find. More than twice that number use firewood, charcoal, straw or cow dung as their main source of energy.[6]

Contrast that harsh reality with the fantasy world of the ultra-rich. The combined wealth of the world's richest 225 people exceeds one trillion dollars.[7] Their wealth exceeds the annual income of the poorest 47 per cent of the planet's population, about 2.5 billion people.[8] Bill Gates alone is worth more than 19 of the world's poorest countries (total GDP), which have a combined population of 375 million people.[9]

Statistics can barely scratch the surface of the polarized world we live in. The global differences in living standards are so extreme that a social reality in one country is completely unthinkable in another. Canadian political economist Thomas Homer-Dixon puts the issue into sharp perspective: "In India, an estimated 60 percent of all newborns are in such poor condition from malnutrition, low birth weight and other causes that they would be immediately placed in intensive care were they born in California. Never in human history have we seen such differentials between rich and poor. And these differentials are the main cause of huge and often disruptive migrations of people around the world in search of a better life."[10]

The magic of liberalized trade is that it increases the total amount of wealth shared between trading partners. But remember the caveat of Chapter 2: the increase in wealth from free trade can be divided between the trading partners in any number of ways, and the laws of economics do not suggest that this distribution will be in any sense "fair." The WTO claims that its trade rules have increased world income by over $500 billion in the seven years after 1995. Unfortunately, poor countries have captured only a tiny fraction of that gain.[11] Developing nations have particularly hard feelings about the last round of WTO negotiations (the Uruguay Round), when they were promised that the playing field would be rendered more even. Two prominent Canadian political economists, Daniel Drache and Sylvia Ostry, report:

> Many (but not all) developing countries remained convinced that the Uruguay Round had been a one-sided deal, involving commitments for major structural reforms on their part in return for market access that had not been forthcoming, and that they were not enjoying the benefits from freer trade that had been predicted.[12]

History repeats this pattern: the rich and powerful countries of the world take most of the gains from trade.

International trade is not the only cause of global inequality, but it is almost certainly a contributing factor. Free trade advocates know this. They acknowledge the inequality, but they believe it does not matter. They have what appears to be a compelling reply. Let's not worry about the thorny issues of distributional justice in the economic system, they say; first, we should concentrate on creating more *total* wealth. The most important thing, the argument goes, is to ensure that trade helps increase the GDP of each nation; the *relative amount* by which each nation's GDP increases is only a "secondary" matter.

Often this argument is ostensibly accompanied by a concern for the poor. If we encourage trade, say free-trade advocates, the evidence suggests that GDP will grow in developing countries. Trade can lift the economy in poor countries, bringing new wealth—and if it should offer the same or more to other nations, should anyone begrudge them? Surely not, say the free traders.

THE IMPORTANCE OF RELATIVE WEALTH

This argument appears compelling. It certainly eases our consciences: it leads us to the happy conclusion that rich countries can help the poor, even as our wealth and standard of living get increasingly more distant from them. The trouble with this is that orthodox economic theory is misleading. Most of modern economics is built on the notion that individuals are isolated "rational" actors, who seek to accumulate wealth for themselves but are oblivious to the wealth of those around them. In fact, our world is considerably more interactive and competitive than that. The notion that "one person does not lose by another's gain" sounds pious and appealing, but it is quite deceptive.

Imagine that you are talking to the head of the military in any nation in Africa, and you asked him* how he would feel if his neighbours were suddenly to become twice as rich as they are now. Give him a moment, and he will reply that their new wealth will give them the power to purchase new weapons, raise new armies and present new threats to the security of his own country. In war, every advantage of one's enemies is a disadvantage to one's own country. Free-trade advocates might think that we should ignore how trade agreements will bring wealth to our trading partners, but this is foolish. Even in the most peaceful times, a country's freedom and security rest upon its position with respect to its neighbours. Moreover, a country's relative standing dictates how much authority it has when it meets other nations on all sorts of matters: environmental negotiations, fishing treaties, investment opportunities, and (of course) trade agreements. The sad truth is that a nation must give constant attention to its relative standing in the international community.

A nation's standing is important in much the same way that our own standing relative to the individuals around us is important. For instance, most working adults would like to have a little more spending money. By the time someone reaches the age of forty or fifty, there are significant social demands on their income: they want to provide well for their family, they want to drive a nice car, and they want to be able to meet friends at nice restaurants. Suppose this situation describes Abigail, who makes $40,000 per year. If we took half of Abigail's income away, she would feel a huge loss. On her new $20,000 salary, she could no longer afford quality meals with her friends or drive an expensive car; she would probably have to move to a cheaper neighbourhood to save on housing expenses.

---

* The use of the male pronoun in this paragraph is not meant to be sexist. Few, if any, African nations have a female military leader.

If Abigail were a student, however, that same $20,000 might look entirely different. Because the social systems of students are very supportive of having little money, it is not a great hardship to have less income than a working adult does. Most students always seem to find enough money to have a little left over for pizza and beer with their friends. Abigail the student would probably live just fine on $20,000 a year.

The point here is simply that economic comparisons to those around you are enormously relevant.[13] If you earn more today than you did yesterday, economists say that you have increased your *absolute income*. If, on the other hand, today you earn more than your neighbour, whereas yesterday you earned less than her, economists say that you have increased your *relative income*. Note that the two concepts are quite independent: you can increase your absolute income (i.e., both you and your neighbour are earning more today than you did previously) even as your relative income is decreasing (i.e., you earn less today compared to your neighbour).

Many free-trade advocates argue that a country should be interested only in improving their absolute income. If globalization makes a country's absolute income rise, then it is a good thing—end of story. After all, they say, a rise in absolute income helps lift the world's poor out of poverty. The problem with this logic, however, is that it ignores the importance of relative income. The amount of income we have relative to our neighbours is nearly as important to us as the amount of income we have relative to yesterday's income.

Free-trade advocates maintain that it is essential for a developing country to gain wealth in absolute terms, even if it means falling further behind the level of prosperity available elsewhere in the world. Imagine for a moment that we applied that argument to highway driving. If absolute income is all that matters, then it is irrelevant what other people are able to afford when they purchase a car. But if all you can afford is a small two-door sedan, and everyone else around you drives an enormous SUV, you are in much more danger than if everyone else were driving a small car like yours. If your two-door sedan crashes with an SUV, it won't be the SUV that gets crushed—it will be you. Clearly, the size of your car, *relative to those around you*, suddenly becomes very important. Moreover, because car size is usually associated with its cost, the relative cost of cars is important too.

It is simply wrong to say that the kind of cars other people can afford should not or does not matter to you. Certainly, absolute wealth is important— without some level of wealth, you would not be able to afford a car at all. But beyond that minimum threshold, the relative characteristics of your car become important—just as your relative wealth becomes important in everyday life. It is not right to accuse you of irrational jealousy if you see those around you grow wealthy while you do not. Your economic position affects what neighbourhood you can afford to live in, where your children will go to school, and a host of other life conditions. The wealth of those around you affects you in a myriad of ways everyday.

Just as relative income is important to individuals, it is also significant for countries. Economic position dictates a country's responsibilities and opportunities within the international community. For instance, countries that are rich relative to others provide the leadership for international institutions like the World Bank and the IMF. Only the seven largest democratic economies make up the Group of Seven, where the pecking order is explicit: each country has influence according to its size. (Canada, being in last place among the seven, wields a commensurately small amount of power.) Likewise, at times of international crisis, countries are expected to provide aid or military force roughly in proportion to their economic capacity.

THE ROLE OF RELATIVE AND ABSOLUTE INCOME IN MANAGING FREE TRADE

Clearly, then, relative income can be as important as absolute income for both countries and individuals. History teaches us that although developing countries have made some gains in their absolute income through international trade, they continue to fall behind in relative terms. Thus, unbridled free trade is *not* necessarily good for each country involved, even if the absolute income in every country is increasing.

It is a mistake to say that economic inequality is merely a "secondary issue" compared to absolute income. Free trade's promise to deliver absolute gains must be weighed against its consequences for global inequality. If free trade causes the divide between rich and poor countries to grow even more extreme, surely this should make an already poor country hesitate to embrace it. A country (especially a poor one) needs to evaluate trade in terms of the way it will affect both its absolute and relative economic standing.

When anti-globalists interrupted the 1999 WTO meeting in Seattle, the next issue of *The Economist* had a picture on its cover of poor people in developing countries, entitled "The Real Losers." The lead article claimed that the international community should be "clear about who would stand to lose most if globalisation really were to be pushed sharply backwards— or, indeed, simply if further liberalisation fails to take place. It is the developing countries. In other words, the poor."[14] Despite what free-trade advocates like to claim, policy makers might do considerably more for the poor by concentrating on a reasonable international distribution of wealth rather than pushing the latest free trade agreement. While steady economic growth indubitably makes it easier to help people out of poverty, there is no reason why trade organizations should be philosophically opposed to policies of redistribution. Sadly, the WTO seems not only unwilling to fight for equality; it seems actively involved in the fight against it.

THE WTO LOOPHOLES: AGRICULTURE AND TEXTILES

The WTO's claim to be working in everyone's interests while advancing free trade needs to be examined in light of its progress on the trade issues that are most important to developing nations. In Chapter 4, we saw how free trade encourages developing countries to specialize in particular economic areas. For much of the world (India, Africa, and most of Latin America), that usually means significant specialization in just two sectors: agriculture and textiles. Unfortunately, it is with regard to agriculture and textiles that the term "free trade" is most misleadingly applied. Negotiations at the WTO and elsewhere are unbalanced, such that even as the rich countries demand trade concessions from the poor, they are unwilling to open their borders to food and clothing exports from the developing world.

Trade in agriculture is anything but "free." Before the trade agreement that gave birth to the WTO in 1995, the rich countries had very high tariffs: 244 per cent on sugar in the United States; 213 per cent on beef in the European Union; 353 per cent on wheat in Japan; and 360 per cent on butter in Canada, for instance.[15] Up to the end of 2000, the WTO required the rich countries to reduce their rates by only 36 per cent on average. This leaves the tariffs still very high, making it virtually impossible for developing countries' exports to gain access to the large markets. The World

Bank estimates that agricultural protection and subsidies in rich countries cost farmers in poor countries an amount equal to 40 per cent of all current foreign aid received by developing nations.[16] As if that were not enough, the trade rules explicitly permit rich countries to impose import quotas on many foods. The rules on agriculture are an example of how "free" trade rules tilt the playing field in favour of the rich and powerful nations of the world.

European farmers get 36 per cent of their income from government subsidies; North American farmers get closer to 20 per cent.[17] Subsidized American corn now makes up almost half of the world's stock, effectively setting the world price so low that many small farmers in developing countries can no longer survive. In 2002, President Bush signed a law to provide $57 billion in subsidies for American farm products over the following 10 years. Contrary to the rhetoric of support for small farmers, nearly 70 per cent of these payments go to the largest 10 per cent of producers. Agricultural subsidies in the US are actually a massive corporate welfare program.[18]

The inequities of this trade system for agriculture are taking their toll. The UN Food and Agriculture Organization (FAO) reports, "Although drought and other natural disasters remain the most common causes of food emergencies, an increasing proportion are now manmade."[19] The number of chronically hungry people around the world, which had been falling during the 1990s, has begun rising again and now stands at more than 800 million people, most of whom live in Africa, the Middle East, and India.[20] Global trade policy is doing little to help this situation, and much to exacerbate it.

Rich countries are also protectionist in the other sectors where developing countries are best able to compete: textiles and clothing. The World Bank reports that as a result, rich countries' average tariffs on manufacturing imports from poor countries are four times higher than those on imports from other rich countries.[21] This imposes a huge burden on poor countries. The United Nations Conference on Trade and Development (UNCTAD) estimated in 1999 that they could export $700 (US) billion more a year by 2005 if rich countries did more to open their markets.[22] The UN Food and Agriculture Organization analysis of past WTO negotiations and regional free trade deals agrees: "most benefits will go to rich countries."[23]

The slim silver lining to this dark cloud is that developing countries are now banding together to ensure that the WTO works harder to instil some sense of justice to international trade rules. While many developing countries signed on to the WTO agreement without fully appreciating what they were getting into, they are ready for change during the current WTO negotiations. As Drache and Ostry suggest, developing countries in 2002 "were much better prepared this time around. And, equally importantly, they were prepared to exercise their new-found clout."[24]

The other piece of good news is that the US may be resuming its leadership on trade matters, in a very constructive way. The Bush administration released a plan in July 2002 to reduce tariffs on farm goods, which would open rich-country markets to poor farmers in Africa, Asia, and Latin America. The plan also called for rich-country governments to stop paying their farmers to export their crops, which would help farmers in developing countries by dramatically raising crop revenues. *The Economist* reports that the overall "effect would be to remove $100 billion in global trade-distorting subsidies and to cut the average global tariff on farm products from 62 percent to 15 percent."[25] While these proposals need to be implemented in a way that is fair and reasonable to farmers in the US, Canada, and elsewhere, this plan represents a major step in the right direction toward fairness in international trade.

UNDER FREE TRADE, INEQUALITY BEGETS MORE INEQUALITY

International inequality will almost certainly rise as global trade increases and the planet continues to integrate. The United Nations' report in 1999 stated that "the top fifth of the world's people in the richest countries enjoy 82 percent of the expanding export trade and 68 percent of the [foreign investment]—the bottom fifth, barely more than 1 percent. These trends reinforce economic stagnation and low human development. ... Economic integration is thus dividing developing and transition economics into those that are benefiting from global opportunities and those that are not."[26] By contributing to future inequality between rich and poor countries, unbridled free trade is doing the world a serious disservice.

Unfortunately, inequality begets more inequality. As the economic disparity between countries grows, so does the difference in their negotiating strengths during trade talks. The vast wealth of the rich countries decreases our dependence on international trade, because the developing world is too poor to offer much that we do not already have. At the same time, a small economy is increasingly dependent on trade access to the large economies, shifting the negotiating balance still further in favour of the rich.

Clearly, this should give a developing country—or even a small industrialized economy, like Canada—pause before rushing to open its borders to unbridled free trade. No one wants to forever weaken their own negotiating position. On the other hand, a single country (especially a developing one) cannot stop this by closing its borders to trade. Doing so would only make things worse by preventing that country from making the small gains in absolute income that trade would offer. It is as if developing countries are to become little more than beggars who seek breadcrumbs as they roll off the rich man's table. What should a country make of these bleak alternatives?

BOTH THE RICH AND THE POOR WOULD GAIN FROM JUSTICE

The rich countries that sit atop the global order, Canada included, have the most to lose if the world trade system self-destructs. Yet market fundamentalists make no apologies for the rising inequality. They insist that so long as everyone benefits from trade at least a little bit, there is no cause for complaint. It is "the market" that divides the gains from trade, they say, and the market promises nothing about "fairness." It's just too bad if the gains are distributed unfairly, they say.

No wonder controversy surrounds the WTO. The fissures in its foundation grow as more and more people are made aware of the unjust advantages that the trade rules grant to the rich countries. In the long run, it is the rich countries that have the most to gain by restoring the legitimacy of the WTO. This chapter, along with the one that follows, should make it abundantly clear that the WTO hands an unequal and unfair deal to small countries. Obviously, small countries would like that to change. What is less obvious is that large countries ought to want to change the WTO, too.

Consider one example from history that shows how marvellous a spirit of cooperation can be, not just for those who are helped, but for those who are helping. At the end of World War II, America looked across the Atlantic and saw Europe pillaged by the ravages of war. Instead of turning a blind eye, the US did a truly remarkable thing. American leaders saw that they needed to broaden their concept of self-interest to include the welfare of others. With wisdom and foresight, America decided to invest in the development of Western Europe—including the people of Germany, a people against whom US soldiers had fought bitterly just a few years before. The US invested billions of dollars, and in so doing they helped guarantee the peace and prosperity that would characterize Western Europe for the next fifty years.

What is remarkable about America's efforts to aid Europe is not that it did so much good for Europe; what makes it remarkable is that it did so much good *for America*. First, a strong Western Europe helped the US to prevent the expansion of Russian communism, and eventually to defeat it altogether. Equally important, America's help to Europe created markets and demand for American-made goods. As a result, the US has its investment in Europe to thank, partially, for the good economic times in the 1950s and 1960s. Such were the benefits that arrived when America began to see its self-interest more broadly than its own backyard.

The US, Canada, and all the other rich nations of the world would be wise to remember the post-WWII era as they consider the global order of modern times. By acting conscientiously now to shift the WTO into a more equitable and fair treatment of the developing world, the rich countries could serve their own self-interest as well as the developing world's. History demonstrates that the gains from trade are very unevenly distributed, with the rich countries reaping most of the rewards. In the long run, this hurts everyone. The rich countries would be far wiser to invest in the developing world today, much as America invested in Europe after World War II.

Not everyone is optimistic about seeing a sense of justice shape trade negotiations. Prominent free-trade advocate Jagdish Bhagwati, for instance, argues that moral rhetoric is used primarily to disguise self-interested protectionism. He writes: "After all, trade negotiations and treaties typically relate to competitiveness; and this aspect will dominate whatever the genuine moralists want. ... At a poker game where men drink whisky and tell dirty jokes, do not expect the players to burst into singing madrigals."[27] After Bhagwati's lifetime of experience in the international trade arena, no doubt this is an understandably pessimistic attitude. Nonetheless, this sets the moral standard far too low. The triumph of human civilization is that deliberative principles are used to inform our actions and our society. For animals, might makes right. Humans can aspire to much more than that. Indeed, we have: the force of morality shapes the laws and institutions of which we can be most proud—democracy, the abolition of slavery, universal voting rights for men and women. Demanding that justice serve as a guide in shaping our laws is not only desirable; it was feasible in the past and it is feasible in the future.

As former US president Bill Clinton once put it, globalization "ain't worth it if we lose the human face of the international community."[28] This does not require a radical jump in foreign aid to the developing world. At minimum, however, the powerful countries should eliminate the basic unfairness of international trade rules, so that the developing world has a better chance of pulling itself up on its own. In so doing, the world's opportunities for peace and prosperity grow enormously. After all, people are far less likely to engage in acts of terrorism if they feel the system offers them a better alternative. Globalization, guided by a spirit of justice, could provide the economic growth in poor nations that would offer just this kind of alternative.

WHAT CAN BE DONE?

Free-trade advocates have controlled the globalization debate by arguing that while unbridled free trade might cause some inequality, it always helps the national economy of trading partners. This argument simply does not hold water. In either absolute terms (Chapter 3) or relative terms (this chapter), it is not at all certain that everyone benefits from unbridled free trade.

Unfortunately, it will not be easy to get rich countries to broaden their view of national self-interest to include the well-being of developing countries. Canada can help by pushing hard to even the playing field for international trade, especially in the areas of agriculture and textiles. Canada may not have great economic stature, but we can command considerable moral authority in the international arena. Canada can coax, coerce and even shame the other rich countries into a more equitable system of international trade. It is not enough for the developing world to see the injustice inherent in the international trade system; the governments of the industrialized world must recognize it too.

Drawing attention to the growing inequality within the WTO can serve a purpose in other areas, too. When it comes time for other international commitments, such as environmental treaties, the rich countries ought to recall their obligations. It is the rich countries who have benefited from the global order, and thus it ought to be the rich countries who act to protect our planet's ecosystem. Industry in the developed countries is responsible for most of the pollution in our skies, the damage to the ozone layer, and the havoc in the planet's climate. The cost of addressing these problems ought to fall to those who have benefited most from the global order.

NOTES

1 T. Pogge, paper delivered for the Charles T. Travers Conference on International Ethics, University of California, Berkeley, March 2001.

2 T. Homer-Dixon, *The Ingenuity Gap* (Toronto: Vintage Canada, 2001), p. 31.

3 Department of Foreign Affairs and International Trade (DFAIT), "International Trade—The Views of Canadians," 23 May 2002. <www.dfait-maeci.gc.ca/tna-nac/presentations/CATIT/menu-e.htm>

4 DFAIT, "International Trade."

5 World Bank, *World Development Report, 2001.*

6 World Bank, *World Development Report, 2001.*

7 Canadian dollars. Homer-Dixon, *The Ingenuity Gap*, p. 33.

8 Exchange rates are used here rather than purchasing power parity (PPP) conversions. Exchange rates measure the value at which goods are traded between countries, whereas PPP is a proxy for the value at which similar goods are traded between individuals across countries. Exchange rates are the appropriate metric to measure inequality in this case because they illustrate the (rapidly growing) differences in economic power between developed and developing countries. This difference in economic power will prove to be an essential obstacle to developing countries' ability to purchase new technology, medicine, and intellectual property in the future.

9 Based on 1999 figures; Bill Gates' estimated net worth is $90 billion (US). The country information comes from the World Bank's *World Development Indicators 2001.*

10 Homer-Dixon, *The Ingenuity Gap*, p. 34.

11 UNDP, *Human Development Report, 1999*, p. 31. Quoted in M. Khor, *Rethinking Globalization*, (London: Zed Books, 2001), p. 33.

12 Drache and Ostry, "From Doha to Kananaskis."

13 For a brilliant explication of this point, see R. Frank, *Luxury Fever* (Princeton, NJ: Princeton University Press, 2000).

14 "The Real Losers," *The Economist* 11 Dec. 1999: 15. To be fair, *The Economist* does note that "Free trade, like freedom in general, is not a panacea." Alas, not all free-trade advocates—including other writers for *The Economist*—are as reasonable.

15 Khor, *Rethinking Globalization*, p. 41.

16 F. McMahon, "Anti-globalists have it wrong," *Saint John Telegraph-Journal* and *New Brunswick Telegraph-Journal* 28 May 2001.

17 OECD, "Agricultural Policies in the OECD Countries: Monitoring and Evaluation 2002," 6 June 2002. See also OECD, "Agricultural Policies in the OECD Countries: A Positive Reform Agenda," 25 Oct. 2002, and J. Saunders, "Wheat dispute goes against the grain," *Globe and Mail* 8 Sept. 2003: B1.

18 Rosenberg, "The Free-Trade Fix."

19 Canadian Press, "Conflict, unfair trade blamed for global poverty," *Globe and Mail* 25 Nov. 2003. <http://www.globeandmail.com/servlet/story/RTGAM.20031125.whunger 1125/BNStory/International/>

20 Canadian Press, "Conflict, unfair trade."

21 "White Man's Shame," *The Economist* 25 Sept. 1999: 89.

22 US dollars. UNCTAD *Trade and Development Report*, 1999.

23 Canadian Press, "Conflict, unfair trade."

24 Drache and Ostry, "From Doha to Kananaskis."

25 US dollars. "Fast track to Doha," *The Economist*, 3 Aug. 2002: 12.

26 UNDP, *Human Development Report, 1999*, p. 31. Quoted in Khor, *Rethinking Globalization*, p. 33.

27 Bhagwati, *Free Trade Today*, pp. 72–73.

28 H. Mackenzie, "US seen as cultural imperialist," *Gazette* 16 March 1999. <http://www. globalpolicy.org/globaliz/cultural/cultimp.htm>

PART TWO
THE SOCIAL CONSEQUENCES OF FREE TRADE

chapter
SEVEN

Trade Rules, the New Weapons of Corporate Warfare

Part I of this book looked at the economics of international trade. We saw that it comes with both costs and benefits. In Part II, we turn to the social effects of trade. Globalization is about so much more than a set of trade rules. It has the power to bring this planet closer together, to connect our homes with people on the other side of the planet. The issues involved—immigrants, genetically modified food, the environment, and more—affect our national culture and touch our daily lives. The implications of this complex phenomenon called globalization are many, and still poorly understood.

The World Trade Organization proudly claims to be extending a "rules-based international trade system," nominally to bring fairness to an otherwise chaotic world. The Canadian government has accepted this at face value, stating:

> Canada is firmly committed to a rules-based system that provides a framework in which to manage international trade relations and the inevitable disputes that arise. In Canada's view, the WTO DSU [Dispute Settlement Understanding] is a key element of this framework. It is based on the rule of law, not power. It is fairer, especially for small and medium-sized countries, and limits the use of unilateral actions on the part of larger countries; consequently, it contributes to the stability and predictability of the international trading system to the benefit of all countries.[1]

Does the international trade system actually do this? If it does, it is not obvious. This chapter looks at four cases that question the ability of the WTO and NAFTA to bring the Rule of Law to the world of international trade.

PUSHING CIGARETTES IN THAILAND

According to the World Health Organization (WHO), there are currently four million deaths per year from tobacco use. The WHO expects this figure to rise to about ten million by the 2020s, making smoking the leading cause of fatal disease around the world. By 2025, 70 per cent of tobacco-caused deaths are predicted to occur in developing countries.[2] While the tobacco industry has long disputed the damaging health effects of cigarettes, the scientific community agrees that tobacco use is among the largest causes of preventable illness and death around the world.

At least partially due to stricter regulation in the US, American tobacco companies have heavily increased their cigarette exports to developing countries. In 1950, the US industry exported 20 billion cigarettes; in 1980, 82 billion, and in 1990, 164 billion. By 1996, the exports soared to 244 billion, thanks, in part, to aggressive action by the US government to lower world-wide tariffs on cigarettes.[3] Still, not every country was willing to cave to US pressure. Thailand was one of the brave few that resisted fiercely, and in 1990, the United States filed a formal trade dispute with the WTO's predecessor, the General Agreement on Tariffs and Trade (GATT) dispute council. Understandably, health advocates were outraged. The American Heart Association argued that "the US government should not be in the business of encouraging exportation of cigarettes. ... Every country including the United States should be doing everything possible to discourage [their] use worldwide."[4] One US politician warned, "Washington is sending Asians a message that their lungs are somehow more expendable than American lungs."[5]

For its part, Thailand pointed out that Article XX(b) of the GATT allows nations to take measures "necessary to protect human, animal or plant life or health." Since the scientific evidence of tobacco's health hazards was well established, Thailand felt it had a right to restrict cigarette imports to protect human health. However, the GATT panel ruled that the measure had to be *necessary*—that is, that the law was the "least trade-restrictive" policy possible to protect human health. Thailand was told that there were other measures it could take to restrict cigarette consumption, and that it had to open its borders to US cigarettes.

The US tobacco industry was delighted, of course, but its enemies grew more and more powerful. US Surgeon General Everett Koop characterized the American position as "unconscionable ... deplorable ... the height of hypocrisy," and described the export of tobacco products as a "moral outrage."[6] The tobacco industry soon found that its victory was hollow. Thai health activists realized the danger that the trade ruling posed to their country, and acted quickly to mobilize public pressure. They soon changed the government's laws to strengthen anti-tobacco policies. For instance, they took advantage of the fact that the GATT council had ruled that a ban on tobacco advertising was permissible; soon a total ban on retail cigarette advertising was in place. The new regulations were so effective that US tobacco companies captured less than three per cent of the Thai cigarette market.[7]

In a sense, this was a real victory for unbridled free trade and globalization. The cigarette case showed that even though a trade panel in Geneva might strike down policies in Thailand, new laws could be constructed to achieve the same public policy goals. In fact, these laws are arguably better than the old ones: they still discourage smoking, but they do not discriminate against foreign competition.

Instead, the Thai cigarette case highlights three major dangers that the GATT and the WTO pose to small countries today. The first is that not all stories will have the happy ending that appears in the Thai case. As luck would have it, Thai activists were able to gather political momentum and pass laws to protect the health of their citizens. But there is no guarantee that it will always be politically possible to replace the laws struck down at the WTO; indeed, it is easy to imagine some that won't. Our look in Chapter 10 at globalization's effect on national culture will provide an example: despite several attempts, Canada has yet to find a politically feasible solution to support its magazine industry and artistic community. If Thailand had not acted so effectively, it would have joined the many countries already inundated with American cigarettes.

Second, the Thai cigarette case itself set some dangerous precedents in international law. Thailand requested that the panel consult with the World Health Organization on a technical matter. Thailand argued that US cigarettes were more dangerous than Thai cigarettes due to certain chemicals added to the American variety. Shockingly, the United States did not believe that the WHO was particularly competent to address the "health consequences of the opening of the market for cigarettes"[8] and urged the WTO to limit the issues that the WHO could address. The panel implicitly agreed, and their final report did not include the WHO testimony on the potential health consequences of the added chemicals in US cigarettes. The implications are chilling: when a powerful nation such as the US finds the scientific findings of an international body like the WHO inconvenient for its political purposes, it simply silences them. It is a dark sign indeed that the WTO would give in to this pressure.

Finally, this case highlights the pitched battle that small countries like Thailand face when confronting large ones like the United States. The WHO experts involved in the case warned that poorly financed public-health programs in developing countries like Thailand would be unable to compete with the marketing budgets of multinational companies. As a result, death and disease attributable to cigarette consumption would increase.[9] Even more poignant is the fact that Thailand had to rely on the WHO for so much of its scientific testimony in the first place. Unlike the US, Thailand cannot afford to maintain a large retinue of lawyers and medical experts in Geneva to argue its case. Indeed, 29 small countries are unable to afford *any* full-time representation at the WTO's headquarters.[10] How can we expect justice for small countries if they are unable to level the playing field at the WTO's legal tribunals?

Greed and corporate profits drove the US government to demand that Thailand open its markets to American tobacco. While ultimately a failure for the US cigarette industry, the Thai case shows three looming dangers for small countries from the WTO: the political infeasibility of replacing each law the WTO strikes down, the US disregard for international organizations, and the inability of small nations to afford proper legal representation. Current international trade rules darken the sky above small countries.

FOREIGN INVESTOR RIGHTS UNDER NAFTA AND THE MAI

In 1993, Canada, the United States, and Mexico signed the North American Free Trade Agreement (NAFTA). One of the more contentious provisions was Chapter 11 of the Agreement, designed to protect foreign investors from actions taken by governments. While the desire for protection from arbitrary discrimination is understandable, NAFTA actually extends foreign investors' rights well beyond those of domestic citizens.

In the US and Canada, domestic citizens have the right to sue the government if they have been directly harmed by a law, but not if they are indirectly harmed. For instance, a citizen whose house is destroyed to make room for a highway is entitled to monetary compensation: this is direct harm. However, if a shopkeeper's sales decrease because a public highway causes fewer people to stop in the neighbourhood, the shopkeeper is not entitled to any compensation: this is indirect harm. Under NAFTA, however, foreign companies have more rights than domestic citizens; they hold the right to sue the government for both direct and indirect harm.

The rise of corporate power in the courts is starting to disturb all three countries, as each sees foreign companies overriding its domestic legal process at NAFTA tribunals. But Dan Price, the lead US negotiator on NAFTA's Chapter 11, says this was the intentional design of the free trade agreement: "NAFTA checks the excesses of unilateral sovereignty." One wonders, what good is national sovereignty if you need the legal permission of foreign multinational corporations to exercise it? But Mr. Price has little sympathy for such concerns. As for anyone troubled by NAFTA's intrusions on national sovereignty, he remarks, "My only advice is, get over it."[11]

At issue here is an ideological battle over the limits of private property, especially when that property conflicts with society's public values. Political conservatives in the US have long argued that the government should be obliged to pay for "regulatory takings." Under this view, a government that wants to regulate the public sphere will be required to pay property owners for any damages caused by the law. In the conservative view, it does not matter whether those damages are direct or indirect. However reasonable this might seem at first glance, consider the enormity of its consequences. It means, for instance, that the government could not pass anti-smoking regulations without first paying the tobacco companies billions of dollars for their lost sales. It means that government could no longer force dirty companies to restrict their pollution, unless tax dollars paid the companies for the cost of the regulation. The "regulatory takings" law would paralyse the social mission of national governments.

While Ronald Reagan was president, US conservatives tried mightily to get this "regulatory takings" view adopted into domestic politics. They failed. Politicians knew that this radical swing to the political Right would never fly with the American public. Instead, the conservatives decided to influence the shape of NAFTA regulations. Edward Graham, a NAFTA expert at the Institute for International Economics, comments about the negotiation, "there was strong advocacy that thinks, whenever the government enacts a regulatory measure, it should compensate. They saw [NAFTA], I am told, as a way of getting such a provision into international law that does not exist in US domestic law."[12] Indeed, Dan Price boasts that the "breadth of coverage and strength of the disciplines [in NAFTA Chapter 11] exceed those found in any bilateral or multilateral instrument to which the United States is a party."[13]

The principle behind Chapter 11 is to defend foreign investors from discrimination by national governments or corrupt courts (the latter being the US's major concern about Mexico). In practice, however, Chapter 11 is not a shield, but a new weapon in the hands of corporate interests. This weapon has its most striking effects in health policy. For instance, when Canada proposed a law to require plain packaging for cigarettes, lawyers from R.J. Reynolds and Philip Morris went on the attack. If the government did not back off from the law, they threatened, Canada would have to pay the tobacco companies millions under NAFTA. Allan Rock, the Canadian Health Minister, talked tough: "No US multinational tobacco manufacturer or its lobbyists are going to dictate health policy in this country."[14] But the government backed off, nonetheless.

Corporate powers, especially from large countries, are using the new rules of international trade as weapons of intimidation in policy making. And it isn't just the corporate interests from big countries that try to ride roughshod over the democratic process. Canada's corporations have used NAFTA aggressively to sue the US government, too. One of the most notable cases is *Methanex vs. the United States*, in which the Canadian firm Methanex is suing over California's environmental laws. California is trying to ban MTBE, a chemical additive to gasoline, which has been found leaking from storage tanks into public drinking water. Californians are understandably upset to find that their drinking water tastes and smells like turpentine, and yet their government is being taken to court because the ban on MTBE would cost Methanex hundreds of millions of dollars in sales to California. The case is still pending, but we can be sure that if California loses the case, the public outcry will be deafening.

Just as social advocates awoke to the awesome implications of NAFTA's Chapter 11 in the mid-1990s, corporate interests pushed to expand it to new horizons. The proposed Multilateral Agreement on Investment (MAI) would have extended NAFTA's tenets of "investor rights" to 29 of the richest countries in the world. By then, however, public activists had mobilized. Citizen protestors, led by Maude Barlow at the Council of Canadians and joined by American activists like Global Trade Watch, raised a storm of critical objections. Facing enormous public pressure, the MAI negotiations collapsed. Nonetheless, the issue remains alive. Many conservatives, both in the US and elsewhere, hope to extend NAFTA's rules on investment to all of Latin America under the proposed Free Trade Area of the Americas (FTAA).

CANADA-US SOFTWOOD LUMBER

Canada has been fighting for fair access to the US softwood lumber market for decades. Unfortunately, local power politics and changing administrations in the US have made this an elusive goal. The US government has repeatedly changed its policy on Canada's lumber exports, each time doing serious damage to our softwood industry. In response, Canada has challenged the US positions at international trade tribunals. The trade tribunals have consistently ruled in favour of Canada and demanded that the US reduce its punitive tariffs on Canada's products. Unfortunately, the Canada-US softwood lumber dispute is a telling example of how powerful countries can flout trade rules at the expense of small ones.

Forestry has always been important to Canada. Covering half of the Canadian landscape, and amounting to 10 per cent of the world's forest cover, our forests are a prominent feature of our economy, culture, and history. Forestry is a $68-billion industry in Canada, providing 384,000 jobs in 1998.[15] Softwood exports to the US alone are worth $10 billion.[16] The industry is important across the country, from BC to Quebec to New Brunswick. It is no wonder, then, that the issue of access to the huge US market is of vital importance to the softwood lumber industry and to the Canadian economy.

In October 1982, US producers filed a petition against the Canadian softwood lumber industry, starting a case known as "Lumber I." The petition alleged that Canadian provincial and federal governments were subsidizing softwood lumber production by selling the right to cut timber on public lands ("stumpage rights") at artificially low prices. The US Department of Commerce (DOC) investigated the allegations. The DOC terminated the case on May 31, 1983, when it determined that the stumpage programs conferred no subsidy.

"Lumber II" started on May 19, 1986, when the American lumber lobby filed a second petition alleging new evidence to support its claim that Canadian stumpage rights subsidize lumber production. In October 1986, the DOC reversed its prior determination in Lumber I, and issued a preliminary determination that a tax should be applied to Canadian softwood. To avoid the expense and politics of continuing the case, Canada agreed to a temporary 15 per cent tariff on exports of Canadian softwood lumber.

After five years of the "temporary" tariff, Canada had had enough. On September 8, 1991, Canada advised the United States of its intention to terminate the agreement. The US responded by initiating an investigation of alleged subsidies—and insisted that Canadian producers post bonds worth millions of dollars on the lumber destined for the US. Almost a year later, the DOC completed its investigation. On May 28, 1992, the US government decided that Canada was subsidizing its lumber production, and imposed a 6.5 per cent tax on Canadian softwood.

"Lumber III" had begun. After trying to settle the matter by negotiations, Canada invoked the panel review process at the GATT council. There was another lengthy delay. On February 19, 1993, the GATT panel found that the US tariff was invalid. The panel also found that the requirement on Canadian producers to post bonds for their products was illegal. Following the ruling, the DOC came to its original conclusion that Canada was not actually subsidizing its softwood lumber industry after all. The GATT panel affirmed that decision on February 28, 1994.[17] Reconsidering, the US decided to appeal the decision, and again Canada won. Despite this, US Trade Representative Mickey Kantor refused to refund the Canadian producers' deposits that the US had collected under their invalidated law. Faced with the loss of hundreds of millions of dollars and threats of a fourth lumber dispute, Canada agreed to the US-Canada Softwood Lumber Agreement on May 29, 1996. The five-year agreement required Canada to impose its own export tax on softwood lumber. At least this way, the Canadian federal government got the tax revenues, rather than the American government.

But that is not the end of the story. In March 2001, the five-year Softwood Lumber Agreement ended. "Lumber IV" started three days later, when the American lumber lobby filed yet another case against Canada. In August, the US government decided to impose a 19.3 per cent tariff on

Canadian softwood, the largest tariff yet in this sordid history. On top of that, the DOC slapped a 12.5 per cent surtax to punish Canada for "dumping" its cheap softwood on the US market. Extremely frustrated and deeply worried about the thousands of jobs on the line, Canada challenged the US position at the WTO. On July 26, 2002, the WTO issued an interim report, ruling in Canada's favour on eight out of nine legal points.

Over the twenty-year history of this dispute, international dispute panels (both NAFTA and at the WTO) have ruled in favour of Canada again and again. Unfortunately, the trade rulings do little to prevent serious damage to the Canadian softwood industry. Each time the US imposes a tariff upon Canadian exports, it takes months or even years for trade panels to hear the dispute and make a ruling. In that time, enormous damage is done to the Canadian forestry industry—particularly when the tariffs add up to over 30 per cent of the price of the wood.

The softwood lumber saga continues. As this book went to press in 2004, Canada was willing to concede to a quota system that would permit duty-free exports so long as Canadian lumber made up less than 31.5 per cent of the US market. If Canadian firms export above their allocated 31.5 per cent market share, they have to pay significant tariffs ($200 per 1,000 board feet) on the additional lumber. In addition, the deal "includes a controversial and unprecedented concession by Canada: to let Washington keep nearly half of the $1.7 billion (US) in duties collected so far," according to the *Globe and Mail*.[18] This deal is made in spite of the economic evidence, and clearly violates the spirit of free trade. In fact, prominent US economist Paul Krugman writes, "George W. Bush has turned out to be quite protectionist. The steel tariff and the farm bill attracted the most attention, but they are part of a broader picture that includes the punitive (and almost completely unjustified) tariff on Canadian softwood lumber and the revocation of Caribbean trade privileges."[19] Doubtless, this is not the last set of negotiations for Canadian lumber producers.

Under the current international trade regime, the most the NAFTA or WTO dispute panels can do is to impose a penalty when its rules have been broken. However, there is often no penalty for the damage already done by the time the panel makes its decision—and that could take years. Meanwhile, an export industry in a small economy like Canada's could be crippled. In addition to the actual tariffs the US imposes, the *threat* of additional tariffs causes uncertainty. That uncertainty scares away investors from the industry, making it difficult for them to raise the capital needed to run their business. Worse still, there is no way to make a trade panel's judgement permanent. The US can abide by the judgement for a few months, and then recommit the same trade violation by recreating the same unfair tariffs.

This leaves Canada with a dilemma. On the one hand, we probably do not want to make NAFTA or the WTO any stronger than they already are; they can already do much to infringe on national sovereignty. On the other hand, it seems that the trade agreements are not strong enough to do the one thing they promised: provide protection from the bullying of large countries. What is the point of making concessions at trade talks if powerful countries are going to perpetually flout the rules?

PHARMACEUTICAL DRUGS, REVISITED

In Chapter 1 we examined what is probably the most egregious example of the use of trade rules to threaten small countries. The pharmaceutical industry ultimately failed in its attempt to prevent South Africa from making AIDS drugs affordable for its people. Nevertheless, international trade rules may soon make the provision of affordable medicines in poor countries increasingly difficult. The controversy at the WTO surrounds the agreement on "Trade-Related aspects of Intellectual Property Rights," or TRIPS.

Admittedly, patents and intellectual property rights are an essential part of the economic incentive system that supports private research and development of new medicines. Without the prospect of financial rewards for medical research, private companies would simply be unable to continue much of their ground-breaking work. However, this reality alone does not justify the current effort by the WTO to extend corporate patent laws to all WTO members, regardless of their level of economic development. The real question is whether poor countries will gain anything by adopting the WTO's patent rules under TRIPS.

When confronted with this question, most TRIPS advocates will make a rather interesting argument. An analyst at the Fraser Institute, for instance, writes, "The TRIPS Council risks altering the basic balance of interests upon which TRIPS is based: greater respect by developing countries for intellectual property rights in return for more access to developed-world markets."[20] Apparently, it is clear that TRIPS is costly for developing countries, but the costs are outweighed by the other benefits they will receive at the WTO. However, this position rests uncomfortably with another common position taken by advocates of unbridled free trade, namely, that lowering tariffs, even unilaterally, is virtually always beneficial to a country. On this view, tariffs are a distortion to the free market and a source of inefficiency in the economy. According to most free-market advocates, this is true *regardless of whether any other country lowers its tariffs in exchange.*[21] But if rich countries will benefit from opening their markets to foreign producers, we should do so willingly—and not demand that poor countries adopt costly intellectual property rules.

The WTO does not share this view. By 2005, most developing countries will have to accept patent rights on medicine developed in industrialized nations. The very poorest nations will follow in 2016. As the *New York Times* puts it, "This regime does nothing for the poor. Medicine prices will probably double, but poor countries will never offer enough of a market to persuade the pharmaceutical industry to invent cures for their diseases."[22] The World Bank calculated that the WTO's intellectual property rules will force poor countries to transfer $40 billion a year to corporations in the developed world.

In South Africa, the moral ramifications of patent rights were reasonably clear-cut. AIDS was killing a thousand people each day the drug companies pursued their lawsuit. That kind of issue grabs headlines and brings public pressure to bear on injustice. But it won't always be so easy: corporations are much more difficult to stop on issues that are not so directly linked to the death of innocent victims.

PREPARE FOR THE NEW WEAPONS OF UNBRIDLED FREE TRADE

From cigarettes in Thailand to softwood lumber in BC, trade rules are being used to threaten the rights of small countries. The NAFTA and the WTO promise to bring the "Rule of Law" into international trade to protect small countries. However, if the softwood lumber dispute is what we can expect under their regime, small countries will continue to suffer. What can Canada do about it? Unfortunately, very little. Perhaps the best we can do is to recognize that occasionally powerful countries will bully us, no matter what the trade rules say. At least this recognition will prevent us from naivety in the next round of trade talks.

However, there are three tangible steps that the WTO can take to improve the international trade system. First, some experts are already pushing for greater flexibility in the international agreement on patent rights (TRIPS). Indeed, the WTO was able to successfully launch the Doha round of negotiations only because the United States demonstrated some willingness to accommodate on the issue of access to essential medicines.[23] Trade experts and social activists alike are working to ensure that giant multinational corporations like the pharmaceuticals are never again in a position to compromise the poor's access to affordable health care, as they were in South Africa. The WTO ought to recognize that any law genuinely aimed at the public good should trump the desire for more corporate profits.

Second, the rich nations should provide significant funding for legal aid at the WTO for developing countries. Renowned trade economist Jagdish Bhagwati supports the growing chorus of supporters for such legal aid. In particular, he has called for an international endowment in the range of $150–250 million (US), the proceeds of which would support an analytical staff to better understand the far-reaching effects of the WTO's agreements.[24] This proposal would help level the playing field within the WTO's halls of power.

Canada ought to stand firmly behind such a proposal. Instead, Canada has donated a paltry $1.3 million for trade-related technical assistance to developing countries.[25] This is barely enough to support a small office for one country for one year. As we saw in the Thai cigarettes case, developing countries are rarely able to afford the well-paid lawyers and medical experts that are necessary to confront the powerful US tobacco industry. Moreover, money is not enough; developing countries need experienced analysts and technical training to prepare them for the next round of trade negotiations. An international effort to provide reasonable resources for developing countries would give the WTO greater legitimacy, and give globalization a brighter future.

Finally, Canada should continue to be wary of any provisions that extend the rights of foreign investors. Even now, the WTO wants to expand the current agreement on international investment (called the Agreement on Trade Related Investment Measures, or TRIMS) to make its rules disturbingly similar to NAFTA's Chapter 11. Canadians should oppose this agreement with the same passion that defeated the MAI. The WTO ought to delay the negotiation of such agreements until everyone is better able to understand the powers it gives to foreign investors to interfere with public policy. As with the other two proposals, the WTO should be guided by the desire to strengthen democratic law in its member countries. Indeed, the very legitimacy of the WTO depends upon it.

NOTES

1 Department of Foreign Affairs and International Trade, <www.dfait-maeci.gc.ca/tna-nac/text-e.asp> Visited 6 Sept. 2002.

2 World Health Organization, *The World Health Report 1999.*

3 See *Tobacco Control and Marketing: Hearings on US Tobacco Export and Marketing Practices on May 17, 1990 Before the Subcommittee on Health and the Environment of the House Committee on Energy and Commerce,* 101st Congress, House of Representatives No. 101–171 at 112 (1990) (statement by Sandra Kristoff, Director, Assistant US Trade Representative for Asia and the Pacific Region). Quoted in Y.D. Park, "The Thai Cigarettes Case: A Current Critique," in E.B. Weiss and J. Jackson, eds., *Reconciling Environment and Trade* (New York: Transnational Publishers, 2001).

4 J. Burgess, "Cigarette Sales Overseas Light a Fire under US Tobacco's Tail," *Washington Post National Weekly Edition* 24–30 Dec. 1990: 21. Quoted in D. Vogel, *Trading Up* (Cambridge, MA: Harvard University Press, 1995), p. 201.

5 P. Schmeisser, "Pushing Cigarettes Overseas," *New York Times Magazine* 10 July 1988: 20. Quoted in Vogel, *Trading Up*, p. 201.

6 P. Magnusson, "Uncle Sam Shouldn't be a Travelling Salesman for Tobacco," *Business Week* 9 Oct. 1989: 61; "Medical Association Assails US Policy on Tobacco Exports," *New York Times* 21 June 1990: A5. Quoted in Vogel, *Trading Up*, p. 201.

7 Vogel, *Trading Up*, p. 143.

8 *Thai Cigarettes Case*, paragraph 58. Quoted in Park, "The Thai Cigarettes Case: A current critique."

9 *Thai Cigarettes Case*, paragraph 52. Quoted in Park, "The Thai Cigarettes Case: A current critique."

10 "White Man's Shame," *The Economist* 25 Sept. 1999: 89.

11 W. Greider, "The Right and US Trade Law: Invalidating the 20th Century," *The Nation* 15 Oct. 2001: 22.

12 Greider, "The Right and US Trade Law," p. 24.

13 Greider, "The Right and US Trade Law," p. 26.

14 Greider, "The Right and US Trade Law," p. 28.

15 Canada's Forest Network, <www.forest.ca>

16 A. Ali and S. Saccoccio, "Softwood Lumber," CBC News—In depth backgrounder, October 2001.

17 "A Brief History of the US-Canada Softwood Lumber Dispute," American Consumers for Affordable Homes, <www.acah.org/history.htm> Visited 6 Sept. 2002.

18 S. Chase, "US, lumber industry agree to terms for ending softwood dispute," *Globe and Mail* 6 Dec. 2003. <http://www.globeandmail.com/servlet/story/RTGAM.20031206.wsoftwood1206/BNStory/National/>

19 P. Krugman, *The Great Unravelling* (New York: Norton 2003).

20 O. Lippert, "Poverty, Not Patents, is the Problem in Africa," printed by Pfizer in *The Economist* 12 Oct. 2002.

21 For instance, see W. McKibbin, "Regional and Multiregional Trade Liberalization: The Effects on Trade, Investment and Welfare," Brookings: The Brookings Institution, Washington DC, 1997. See also E. Berglas, "The Case for Unilateral Tariff Reductions: Foreign Tariffs Rediscovered," *American Economic Review* 73.5(1983): 1141–42; and S. Edwards and D. Lederman, "The Political Economy of Unilateral Trade Liberalization: The case of Chile" Cambridge, MA: National Bureau of Economic Research, 1998.

22 Rosenberg, "The Free-Trade Fix."

23 Drache and Ostry, "From Doha to Kananaskis," p. 5. Alas, the United States later showed remarkable stubbornness in refusing to join to an agreement by the other 143 nations of the WTO whereby inexpensive drugs could be made more accessible to the world's poor. See BBC News, "US blocks cheap drugs agreement," 21 Dec. 2002. <http://news.bbc.co.uk/2/hi/health/2596751.stm> Visited 13 June 2004.

24 Bhagwati, *The Feuds Over Free Trade*, p. 15.

25 "Canada contributes $1.3 million in trade-related assistance to developing countries," Department of Foreign Affairs and International Trade, 10 March 2002.

EIGHT

MORALITY, GENETICALLY MODIFIED FOOD, AND FREE TRADE

Through the generations, we have coaxed Nature into providing for us; now we are beginning to collar Nature herself. Modern science is creating genetically engineered food, known to the world as "GMOs," or genetically modified organisms. Biotechnology, pioneered by giant multinational firms such as Monsanto, is creating new plants to serve as genetically superior crops. GMO technology poses a host of new bio-ethical questions for modern society to answer, and we are only beginning to grapple with the issues. Into this crossroads of science and morality, the international trade system interjects itself.

Sceptics have good reason to be concerned about the World Trade Organization's power to interfere with our country's democratic process. Moral issues, particularly those involving bioethics, are exceedingly complex. It takes years to build a social consensus from which lawmakers can legitimately form national policy. Unfortunately, the WTO has already shown itself to be impatient in the resolution of trade disputes, and it does not hesitate to overrule national standards of food safety and acceptability.

In this chapter we will consider the ethical issues surrounding GMO foods in order to explore how international trade rules affect a country's democratic policy process. Are small countries capable of upholding policy decisions on moral grounds, especially when those decisions are different from international norms?

THE GREAT GENETICALLY MODIFIED FOOD DEBATE

In North America, GMO foods have already reached the dinner plates of virtually every household on the continent. Most people don't know it. Canadian and American farmers already use GMO crops routinely, since there are some rich rewards to doing so. For instance, GMO crops can be engineered to resist herbicides and pesticides. This allows farmers to spray powerful toxics directly onto their fields, killing virtually everything that wasn't born in a laboratory. By keeping the fields free of pests and weeds, the toxic sprays provide the farmers with richer harvests.

The proponents of GMOs see this as a realization of the promise of biotechnology. With the increases in farmers' yields, food is cheaper and more abundant. In a world where hundreds of millions of people are undernourished, no one should underrate the prospect of making food available more cheaply. Consider the tangible benefits that biotechnology offers to poor farmers in developing countries. In 2001, Kenyan farmers harvested their first crop of sweet potatoes engineered for resistance to a disease that previously killed up to 80 per cent of their crop.[1] GMOs could offer more food to the world at better prices than ever before, while at the same time increasing farmers' revenues and profitability.

GMOs could also be a boon to the environment. By creating crops that are resistant to toxics, biotechnology allows direct application of pesticides and herbicides to the farmers' fields. This direct spraying means that lower doses can be used than traditional crop farming, resulting in less toxic run-off into local streams and ponds. Having fewer toxic substances in our environment is good news for everyone.

Thus, GMOs hold the promise of both environmental protection and cheaper food. Governments in North America have been so supportive of GMOs that they appear, unlabelled, in many of the foods available in supermarkets. So far, North Americans have barely noticed their presence: one survey found that 37 per cent of grocery shoppers said they had heard nothing at all about genetically modified food, and only nine per cent said they had heard a lot about it.[2]

Across the Atlantic Ocean, however, the prevailing attitude is quite different. An opinion poll published by the European Commission in December 2001 showed that over 70 per cent of European consumers do not want GMO food in any form.[3] The European Union has banned GMO foods for human consumption. Europe also resists all attempts by North

American producers to open up its borders to GMO imports. It is only because Europe is powerful that it is able to resist the North American pressure for the free trade of GMOs; if a small country, especially a poor one, tried to take Europe's stand against North America, it would not last for long. To this issue, we will return. First, we should try to understand why Europeans are so opposed to GMO crops.

Most Europeans see GMO technology as a mixed blessing at best, and a moral abomination at worst. They are sceptical of assurances from industry or scientists that GMO food is safe. This should come as no surprise; after all, authorities were assuring Europe that there was no danger of mad cow disease from British beef as recently as 1997. When those assurances turned out to be horrifically wrong, it is no wonder that Europeans thought long and hard about what food they wanted to put before their families.

The case against GMO food includes at least three different arguments. The first is that genetic modification is an inherently risky business, and its dangers to humans outweigh the prospective benefits. In the process of creating crops that are superior in some technical sense, scientists run the risk of creating dangerous side-effects, such as allergenic properties. Scientists have already created soybeans with genes inserted from Brazil nuts, creating a health hazard for people with allergies to nuts. [4] In another instance, the US Environmental Protection Agency approved "Starlink" corn for animal feed but did not consider it safe for human consumption. When Starlink corn later showed up in taco shells, consumers were outraged. Imagine the consequences if "contraceptive corn"—a product genetically engineered to produce antibodies that attack human sperm—got mixed with sweet corn on its way to dinner tables. [5] Despite the best intentions of GMO producers and farmers, these risks will always be present.

The second argument is that this technology is a big step down a slippery slope, and that it could lead to genetic selection of animals and even humans. Given the massive financial incentives for developing GMOs, biotech companies are not going to limit themselves to new plant varieties; indeed, they are already pursuing far more lucrative profits in the market for animals. [6] Cloning opens the door for scientists to design herds of animals with identical characteristics: lobotomized animals, for instance, to make them docile and easier to handle.

Aside from the moral considerations of the animals themselves, this technology could do significant damage to biological diversity. Genetic modification includes screening of embryos, and those considered "defective" would be discarded. In making this selection, however, scientists rob nature of its opportunity to bring hidden miracles. In some tiny fraction of sheep embryos, for instance, there may be the biological material that would provide the cure for cancer. To put this in human terms, consider Stephen Hawking, the brilliant Cambridge physicist who is afflicted by Lou Gehrig's disease. If Dr. Hawking's mother had been screened for genetically "unsuitable" eggs, he might never have been born, and the world would have lost one of its most eminent physicists.[7]

Finally, GMO opponents argue that even if GMO foods prove safe for humans, they pose a threat to the environment. Biology teaches us how plants can naturally cross-pollinate, thus sharing genetic materials from one plant to another. Unfortunately, natural cross-pollination means that once a GMO crop is planted in a farmer's field, the artificial gene has the potential to spread to neighbouring plants in the wild. The artificial gene, which might have been beneficial in the original crop, could do considerable harm once spread to wild plants. In fact, research at the University of Nebraska and Indiana University has already found "that genes introduced into plants can migrate to nearby weeds, possibly making them stronger and more resistant to chemicals."[8] These new "super weeds" could wreak havoc, spreading to neighbouring fields and beyond.

For all these reasons many people view GMOs with considerable scepticism. The danger posed by allergenic foods, the loss of biological diversity, the moral consequences of designer animals, and the potential for GMO-pollinated "super weeds" add up to considerable uncertainty about the long-term consequences of biotechnology. However, we should not forget about the benefits of GMOs. They hold enormous potential to provide abundant, inexpensive food to the world's poor, as well as greater revenues to farmers. Already, most North Americans consume food containing GMOs, and as far as we know, not one person's health has suffered from it. Moreover, GMOs may actually be safer for the environment than the toxic pesticides already in use. With powerful arguments on both sides of the debate, it is no wonder that GMOs are so controversial.

Indeed, because of the uncertainty about GMOs and the environment, some people argue that governments should apply the *precautionary principle*. Loosely speaking, the precautionary principle says that in cases where we suspect the possibility of catastrophic damage to the environment, we should take extra measures to avoid that catastrophe. After all, history teaches us that the precautionary principle could have been useful in dozens of situations: mercury, tobacco, ozone-depleting chemicals, and radioactive materials were all once thought quite safe. Tobacco, in particular, is a great example of the need for precaution: for years the cigarette industry's scientists maintained that tobacco posed no health hazard.

Applied to the case of GMOs, the precautionary principle suggests that we should delay using GMOs outside of the laboratory context until we are virtually certain that they do not pose a significant danger to human health or the environment. The precautionary principle is a major tenet of international law within the European Union, but the World Trade Organization has yet to accept it. Largely because of American opposition, the precautionary principle unfortunately stands outside all of the major international trade agreements to which Canada is a party.

GMOs AND FREE TRADE

The environmental health risks and the ethical consequences of genetic modification are serious, and as a society we have yet to fully confront them. As the issue makes its way into the public forum, however, it runs headlong into conflict with the WTO's international trade regulations.

So far, Europe's opposition to GMOs has kept American producers from pursuing the issue at the WTO. Europe is so powerful, and its opposition to GMOs is so strong, that the WTO has not yet dared to touch the issue. Indeed, if its trade rules forced Europe to lift its ban on GMOs, Europe might decide to pull out of the WTO altogether, causing the WTO to collapse. Such is the economic power of Europe. If it were a small country, however, the issue might be decided in a rather different manner. In fact, apart from the US, the European Union is probably the only economic entity in the world powerful enough to resist the pressures that are brought to bear by the WTO. Rich but small countries like Canada and Australia could not do it; small and poor ones like Kenya certainly couldn't; even mighty Japan would probably have to bow to the WTO. Canada should be concerned about the WTO's awesome power to impose upon public policy in small countries.

The WTO claims that its mission is to enforce the Rule of Law in the world of international trade; instead, it may be providing business interests with new ways of legitimizing their tactics against national sovereignty. Imagine for a moment that the European Union, in time, comes to accept GMO foods.

If this happens, the pressures that will be brought to bear upon the rest of the world to accept GMO foods into their markets will be irresistible. With both Europe and North America blessing the use of GMOs, the trade rules of the WTO would provide business interests in the rich countries with new ways of bullying the small countries.

For instance, suppose a small country like Costa Rica—or even a group of small countries—tried to take a moral stance against the marketing of GMO meats within its borders. Foreign producers of synthetic meat would see this as a potential market that is barred to them. They could demand the right to sell genetically modified meat in Costa Rica's food market. If Costa Rica refused, the issue could go before the WTO's dispute panel. And if the WTO ruled that Costa Rica's moral position was not sufficient to justify a ban on GMO meats, it could impose economic sanctions upon it, costing millions of dollars. Unfortunately, the WTO might do exactly this. The history of the WTO gives good reason to be sceptical about its respect for moral decisions by sovereign nations.

WTO rules do nominally give a country the right to enact laws designed to protect public morality. The GATT Article XX, subsection (a), allows a country to make laws designed to protect public morality. Unfortunately, the WTO rules are worded so vaguely that no country has ever sought to defend its laws under Article XX(a). A rule this vague and untested provides little protection for a small nation in an issue that is as hotly contested as the debate surrounding GMOs. Even Europe was wary of using the XX(a) defence at the WTO when it faced a similar situation: the beef hormone dispute.

THE BEEF HORMONE DISPUTE

In the 1990s, Europe banned North American meat imports containing artificial beef hormones. Recall that at the same time, Europeans were dealing with the horrific effects of an outbreak of mad cow disease among humans, even after European governments had assured citizens they were safe. They were understandably concerned about their food and sceptical of scientific "authorities." Nonetheless, Canada and the US opposed the ban on beef hormones and took the Europeans to court at the World Trade Organization.[9] In 1997, the WTO ruled against Europe.[10]

Consequently, the WTO allowed the US to impose a severe set of economic sanctions.

The key issue in the European beef hormone case was the question of whether there was a plausible threat to human health from North American meat imports. The WTO demanded that the Europeans provide scientific evidence for the existence of such a threat. Unwilling to conduct a scientific risk assessment, the Europeans argued they had the right to ban artificial beef hormones even without scientific study. They contended that caution was required, given the possibility of enormous danger to human health. After all, the governments' own scientists had assured them that mad cow disease could never reach humans, and sure enough, it did.

As discussed above, Europeans want to incorporate the *precautionary principle* into international law. The WTO, however, has never formally accepted it. It says that the "spirit of the precautionary principle" is already embodied in the trade rules, particularly in a clause called SPS Article 5.7. Unfortunately, that key clause was *never applied* in this case. Moreover, the WTO explicitly ruled that it did not have a duty to defer to national sovereignty, and that it could overrule a country's own standards in deciding how food safety applies in a trade context. As a result, it ruled against the Europeans and allowed the US to impose $117 million in punitive tariffs.[11]

The WTO made a bad decision in this case. Instead of punishing the Europeans, the WTO should have reserved judgment, granting them a temporary reprieve. In that time, the scientific study of the health effects of beef hormones could have continued. Even more important, in practical terms, a temporary reprieve would have given the European scientific community time to regain the public's trust after the mad cow outbreak. At the same time, the WTO could have put the Europeans on notice that they had a responsibility to rational policy making in light of long-term scientific evidence. If no health hazards had emerged, Europe would have been obliged to allow the North American beef. Unfortunately, the WTO focused on a narrow and legalistic application of the trade rules. In doing so, it provoked justifiable fears that it will thwart the democratic processes of countries worldwide.

GMO LABELLING

The controversy over food and trade is a layered issue. On one level the debate is whether certain products be traded at all. Concurrently, there is a second debate about the extent to which food products should be labelled, if they are traded. The promise of free trade is that it will open up more options for consumers at the market place. The trouble is that the promise of greater choice is betrayed if consumers are not given the information they need to make an informed choice. In the context of GMO foods, the key information is a label.

Regardless of one's opinion of GMOs, it is only proper to recognize that differences of opinion will continue to exist and that people ought to be able to make informed decisions about the issue. If GMO foods were clearly labelled, consumers would have the option not to buy those foods. Normally, the WTO has been supportive of labelling, as it is consistent with the free-trade philosophy of greater consumer choice. So why, then, is there a debate about allowing governments to label food, distinguishing products that contain GMOs?

Like everything else about GMO foods, the labelling issue is not quite so simple. Market research by agriculture producers suggests that most people would choose not to consume GMO foods if they had a choice. According to a poll conducted for the Council of Canadians by Environics Research Group, 75 per cent of Canadians familiar with GMO foods are worried about their safety and almost all (95 per cent) want GMO foods labelled as such. A similarly high number (95 per cent) want to be able to buy non-GMO foods, and over two-thirds (71 per cent) would even be willing to pay more to get them.[12] *The Economist* reports, "Only 4 percent of Americans would actually be more likely to buy foods because they are genetically modified. By contrast, 57 percent would be less likely to buy them."[13]

Knowing that the labels would devastate their revenues, GMO producers oppose the use of labelling, saying that it is almost as effective as an outright ban. According to the biotech lobbyists, "two out of three [US] consumers support foods produced through biotechnology and have confidence in the Food and Drug Administration's policy for labelling biotech foods."[14] On this view, GMO labels are unnecessary. In fact, biotech advocates claim that, rather than requiring GMO labelling, 81 per cent of consumers agree that, "it would be better for food manufacturers, the government, health professionals and others to provide more details through toll-free phone numbers, brochures and web sites."[15] Of course, this stands in stark contrast to a *Time* poll that claimed that the same proportion of Americans (81 per cent) wanted genetically engineered food labelled.[16]

GMO labels could also mislead consumers' beliefs. Currently, there is no scientific evidence that GMO foods have had any public health consequences. Biotech advocates contend that labels will send the wrong message about the food's health effects. The matter becomes even more complicated when one considers the product's effect on the environment. For example, if farmers grew a GMO crop using far fewer pesticides than the traditional alternative, consumers might want to know this. On the other hand, genetically engineered crops carry their own risks for the environment. A simple "GMO" food label could lead to considerable consumer confusion about both environmental and health effects.

The agriculture business has successfully lobbied the Canadian and US governments on this issue. Already, GMO labelling in both Canada and the US is illegal. Moreover, the US government is vociferously opposing any new trade rules at the WTO that would allow other countries to have GMO labelling requirements. However, the US position is not only contradictory to the principles of a free market, it is inconsistent with the US's own laws domestically. The US government already allows mandatory labels based strictly on consumer concern—without regard to actual health effect. For example, labelling of protein hydrolysates is allowed because it indicates that a product is derived from animal sources, which has religious significance to some consumers. One can easily see a parallel to GMO labels—many people have very strong ethical beliefs about GMO foods, and they ought to have the information they need to act according to their moral position.

The fact that science has not yet found any negative health effects caused by GMO foods is not a valid reason to ban proper labelling. In 1986, the US Food and Drug Administration (FDA) declared that food irradiation is safe and allowed the treatment as a way to destroy bacteria on produce. However, many consumers strongly opposed irradiation, often simply with the sense that irradiation is unnatural, and therefore undesirable. Without backing down from its position that the practice is safe, the FDA mandated labelling of irradiated food to give consumers the choice not to buy it.[17]

Canada's position on GMO labelling is also mainly negative. According to the Department of Foreign Affairs and International Trade, "Canada does not believe the issue of 'eco-labelling' or labelling more broadly is an appropriate subject for negotiations. However, we do support a broader policy-based discussion on labelling in the TBT [Technical Barriers to Trade] Committee."[18] Apparently, our government would be satisfied if this issue were handed off to a subcommittee, away from the main negotiations. This is a mistake—trade bureaucrats should not treat informed consumer choice as a secondary issue.

The principles of a free-market economy suggest that consumers should be given the information they need to make educated purchasing decisions. From this perspective, it is hard to see how GMO advocates can oppose labelling in any ethically consistent way.

GMOs, BEEF HORMONES, AND LABELS: PRECEDENTS FOR SMALL COUNTRIES

Each of the controversies covered in this chapter presents a perspective on the threat that the WTO poses to the sovereignty of small nations. In the GMO debate, the enormous economic might of the European Union has thus far prevented American producers from filing a trade dispute at the WTO. Only the fear of the total collapse of the WTO keeps North American business interests from trying to repeal Europe's ban on GMO foods.

No small country has this power. If US and European interests were aligned on GMOs, their powerful agriculture industries would almost certainly demand that their rules and standards be recognized by the WTO as the "right" ones. Even if international standards were set with perfect integrity, the debate about GMO food is about so much more than just science. This is a policy debate that affects us at our dinner tables; it presents risks to our health and our environment; it touches upon our core values and beliefs. It is no wonder that it is so hotly contested.

No confidential WTO trade panel in Geneva should be able to dictate the GMO policy of any nation, large or small. If ever an issue ought to be open for debate in the public forum, surely this is it. The questions raised by GMOs confront us both as national communities and as individual consumers in the marketplace. This is not a debate merely about consumer preference; it is about the extent to which we will allow technology to guide the development of living creatures. On an issue of this breadth and this importance, every country should have absolute sovereignty. Sadly, the WTO appears to guarantee that sovereignty only to powerful economies like the European Union and the United States of America.

WHAT CAN BE DONE?

The beef hormone dispute speaks volumes about the WTO's impact on a nation's ability to plot its own course. Caught in the midst of an outbreak of mad cow disease, Europe had every interest in the safety of its food. Despite a lack of scientific evidence that beef hormones could be hazardous to human health, the Europeans wanted to apply the precautionary principle—better safe than sorry. The WTO, however, had other ideas: without scientific proof that beef hormones were dangerous, Europe's decision was going to cost them over $100 million each year in trade sanctions. If the WTO is willing to enact this sort of penalty against Europe, it will certainly do it to a less powerful economy.

Unfortunately, the Canadian government is moving in exactly the wrong direction on the issue of the precautionary principle. In its public statement before the most recent round of negotiations at the WTO, the Department of Foreign Affairs and International Trade argued, "On *precaution*, Canada believes that the existing WTO rules provide sufficient science-based scope for precautionary action when it is deemed necessary to address a serious and proven risk. We do not believe there is a need for negotiations on precaution at the WTO."[19] Unfortunately, the WTO's actions on the beef hormone case undermine this faith.

Canada should demand that the WTO explicitly recognize the debate over GMOs as an issue of national policy, one that will not be decided behind closed doors by trade bureaucrats. The WTO ought to defer to national policy, including the right to label and even to ban GMO foods. Advocates of unbridled free trade oppose this, lobbying for as little regulation of the marketplace as possible. Managing free trade appropriately, however, demands that policy makers should act to disarm the threat of trade sanctions. Until the WTO adopts an explicit statement recognizing national sovereignty over GMO policy, that threat will remain ever present.

NOTES

1 D. Victor and C.F. Runge, "Farming the Genetic Frontier," *Foreign Affairs* 81.3(2002): 107–121.

2 "Trends in the United States: Consumer Attitudes and the Supermarket, 2000," survey by Research International USA for the Food Marketing Institute. Quoted in B. Murray, "GMO-Free Zone," *Supermarket News* 14 May 2001. <www.biotech-info.net/GMO_free.html>

3 Eurobarometer 55.2, "Europeans, science and technology," European Commission, Dec. 2001. <europa.eu.int/comm/research/press/2001/pr0612en-report.pdf>

4 M. Specter, "The Pharmageddon Riddle," *The New Yorker* 10 April 2000: 58–71.

5 Victor and Runge, "Farming the Genetic Frontier."

6 The first patented mammal, known as the "Harvard Mouse," made its way into Canadian law in 1985. David Gambrill, "Court allows patent for Harvard Mouse," *Law Times*, Canada Law Book, 2002.

7 The Hollywood film *Gattaca* vividly portrays this futuristic nightmare.

8 O. Moore, "Super Crops Lead to Super Weeds," *Globe and Mail* 8 Aug. 2002. <http://www.globeandmail.com/servlet/ArticleNews/front/RTGAM/20020808/wmodi0808/Front/homeBN/breakingnews>

9 Technically, the WTO is not a legal "court." However, it holds trade "dispute settlement panels" that listen to the arguments of each country, and then delivers a judgment that is enforceable by WTO law.

10 World Trade Organization, Appellate Body, "EC Measures Concerning Meat and Meat Products (Hormones)," AB-1997-4, Geneva, 1997.

11 US Trade Representative, "US Response to EU Beef Import Ban," *USTR Fact Sheet*, July 1997.

12 "National poll and cross-country protest demonstrate consumers won't be fooled by GE foods," Canadian Press Release, 31 March 2000, <www.biotech-info.net/canadian_poll.html>. This poll is supported by others, including one by the Consumers' Association of Canada, described in "Poll shows huge support for GMO labeling," *Globe and Mail* online edition, 3 Dec. 2003.

13 "Economist GM poll— 57% of US citizens less likely to buy GM foods," *The Economist* 15 Jan. 2000.

14 International Food Information Council, "Americans Remain Positive on Food Biotechnology," Oct. 1999.

15 International Food Information Council, "Americans Remain Positive on Food Biotechnology."

16 Quoted in M. Guru and J. Horne, "Food Labelling," Kerr Center for Sustainable Agriculture, <http://www.kerrcenter.com/publications/FOODLABEL.pdf>

17 K. Eiseman, "Food labelling: Free trade, consumer choice, and accountability," in Weiss and Jackson, eds., *Reconciling Environment and Trade*.

18 Department of Foreign Affairs and International Trade, "2001—WTO Consultations: Trade and Environment— Information Paper," 25 Sept. 2001, <www.dfait-maeci.gc.ca /tnac/env-info-e.asp> Visited 14 Sept. 2002.

19 DFAIT, "2001— WTO Consultations."

chapter NINE

FREE TRADE AND THE BRAIN DRAIN

In today's intense global economic rivalry, talented and educated people are critical for a nation's competitiveness. As humanity's mastery of natural resources grows, the key to economic success increasingly lies in the management of people and information. At the same time, globalization and modern travel have made it possible for millions of people to cross international boundaries each year. The dramatic rise in human mobility makes the development and retention of a highly skilled workforce a national challenge for virtually every country on the globe.

"Brain drain" refers to the international flow of highly educated individuals who migrate to new countries to find better job opportunities. Since these talented people are so important to a country's global competitiveness, this chapter will focus on how free trade affects brain drain.

Most international trade agreements, designed by advocates of the free market, reduce the ability of national governments to influence the labour market. Many economists want trade to be unfettered by labour regulations, which they see as an undesirable deviation from market principles. This is dangerous, however, because unbridled free trade actually reduces the high-quality job opportunities for people in small and developing economies. National governments need to be involved in protecting job opportunities.

Historically, Canada has played a dual role in the migration of highly skilled workers. Each year, Canada draws thousands of doctors, engineers, and technicians from developing countries ("brain gain"); on the other hand, we also lose thousands of similarly educated people to the United

States ("brain drain"), where companies often offer significantly better pay. Think of Canada's position as similar to one of the Great Lakes: it has an inflow of water (skilled workers) on one end, and an outflow of water (skilled workers) on the other end. The brain drain is particularly relevant for Canada: 17 per cent of Canada's population was born in another country, compared with an average of 8 per cent among the major industrialized nations.[1] Moreover, we have one of the most highly educated workforces in the world. The portion of the Canadian workforce that has a post-secondary education is nearly double the average of industrialized (OECD) nations.

Canada is deeply affected by both the "brain drain" and the "brain gain," so it is important that we understand how free trade influences international migration. Equally important, Canada needs to work to establish international safeguards for a government's ability to create high-quality opportunities for its people.

SKILLED AND UNSKILLED LABOUR

Remember the situation we looked at in Chapter 2, where countries were trading just two products, carpets and videotapes. Imagine for a moment that these two products represent two kinds of jobs that a person might have. The first kind of job is called *unskilled* and requires relatively little education. The work might be exhausting, but it is not very complicated, and almost anyone can do it with a little training. The other kind of work is, of course, *skilled* labour. Like the engineering required to design and manufacture videotape and VCRs, skilled jobs involve mentally complex work, usually requiring years of education and training to perform.

Naturally, any economy needs a certain amount of both kinds of labour. Even in the most primitive countries, for example, there is a need for people who can design the law and manage the business affairs of the country. Likewise, the most advanced economies still have jobs for ditch diggers and garbage collectors. The difference is that not every country needs the same amount of each kind of labour. For instance, we know that international trade encourages each country to specialize in what it does best. It follows that as each country specializes, the number of skilled and unskilled jobs is going to change. When a country pursues free trade and specializes according to its trade advantages, there could be either more or fewer skilled jobs in the country, depending on what type of business it specializes in.

In theory, then, free trade could mean that more skilled jobs are available for the people of any country. In reality, however, unbridled free trade tends to reinforce the fact that the best job opportunities are available in industrialized countries. Why? The countries that are already developed have a well-educated workforce. Their biggest trade advantage is in industries that require skilled labour. Trade motivates countries to specialize according to their trade advantage, so this creates a positive feedback cycle: countries that already have a skilled workforce choose to specialize in complex industries, which in turn demands more skilled workers. Developing countries, on the other hand, have a workforce that is relatively unskilled. Their trade advantage is in industries that use unskilled work at very low wages. Therefore, unbridled free trade encourages developing countries to specialize in industries that require lots of cheap, unskilled labour.

Some specialization in any economy is a good thing. However, the danger facing many small countries is that, with overspecialization, free trade destroys opportunities for promising people and their communities. Market fundamentalists will say that the best thing any government can do is to stay out of the market place altogether. They will say that developing countries should sign up with the WTO and place their faith in the market to guide their economies. This is an extremely dangerous view.

Imagine that you are the ruler of a small developing country: Cambodia, for example. You decide to follow the advice of free-market advocates, liberalizing trade and agreeing to the WTO's conditions on your policies. Over time, the economy will adjust to your country's comparative advantage, and firms that specialize in unskilled labour will prosper. At the same time, however, firms that use highly skilled labour will face competition from abroad, and some will surely be forced to close down. As those firms close down, opportunities for the most talented of your people will be eliminated.

Now focus on what this means for people and communities. Imagine that today there is an engineering firm in a town not far from Cambodia's capital city, Phnom Penh. The engineering firm has a policy whereby it hires the brightest student from the local high school as an apprentice draftsman. If the apprentice does well, the engineering office encourages the student to go to university to study engineering. This benefits both the firm and the student, since those students typically return to become permanent employees after graduating from university.

Now imagine the future of that engineering firm. Under trade liberalization, Cambodia opens its borders to foreign competition and, in return, is able to export its products to foreign markets. As a result, the industries that employ lots of unskilled labour, such as carpet making, prosper from the international trade. The engineering firms, however, do not fare nearly as well. Increased trade means that large multinational corporations are setting up shop in Cambodia, and they don't use the services of the local engineering company. Instead, the foreign firms tend to get their engineering services from corporate headquarters, in North America or Europe. As a result, the engineering firms in Cambodia suffer, and some of them shut down. Our hypothetical engineering firm is one of those forced to close up shop.

Note that by the standards of most economic thinkers, especially free-trade advocates, there is nothing wrong in all of this. Market competition is essential to economic efficiency, and that means that some industries will prosper while others suffer. Thus it is quite possible that, in our example, Cambodia's economy is growing and its GDP rising. The industries that have benefited from trade, such as carpet making, might have such dramatically increased sales that Cambodia is more prosperous than ever before. Nonetheless, the local engineering firms have paid a price—they cannot compete with the foreign firms.

We need one more character to complete our story. Imagine the case of Koy, the daughter of a carpet-making family in the same town as the engineering firm. Koy is very smart, and has always been at the top of her class in school. She is just about to graduate from her secondary school, and must soon decide whether to take over her family's carpet business. If she does so, she might earn more money than her parents did by making carpets. In this sense, trade liberalization has helped her family.

On the other hand, Koy is very bright. If she became an engineer, she could earn a better income than she ever could making carpets. Even with the benefits of globalization, carpet weaving is not going to offer the kind of standard of living Koy could achieve in a skilled job such as engineering. The trouble is that unbridled free trade means that there are no jobs for engineers in Cambodia now. She is at the top of her class, but the local engineering firm that would have hired her has closed down. Carpet making has become so popular that there really is no opportunity to do much else. If Koy wants to be an engineer, she has to leave her hometown, maybe even leave Cambodia altogether.

This story doesn't apply just to Koy. She represents an entire segment of her generation—those who are bright, talented, and capable of earning a high wage if they are able to enter the right sort of profession. The trouble is, a strict program of trade liberalization has practically eliminated high-quality jobs in Cambodia. The best-paying jobs aren't available anymore, because the economy has specialized in unskilled industries like carpet making. Cambodia's best talent is going to leave the country.

THE DAMAGE WROUGHT BY THE BRAIN DRAIN

This example is only hypothetical, of course, but it bears an unfortunate resemblance to the real world. Many countries, like Jamaica, China, and India, are experiencing exactly this kind of brain drain. As these countries specialize in jobs that require relatively unskilled labour, they may be slowly destroying opportunities for the brightest and most educated part of their workforce. In the 1990s, over 150,000 Jamaicans, or 6 per cent of their population, emigrated to the United States. Most of those who were allowed in by the US government were Jamaica's educated elite—the engineers, lawyers, and doctors of the future. What is most disturbing is the loss this represents for Jamaica. This is a country in which less than 7.5 per cent of the population has any form of post-secondary education. The loss of over 6 per cent of a nation's people, most of them educated, would be cause for concern in any country; for Jamaica, it is devastating.

Jamaica is torn by corruption and violence. No one could blame the individuals who decided to go to the US for wanting safe homes and better opportunities for their children. At the same time, the mass exodus of Jamaica's educated elite leaves their home country in even greater peril. Who knows what difference these talented individuals might have made as leaders in their community.

Of course, Jamaica is just one example; there are many others. Developing countries in general lose many of their best-educated workers to rich countries. For instance, three-quarters of all US immigrants from India who enter the labour market fall in the "professional and technical workers" category.[2] Even in 1980, a study by the World Health Organization described India as "the world's largest *donor* of medical manpower."[3] In this, India is not alone. At one time, there were more US-trained Iranian doctors in New York City than in the whole of Iran.[4] As a group, developing countries export far more doctors than they take in: more than half of the world's emigrant doctors leave from developing countries, and only one in ten immigrant doctors settle there.[5]

Brain drain represents a triple loss for the home country. First, these high-potential individuals are no longer working for, and creating wealth for, their home country. In this sense, the loss is one aspect of a more general situation described earlier. In Chapter 4, we looked at how trade liberalization might produce economic gains in comparison to today's economy, but at the loss of today's potential for future growth. Brain drain is a specific case of that general situation: even as a country's GDP rises in the short term, it loses its most talented people to another nation.

Brain drain causes a second loss to the home country. The people who leave as part of the brain drain are usually pursuing an opportunity to live better financially. In doing so, however, they pay a huge emotional price: they leave behind their family, friends, and loved ones. It is impossible to know how many of those immigrants would have preferred to stay in their home country if the right opportunities had been available for them there, but one cannot help thinking the number must be high. This is a loss for the individuals, and a loss for the community they leave behind. Economists never measure this kind of loss.

Finally, brain drain hurts a country in a third way. Removing the best and brightest from a community costs the local economy more than just that one individual's potential income. The community also loses what that person might have taught to others. The community loses the leadership that person might have provided, and the benefits to the entire group that would have accrued because of what that one talented individual could have done. Communities are not simply the sum of their individuals; rather, they are living organisms that are built on the strengths of each of their members. A talented individual in a community can be like the keystone in an arch, or the foundation in a house of cards—without that individual, the whole structure collapses.

This is not to say that every individual who leaves their home country causes irreversible damage to the communities they leave behind. The point is that the impact of their leaving is almost certainly greater than the economic measure of their individual income. The talented members of a community mean so much more than that. The brain drain is robbing their home country of their potential.

CANADA AND THE BRAIN DRAIN

Canada has traditionally suffered a brain drain to the United States and benefited from a brain gain from the rest of the world. On one hand, Canada suffered a net loss of almost 20,000 professionals to the US between 1982 and 1996, in addition to more than 14,000 managers and 3,000 skilled workers.[6] Statistics Canada reports, "[Canadian] [e]migrants to the United States are more than twice as likely to hold a university degree than are immigrants to Canada. However, because of the overall greater number of immigrants, there are four times as many university graduates entering Canada, from the rest of the world, as there are university degree holders of all levels leaving Canada for the United States."[7] In fact, immigrants to Canada tend to be very well educated: "At ages 24–44, 28 percent of recent male immigrants had university degrees, compared with 17 percent of the Canadian-born."[8]

One might be tempted to conclude that since Canada is both a winner and a loser in the brain-drain game, on balance we should not be too concerned about it. On the contrary: there are at least three reasons why the "brain flow" is hurting our country deeply. First, the brain flow does not necessarily provide Canada with the right mixture of skilled professionals for our society's needs. In particular, Canada is losing thousands of health-care professionals to the US each year. These medical professionals are not being adequately replaced by immigrants from the rest of the world, creating a looming crisis in the Canadian health-care industry.

Second, even if Canada's migration flow kept a desirable professional balance, the cost of replacing Canadian emigrants with newly arriving immigrants is considerable. There are the public expenditures for the processing and settlement of the new immigrants, and at $13,400 per immigrant, these are not inconsiderable. Even more important, however, is the cost to Canada's productivity while the immigrants are given workforce training. Economists call this "deadweight productivity losses," which they estimate at $229,000 per immigrant arrival.[9]

Third, Canada ought to be deeply concerned about the ethical problems of using the rest of the world to make up for our brain drain to the United

States. India and China are major source countries for Canadian engineers and graduate students. This means that Canada is essentially asking taxpayers in these two poor countries to reimburse Canadians for human resources which have flowed to the United States.[10]

For all these reasons, brain drain is a serious issue for Canada. What makes it especially important in the era of globalization is that free trade accelerates the migration of highly skilled workers. Even though there has always been migration between the US and Canada, trade liberalization has arguably had a greater effect on Canadian labour mobility than any other factor. Unbridled free trade creates both the economic incentives and the immigration policies necessary to hasten the brain drain.

In 1993, NAFTA inaugurated the "TN" visas for work in the US, specifically for Canadians with a Bachelor's degree or higher. The explicit purpose of this policy is to draw Canadian talent into the US workforce. As an increasing number of Canadians move to the US, Canada finds itself with an increasing need for highly educated workers from the developing world. This comes at an enormous cost: "For the 50,578 replacement immigrants who arrived circa 1989–96, the total cost from productivity loss, settlement and educational replacement ... is $11.8 billion."[11]

The brain flow is costing Canada billions of dollars. This is made worse by the immigration rules that accompany NAFTA. Moreover, free trade also encourages the brain drain by causing fundamental changes in the Canadian economy. As a nation, we have one of the highest proportions of foreign corporate ownership in the world. This fact has powerful implication for Canada's workforce migration.

FREE TRADE AND THE NATURE OF BRANCH PLANTS

Trade liberalization reinforces the brain-drain effect by encouraging the spread of large multinational firms. The history of globalization is a pattern of large corporations establishing satellite companies in small countries. To see why, we need to revisit the theory of comparative advantage laid out in Chapter 2. The classical theory of comparative advantage is based on the notion that the advantage of one country cannot be transported to another country. When David Ricardo first formulated the theory of comparative advantage in the early nineteenth century, that premise closely reflected reality. Since then, however, local conditions (like land quality and climate) have become a lot less important in the industrialized world. Other elements of production, like financial capital, management skills, and information technology, have become far more important than they were in Ricardo's day. Significantly, these factors can be moved into another country.

Before free trade became popular all over the industrialized world, high tariffs and other barriers to trade encouraged foreign companies to set up *branch plants*: foreign-owned operations to manufacture products locally. This way, a company could participate in another country's market, without having heavy tariffs imposed on its goods.

As the process of trade liberalization dismantles national tariffs, an interesting thing happens to branch plants. On the one hand, branch plants are less desirable under free trade: the "parent" companies no longer need to produce locally to avoid tariffs. Free trade allows the companies to produce in their home territory, and ship their products internationally. The companies can now take advantage of the efficiency of mass-production in one location. Considering this, one might think that branch plants would start to disappear as a result of free trade.

However, free trade also works in another way. True, businesses have an incentive to use mass-production techniques in one location, but that location does not necessarily have to be its own country. Free trade gives them an opportunity to build branch plants in foreign countries, in order to manufacture goods for export back into their home market. Rather than closing down their foreign branch plants, some major corporations in large countries have decided to shut down the manufacturing wings of their own headquarters. In this way, corporations can build industrial "muscle" in foreign countries while keeping their business "brain" in their home country.

Free trade means that branch plants are actually increasing in number, but their character is changing. A good example of this change is the North American car industry. As Holmes notes, "Prior to the mid-1960s, production throughout the international automotive industry was organized on an essentially national basis. ... Major changes occurred in 1965, when the Auto Pact forced the rationalization of the Canadian auto industry and its integration with the US industry on a continental basis."[12] After the Canada-US Auto Pact liberalized trade within the auto industry, "Canadian branch plants develop[ed] specialized niches in their transnational parents' corporate global strategies."[13]

Branch plants are no longer focused on creating locally demanded goods. In a globalized world, branch plants employ local people to produce foreign-demanded goods. This causes a subtle but very dramatic change in the nature of the branch plant. Without free trade, the foreign management needs local expertise for the marketing and strategic direction of the branch plant and its products. With free trade, the management is now designing its products with global markets in mind. Branch plants no longer have much use for local marketing and local expertise.

The fact that unbridled free trade changes the nature of foreign-owned branch plants has striking implications. The foreign parent firm is no longer interested in making a product designed for the local populace.* This eliminates the need for educated locals in management positions. Instead, the branch plant is now merely a node in a larger corporate network designed to produce goods that suit the tastes of the largest possible market. The home corporate headquarters, of course, will usually manage this network.

THE ROLE OF MULTINATIONAL FIRMS

As far as foreign-owned branch plants are concerned, it does not matter whether a small country is developed, like Canada, or developing, like Cambodia. In either case, the satellite companies in small countries get their financial backing—and their orders—from the parent company, which is usually headquartered in a powerful economy like the European Union or the US. The fact that the satellite companies get their marching orders from elsewhere can hurt small countries like Canada in a number of ways.

Globalization scholars are convinced that while industrial "muscle" is being built in the developing world (e.g., in the form of factories), rich countries increasingly specialize in the "brain" functions of industry[14]. The rich countries do this by providing finance, technology, capital goods, and management skills as needed to the rest of the world. For those who think that industrialization might be a way for the developing world to eventually achieve some sort of parity with the rich countries, these scholars have bad news: "The industrialization of the [developing world] has ultimately

---

* This is all too obvious when one sees white-skinned dolls made for children in East Asian countries and elsewhere.

been a channel, not of subversion, but of reproduction of the hierarchy of the world economy."[15] In other words, history demonstrates that trade liberalization allows the rich countries to entrench their status and control over the developing economies.

Consider how foreign ownership affects the management staff in the satellite companies of small countries like Canada. Employees realize that headquarters makes most of the big decisions. This means that Canada's talented managers in foreign firms will eventually face a tough choice. If they really want to rise within the company, they will need to leave Canada and go to corporate headquarters. This is just another form of brain drain. Since trade liberalization could mean that more and more of Canada's leading companies will be replaced by the arms of foreign corporations, this corporate version of brain drain has the potential to get very much worse.

THE ROLE OF NAFTA AND THE WTO

Free-market fundamentalists say that the best thing a government can do is to try to stay out of the market place. Their blinding faith in the market, however, can lead a small country into great danger: trade liberalization can stifle the opportunities for the most promising workers. For instance, NAFTA's regulations on foreign investment[16] are specifically designed to prevent Mexico and Canada from requiring multinational firms to create quality job opportunities for local communities. NAFTA tribunals can penalize any country that tries to create labour laws that require local participation. This means that a government cannot require a minimum percentage of managers or corporate directors to be hired locally. Increasingly, regional free trade agreements, such as NAFTA and the EU, make the protection of opportunities for local people difficult.

As difficult as this situation is for Canada, it is considerably worse for Mexico. Despite decades of foreign-owned branch plants, particularly in car manufacturing, Mexico has never required companies to transfer technological expertise to locals. Now, under the rules of the NAFTA, it will never be able to. "We should have included a technical component in NAFTA," says Luis de la Calle, one of the treaty's negotiators and later Mexico's under-secretary of economy for foreign trade. "We should be getting a significant transfer of technology from the United States, and we didn't really try."[17] As a result, NAFTA will only encourage low-skill jobs in Mexico, and deepen the Mexican brain drain to the United States.

International trade rules should not forbid governments in small countries from guiding the market to create quality career opportunities for their citizens. No country can afford to squander its human resources, especially its most highly skilled workers. Canada cannot let the forces of unbridled free trade push us into the experience of Jamaica, and India, where brain drain is endemic.

In theory, a country has a number of options to promote job opportunities for its people. For instance, a government could insist that when a foreign company wants to build a factory in its territory, a local engineering firm must design the building. Alternatively, the foreign company might agree to hire local firms to maintain its equipment, even though the company would otherwise want to have foreign labour do the maintenance. A government could even stipulate that a certain percentage of the factory's management need to be domestic citizens. If this percentage started low, and was increased over the lifetime of the factory, it would give the company an incentive to train the local workforce in world-class management skills. This kind of job creation could be a powerful tool for the country's economic development.

Of course, in today's world, all of these suggestions would be subject to attack under international trade rules. Foreign companies can use trade regulations to pressure a national government into abandoning its role in protecting job opportunities for its citizens. If threats are not enough, foreign governments can contest any of the measures proposed in the previous paragraph at a WTO or NAFTA tribunal. If free-trade advocates have their way, the defending government will lose.

WHAT CAN BE DONE?

Despite the danger that unbridled free trade poses, we should be careful not to jump to the conclusion that the best solution to brain drain is simply to restrict trade. As in other chapters, we must also ask here, "Would it be any better if we didn't have trade?" If we close Canada's borders to trade, history suggests that our economy will suffer, like so many other countries that have tried the same strategy.[18] If that happens, and our most talented people do not have opportunities to rise into skilled positions, many of them will surely go elsewhere (especially south of the border). If, on the other hand, our economy grows and provides such opportunities, Canadians will be far more likely to stay, and we will continue to attract talented individuals from other countries.

Unbridled free trade sets up a positive feedback cycle whereby countries that already possess a well-educated workforce continue to acquire more and more of the developing world's most valuable workers. Moreover, free trade changes the role of multinational corporate branch plants and exacerbates brain drain in small countries. Still further, current free trade agreements like the WTO and the NAFTA prohibit national governments from intervening to encourage the transfer of skills and technical know-how to local populations. Together, this creates a perverse situation: small countries face enormous challenges in creating quality career opportunities for its labour force.

Nonetheless, abandoning international trade is not the answer. Instead, Canada should move toward *managed* free trade. The WTO actively works against this kind of regulation, but the power to manage trade is essential. All countries, especially developing ones, need to be able to negotiate with foreign-owned companies to ensure that when they invest, they create high-quality opportunities for local people.

Can any government policy stem the tide of brain drain? The answer is yes. In the decade after 1965, for instance, Canadian immigration policies, coupled with unpopular US foreign policy, briefly reversed the "brain drain" into a "brain gain" for Canada.[19] Back then, the government offered Canadian professionals in the US a three-year federal tax rebate, which they received in the fourth year after they returned. The loss of three years of federal taxes was a small price to pay for successfully luring Canadian professionals back home: the returned émigrés paid taxes in Canada for the rest of their lives.

As a society, we have a choice about the way we treat our highly skilled workers. We do have options to make Canada an attractive place for professional workers, so that we can attract—and retain—the vital human capital that our society needs.

NOTES

1 M. Bordt, "The Measurement of International Migration to Canada," Chapter 4 in *International Mobility of the Highly Skilled* (Paris: OECD, 1999).

2 B. Ghosh and R. Ghosh, *Economics of Brain Migration* (New Delhi: Deep and Deep Publications, 1982), p. 81.

3 Ghosh and Ghosh, *Economics of Brain Migration*, p. 85. The WHO study quoted is cited in D.E. Bhagwagar, "Reversing Brain Drain," *The Economic Times* 24 Nov. 1980: 4. Emphasis added.

4 Ghosh and Ghosh, *Economics of Brain Migration*, p. 75.

5 A. Mejia, "World Physician Migration," in *The Arab Brain Drain*, proceedings of a seminar, 4–8 Feb. 1980, ed. A.B. Zahlan. Published for the United Nations (London, Ithaca Press), p. 212.

6 "A survey of Canada: Where the grass is greener," *The Economist* 24 July 1999: S7–9.

7 R. Shillington, "Canada's 'Brain Drain' a trickle not a flood," *Analyze This* 7 June 2000. <www.straightgoods.com/Analyze/0018.asp>

8 T. Chui and M. Devereaux, "Canada's newest workers," *Perspectives* (Ottawa: Statistics Canada, Spring 1995): 17–23.

9 D.J. DeVoretz, "The Brain Drain is Real and It Costs Us," *Policy Options*, Sept. 1999, pp. 18–24. The dollar figures given are in 1994 Canadian dollars; the latter figure represents the difference between the lifetime earnings of immigrants with post-secondary training and those of comparable Canadian-born residents.

10 DeVoretz, "The Brain Drain is Real and It Costs Us."

11 DeVoretz, "The Brain Drain is Real and It Costs Us." Emphasis added. The dollar figure is in 1994 Canadian dollars; it represents the cumulative difference between the lifetime earnings of immigrants with post-secondary training and those of comparable Canadian-born residents.

12 J. Holmes, "The Globalization of Production and the Future of Canada's Mature Industries: The Case of the Automotive Industry," in Drache and Gertler, eds., *The New Era of Global Competition*, p. 156.

13 S. Clarkson, "Disjunctions: Free Trade and the Paradox of Canadian Development," in Drache and Gertler, eds., *The New Era of Global Competition*, p. 113.

14 G. Arrighi and J. Drangel, "The stratification of the world-economy: an exploration of the semiperipheral zone," *Review* 10.1(1986): 9–74.

15 G. Arrighi and J. Drangel, "The stratification of the world-economy: an exploration of the semiperipheral zone," *Review* 10.1(1986): 9–74.

16 NAFTA Chapter 11.

17 Rosenberg, "The Free-Trade Fix."

18 The Latin American countries that focused on "import substitution" are the classic example of this. Economists believe that by restricting trade in the 1930s–1960s, these countries did significant damage to their economies. North Korea is a more recent example. Isolated from the rest of the world, North Korea's economy stagnates and famine has cost the lives of millions its people.

19 DeVoretz, "The Brain Drain is Real and It Costs Us."

chapter TEN

FREE TRADE AND THE ARTS

For decades, Canada has been trying to protect its magazine industry from American competition. Well-known magazines such as *Saturday Night* make only marginal profits, and almost half the Canadian market is dominated by US titles.[1] The federal government—concerned about the future of the Canadian magazine industry—has tried several policies over the years to protect homegrown periodicals. As early as 1965, Canada was trying to fight *split-runs*—the "Canadian" editions of US magazines. Unfortunately, it did not take long for American companies to find ways around these rules, and Canada went back to the drawing board.

Eventually, in 1995, Canada banned split-runs altogether. Almost immediately, the US took the Canadian ban to court at the World Trade Organization. The WTO did not hesitate; it ruled that Canada's laws contradicted its obligations to free trade, and that its laws would have to change. In 1997, Canada appealed the decision, and once again the WTO told Canada to change its laws. In fact, the WTO went further; it ruled that Canada would have to remove the postal subsidies provided to Canadian magazines.[2] With each step, unbridled free trade is dismantling Canada's protection for its magazine industry.

The federal government's struggle to protect the domestic magazine industry is symbolic of the dilemma that Canada faces under unbridled free trade. American cultural exports, especially from Hollywood, have swamped the global marketplace. In doing so, American cultural hegemony undermines the promise of globalization to provide consumers with more choice in the products they want. Unbridled free trade creates an uneven playing field for cultural products, posing real challenges for the protection of cultural sovereignty in small countries.

IS CANADIAN CULTURE WORTH PROTECTING AND PROMOTING?

For a moment, suppose that the economic market for the arts gave American cultural products an advantage over their Canadian equivalents. As that advantage took hold, and Canadians consumed more and more American culture, a distinctive Canadian culture would cease to exist. One might ask, is this really so bad? Is a unique Canadian culture worth protecting?

Canada is a massive country with a relatively tiny population, spread out thinly across a strip of land 5,000 miles across. The geography, climate, economy, and even language vary dramatically across the expanse. In order to remain a unified country, Canada depends on a shared set of cultural experiences to bring its people together. Mass media plays an important role in forming the national bond that makes Canada a cohesive community, despite the innate challenges of our geography and distinct cultures.

Consider professional sports as a cultural product. When one man watches a hockey game, he might enjoy it on his own. If he watches it with his friend, however, it will almost certainly become more enjoyable. The two friends could enjoy the highs and lows of the game together; they could boo, comment, and laugh as appropriate. In a sense, the very fact that someone else is watching with them adds to their enjoyment. Now imagine extending this example to a small town, or even a country. As more and more people watch the same event, they share its enjoyment. Perfect strangers could meet on the street and comfortably discuss last night's hockey game. (Anyone who thinks that this is strange hasn't been to Canada.) Nowhere is this more evident than during the Olympics—Canadians come together as a national community to share in the efforts of our nation's athletes. Who can forget the excitement in the streets in after Canada won both gold medals in men and women's hockey in the 2002 Winter Olympics against our old rivals, the United States? As simple as shared experiences like these might appear, Canadian identity is built on the basis of these common bonds. As more people across the country share these experiences, the community bond becomes more deeply unifying.

Anyone who watches Canadian politics is surely aware of the enormous tension that exists between the different regions of Canada. Atlantic Canada does not want to be treated as the poor cousin of Ontario; the western provinces feel that Ottawa's attention never reaches past Thunder Bay; Ontario feels that it carries the financial burden of Canada on its back; Quebec even flirts with separation. In a political climate that is so fraught with difficulties, national unity is essential to Canada's survival. National unity and national culture go hand in hand. Canada's survival as a functioning national community depends on its ability to resist becoming a cheap imitation of American culture.

Indeed, if the full Americanization of Canadian culture appears acceptable, we might go farther down this track. If we are to have an American culture, we might as well let our political situation reflect it, and merge with the US. After all, there are economic and political benefits to being a part of the world's only superpower. No longer would Canada need to worry about trade disputes on softwood lumber or steel imports; ex-Canadians could have full representation in the US Congress and the presidential elections. Of course, this goes against all evidence about Canadians' desires. Most Canadians do not want to merge with the US, nor become absorbed by American culture. On the contrary, most Canadians feel that protecting a distinctive national identity is important for Canada.

Unfortunately, Canada's cultural sovereignty is under assault from the effects of unbridled free trade. The economics of mass media has made it easy for artists and producers in large markets like the US to overwhelm local artists in small economies like Canada.

THE REWARDS AND RISKS OF MASS MEDIA

One of the revolutionary features of mass media is that it is able to touch so many people so easily. Once a book is written, a film produced or a television show created, the cost to distribute it is almost nothing compared to the initial cost of creation. In the electronic age, especially with the creation of the Internet, the costs to distribute mass-media products have never been cheaper. As we will see, the fact that the *production cost* far outweighs the *distributional cost* of mass-media products has profound implications for the cultures of small groups and minorities.

153

In many ways, this change in the cost of cultural products is wonderful. Globalization offers a dizzying array of products to choose from. It often means that wherever you are in the world, you can find a newspaper written in your language (especially if your language happens to be English). On the Internet, you can access digital images by Monet and da Vinci or electronic copies of Mozart and Bach. Foreign television broadcasts, movies, or just ordinary radio—most of these cultural goods were simply unavailable to our great-grandparents' generation. Few of us want to go back to the days when little of this fantastic range of talent and high-quality work was accessible.

For this reason, free-trade advocates, particularly in the US, push hard for trade liberalization of cultural products. The creation of a Hollywood movie, they say, is no different from the creation of any other economic good, such as a car or a coffee mug. Free trade advocates argue that those who have the most talent will have a competitive advantage over those who do not, and the market will encourage the best performers to rise to the top. Globalization allows people all over the world to access the art and music of these exceptionally talented artists.

However, unbridled free trade of cultural products has a much darker side to it than its advocates are willing to admit. Hollywood movies are *not* regular economic goods like cars or coffee mugs. The reason that trade creates wealth through the magic of comparative advantage is because *it is assumed that it does not matter where the goods are made*, and it is assumed that the goods are identical wherever they are made. This is a very reasonable assumption for most economic goods. For most people, it is unimportant whether a Chevrolet Cavalier is made in Detroit, USA, or across the border in Oshawa, Canada. What matters to the car buyer is the quality of the car, its price, and perhaps its reputation. This is true for most goods—as consumers, we tend to care more about the product itself than about where it was made.

Cultural products, however, are quite a bit different. For most of us, it matters where a movie was made or where a story took place, because the arts are part of the way in which we form our identity. It matters to Australians whether they listen to a British accent or an Australian one; it matters to a Canadian whether the story is set in Toronto or Chicago; it *certainly* matters to the French whether a movie was made in Hollywood or Bordeaux. The point is simply this: we usually value the arts that were designed to speak to our national identity far more than arts designed to speak to a different national identity.

That is not to suggest that we are interested only in our own community. Sometimes we are excited by the exotic and would much rather hear a story of a foreign land than our own backyard. Sometimes, a story from overseas can teach us truths that we would not have seen otherwise. Normally, however, our identities are quite rooted to a specific place, to a specific community, and usually, to a specific nation. Our identities shape our tastes in the cultural arts, and that means we often prefer local stories.

The fact that we have this preference has profound implications for globalization and international trade. As noted above, comparative advantage works its magic only on the condition that it does not matter where a product was made; but for cultural products, this is not true. When it comes to our culture, we often want goods that are designed to speak to our own national identity. And that means that for the arts, unbridled free trade may not lead to a broader range of goods; instead, it may actually lead to a narrowing of the consumer's choices.

Imagine for a moment that you are a film producer. You want to create a movie, and you have two options, both of which will produce a high-quality product. The first option is a compelling drama, set in Chicago and designed for an American audience. The second option is an identical drama, except the movie is set in Toronto and designed for a Canadian audience. Depending on which option you pick, the actors will make subtle adjustments for the cultural differences between Canadians and Americans—they will even say "out" and "about" differently. For the most part, however, the two options are identical, and either option will produce a movie of similar quality.

Suppose the cost and the quality of the two possible movies are identical. The only real difference between the two movie options, in fact, is their appeal to the audience. Because people's national identity affects their preferences in cultural arts, the two movies will bring in different revenues. For this example, let's say that if the movie were set in Chicago, it would attract 10 per cent of Canadians. If the movie were set in Toronto, however, 15 per cent of Canadians would go to see it. Likewise, American audiences prefer the Chicago setting. If the movie were set in Chicago, 15 per cent of Americans would see it; if it were set in Toronto, only 10 per cent would go to watch the movie.

So you, the film producer, must decide: will you set your film for an American audience or a Canadian one? You realize that because Canada's population is only a tenth that of America's, your movie would earn a *lot* less money if you set it in Toronto. If it's set in Toronto, 4.5 million Canadians and about 30 million Americans will watch it, for a total of about 34.5 million people. But if you set it in Chicago, your audience will have fewer Canadians, but many more Americans—for a total of about 48 million people! And those extra 13.5 million people who watch your movie are going to make a huge difference for your bank account—and your reputation. With that boost in both your finances and your fame, the outlook for your next movie is terrific. So, where would you choose to set your movie, Chicago or Toronto? With unbridled free trade, it's barely a choice.

This is the terrible dilemma that faces small countries such as Canada. On the one hand, globalization promises to open new possibilities for consumers. Lower trade barriers mean a broader range of movies, music, and books from all over the world, which expands Canadian artistic horizons to the tastes of the entire world. On the other hand, Canadian artists are forced to compete with foreigners, chiefly Americans. American artists appeal to a US audience, which is far larger than the one in Canada. Because audience size is so important for their profitability and even creative success, both Canadian and American artists will tailor their work to the larger American audience.

Actors know this. Pamela Anderson, Jim Carrey, Mike Myers—all of these Hollywood superstars were once struggling Canadian actors. As their careers took off, there was little question that they would go to Hollywood; even within Canada, success in the US is essential for credibility as a big-name star. For all intents and purposes, Canada and America form one unified labour market for actors. That means that if a Canadian film producer wants to air a film starring Mike Myers, the producer needs to pay Mr. Myers a salary similar to what he would receive in Hollywood. Is this unpatriotic of Mr. Myers, or any other actor? Of course not. They can hardly be faulted for wanting to be paid their worth in the market. But it does have consequences for the arts in Canada.

So, regardless of the audience to which a movie is targeted, a film producer will have to pay top salary for top-notch talent. As we have just seen, however, a movie tailored to Canadian audiences will attract a smaller total North American audience than one suited for Americans. Thus, a Canadian producer cannot make the revenue needed to pay for the most talented (and most expensive) actors on the market. The logical choice for our hypothetical Canadian producer might be to trim costs and work with second-tier actors. In practice, this is exactly what happens—to the great harm of the Canadian film industry, which is unable to compete commercially, not because of a lack of Canadian talent, but instead because of the relative size of the Canadian audience and open competition with the United States.

Of course, one might think that, apart from actors' salaries, making a movie is far cheaper in Canada than it is in the US. Don't these low production costs compensate Canadian producers for their other disadvantages? Sadly, this is no protection for Canada's movie industry. Lower film production costs in Canada mean only that more producers will shoot movies in Canada. This does not in any way guarantee that producers will make those movies for Canadian audiences! In fact, more and more American movies that are set in American cities and designed for American audiences are made in Canada. As just one example, witness Jackie Chan's movie *Rumble in the Bronx*, actually shot in Vancouver, Canada. (If you look closely, you can see Vancouver's mountains in the background as Jackie fights his way through the "Bronx.")

The bottom line? Artists who produce mass-media products for small markets like Canada are at a huge disadvantage because of unbridled free trade. Canada's open border with the United States means that North American actors, musicians, and authors will virtually always be better paid if they perform for an American audience rather than a Canadian one. The market will punish those who decide to perform for a niche market like Canada's.

The great promise of globalization is that the future will offer ordinary consumers an ever-expanding selection of top-quality goods for low cost. The Canadian film industry experience, however, refutes this promise. True, Canadians will have access to a dizzying array of American movies and music. But the truth is that unless something is done, the market will offer Canadian consumers progressively *fewer* choices for Canadian movies, music, and books. Moreover, liberalized trade, as it is currently designed by the WTO and NAFTA, gives the Canadian government almost no power to change this harsh reality.

AMERICANIZATION: THE PRICE OF FREE TRADE?

The United States is taking full advantage of the fact that its trade agreements give it unprecedented access to worldwide cultural markets. Hollywood makes an enormous amount of money selling its products overseas: by the late 1990s, about half of Hollywood's total film revenues came from outside America.[3] Overall, the entertainment business brings in $60 billion in export sales to the US each year. These are boom times: in 1996, the industry grew three times faster than the rest of the US economy. Entertainment has overtaken the automotive, agriculture, and even aerospace industries to become the single biggest US export sector.[4] As one French observer put it, "Cinema used to be side salad in world commerce; now it's the beef."[5]

For decades, Hollywood studios have controlled 85 per cent of the Canadian film distribution market.[6] European theatres, too, are dominated by the relentless expansion of American film. In 1991, the top eight films in terms of gross revenues in Hungary were all American. Even in France, where cultural sovereignty is passionately defended, almost 60 per cent of film revenues go to America. On its opening weekend, the American blockbuster *Jurassic Park* took over nearly one in four movie screens in France's major cities, provoking an outcry from defenders of French culture. The US now controls over 80 per cent of the European film market, while Europe has less than 2 per cent of the American market.[7]

American cultural influence spreads all over the globe. Even in revolutionary Iran, where zealous censors ban most imports, authorities permitted entry to *Dances with Wolves* and *Driving Miss Daisy*, both of which found a large audience.[8] The majority of Indonesian movie theatres show foreign films, especially American ones. One critic writes, "The presence of so many American films has led an entire generation to believe that Indonesia is incapable of producing great movies."[9] The BBC estimates that American-made films occupy about 85 per cent of movie screens worldwide.[10]

American big business enjoys the advantage that the current international trade rules give to it. Until now, small countries have accepted the unfairness of this US advantage as the price they had to pay for more stable access to the markets in large countries. However, this situation is unsustainable. Although most will not admit it publicly, many trade officials can see that the injustice present in the rules of globalization will eventually undermine the legitimacy of the WTO. "The US should do more than heed these warnings; it should recognize that strong cultures are in America's self-interest,"[11] writes Jeffrey Garten, dean of the Yale School of Management, a former investment banker and under-secretary of commerce for international trade in the Clinton administration. "If societies feel under assault, insecurities will be magnified, leading to policy paralysis, strident nationalism and anti-Americanism," Garten adds. Garten proposes that corporate America and free trade advocates encourage cultural diversity around the globe. Slowly, it would seem, even those in the mightiest country are beginning to see that fairness over cultural sovereignty is beneficial to all.

THE CASE FOR MARKET INTERVENTION

If Canada had not made commitments to the WTO's trade rules, it would have considerably more freedom to protect and foster its culture. One way the government could accomplish this is to subsidize cultural activities in Canada. Subsidies would intentionally favour domestic artists over foreign ones in the Canadian market place.

Let's suppose that Canada was not restricted by its trade agreements from providing a subsidy to its aspiring artists.* One might ask, why should the government use tax money for this? Why not simply let the market work? If Canadian artists have a smaller audience, they could make up for it by charging more money for their work. After all, if Canadians truly want Canadian movies, shouldn't they be willing to pay more for them than American movies?

This is a good question. To answer it, we need to return to the sports example discussed earlier in this chapter. Recall that when two people shared the experience of watching a hockey game, it was better for each of them than if they had each watched the game alone. If we think of the two friends as consumers, the hockey game they are watching is the cultural product that they are consuming. The fact that one person's consumption affects another person's—i.e., the fact that sharing the hockey game with a friend makes it more enjoyable—is referred to as an *economic externality*. Economists recognize that markets with externalities, like the cultural arts, are instances when the free market will not necessarily deliver the best

---

* To be clear, trade agreements do not forbid all funding for cultural activities. Canada can and does provide considerable funding for culture at present; however, it is restricted in its choice of funding goals.

social outcome. Often when an economic externality is present, the government needs to step in and guide the market to a better solution than it otherwise would provide.

For instance, public health contains an economic externality. If all of the people around you have the flu, there is a very good chance that you will get the flu, too. However, if the government provides flu vaccines to the people around you, it will help prevent the flu for everyone: both for other members of the public *and* for you. In this sense, the value of a flu vaccine to society is greater than its value to any individual. In financial terms, the price that any single person is willing to pay for a flu vaccine is only part of the full value of that vaccine to the entire community. The remaining part is the economic externality. This is the part of the cost the government often tries to fund.

The free market does not handle economic externalities (e.g., public health or national culture) very well, so as a society we need the government to compensate for what the market cannot do. In the case of public health, the government might pay for flu vaccines; in the case of culture, the government could subsidize the national arts. Government intervention would help Canadian society as a whole reach a preferable outcome than the one produced by a purely free-market approach.

Of course, the process of building a national community by encouraging a common set of cultural references is only possible if the government is able to intervene in the marketplace. Our look at the North American movie industry shows how film producers in small countries are constantly struggling on an uneven playing field. So are the Canadian magazine publishers. Publishers, producers, and artists who perform for large countries can afford to charge low prices and reap the financial rewards of having large audiences. Artists in small countries are not so lucky: to cover their costs, they will have to charge much higher prices; higher prices will make them unattractive to potential audiences. The only way out of the Canadian artists' dilemma is through government intervention in the market: either direct financial support or protection from foreign competition by import tariffs. Alas, our trade agreements currently make such policies impossible.

The real issue here is that Canadians should no longer be barred from encouraging participation in their own culture. History shows that unbridled free trade stands in direct opposition to Canada's cultural sovereignty. The experience of the magazine industry in Canada is telling: on each occasion, the WTO ruled that Canada's policies were in violation of its trade commitments. Gradually, but with increasing speed, unbridled free trade is forcing Canada to abandon its efforts to protect its culture.

Ultimately, of course, Canadians may decide that they do not want to subsidize Canadian culture and heritage. Perhaps the voters will conclude that subsidies to the arts are not worth the cost, regardless of the effects of trade. Alternatively, Canadians may be willing to support some cultural programs (the National Art Gallery in Ottawa, for instance) but not others (tax shelters for NHL hockey teams). These are reasonable choices for Canada to make.

What is critically important, however, is that Canadians have the freedom to make those choices on their own terms. A subsidy for well-paid hockey players was understandably unpopular, but government funding for local artists and authors finds considerably greater support. Ultimately, this is an issue of public policy that should be decided by the people of Canada, not by the unaccountable bureaucrats of the WTO. Small countries like Canada should not have their cultural sovereignty limited by the forces of globalization.

Even trade advocates are beginning to realize this. Economist Jagdish Bhagwati is well known for his pro-trade stance. Nonetheless, he acknowledges that subsidies for cultural goods are an appropriate response to concerns with globalization's increasing encroachment on national identity. Indeed, he warns us that "the desire to preserve one's cinema is better addressed by subsidies to the local production of movies rather than by restrictions on the showing of foreign films."[12] In this way, Bhagwati espouses a position that allows the consumer the greatest range of choice in cultural goods while maintaining the power of policy makers to support national identity.

Modern international trade rules are increasingly powerful in binding the hands of national governments. Of course, that is exactly what those rules are designed to do. For the right purposes, such as eliminating arbitrary discrimination, this can be a good thing. Using trade rules to destroy cultural sovereignty, however, is hardly a good purpose.

DOES NAFTA PROTECT NATIONAL CULTURE?

As the Canadian magazine case illustrates, the WTO does not protect cultural products from international trade rules. NAFTA, on the other hand, does contain a provision to exempt Canadian cultural products from trade obligations.[13] Mexico is not granted the same protection, since NAFTA rules maintain only the exemption previously negotiated under the Canada-US Free Trade Agreement.[14]

However, NAFTA's exemption for cultural industries provides weak protection. While the Article provides cultural exemption for Canada, it also allows a NAFTA party to retaliate against the use of the cultural exemption by taking actions of "equivalent commercial effect." Thus, if Canada protects its cultural industries from the US, the US can retaliate by imposing tariffs on another industry like softwood lumber or wheat. Moreover, NAFTA does not allow Canada to contest the measures taken as "equivalent commercial effect" before the NAFTA Free Trade Commission, as otherwise provided for in NAFTA.[15] This opens the door for a harsh retaliation against any attempt to protect Canada's cultural industries.

In effect, NAFTA fails to provide real protection of national culture. As if to confirm their intention to render NAFTA's cultural exemption impotent, the US Congress has publicly stated it will be carefully monitoring Canadian actions. By law, "the United States Trade Representative [is required to] look out for any act, policy or practice that is adopted by the government of Canada that affects American cultural industries."[16] In addition, regardless of what the NAFTA says, each government also has WTO trade obligations. Even if Canadian magazines or other cultural products are exempted from NAFTA obligations, they are still subject to the WTO ruling against government financial support. Effectively, the international trade system is in conflict with support for the arts on a local and national level.

WHAT CAN BE DONE?

There is an element of tragedy in the conflict between free trade and the arts. It is a tragic problem because its solution, far from being difficult, is readily available within the existing framework of trade rules. Unfortunately, far too much money is at stake for Hollywood to allow a simple solution, however reasonable it might be.

The WTO already has a clause that specifically allows for exceptions to free trade for cultural purposes. Unfortunately, it focuses only on the film industry, even though its logic could easily be (and should be) applied to other cultural products, like magazines. It also contains a huge loophole:

"Screen quotas shall be subject to negotiation for their limitation, liberalization or elimination."[17] Hollywood lobbyists have used this loophole to ensure that the cultural clause is effectively useless for most major countries. Nonetheless, the very existence of this clause presents a model for an easy solution to manage the conflict between trade and cultural sovereignty: simply allow an exception to WTO rules for national policies that support cultural products. This new provision could close the current loophole and extend its protection to other cultural products, like books and magazines. In this way, the WTO could provide the protection that nominally exists under NAFTA.

There might be disputes about what exactly constitutes a "cultural product." This, however, is a technical issue that trade experts can address by good judgment and rational argument. In fact, arbitration of such disputes is the one thing the WTO is supposed to be very good at; after all, this is what keeps trade lawyers in business. No, technical issues are not a problem for a cultural exemption clause. The real problem lies in the lack of political will from the governments of large countries to acknowledge that globalization poses a threat to small countries. Large countries, particularly the US, enjoy the benefits of an uneven playing field for mass-media products like books and movies. As one NGO puts it, the US trade position "is not entirely divorced from the fact that the single biggest export industry of the United States is the entertainment industry."[18] Hollywood's stake in the matter means that it will take a powerful force to move the American negotiating position into accepting a more reasonable set of rules for cultural products.

There is hope that such a force may be gathering. It is worth noting, for instance, that Bhagwati's position on culture and trade has direct implications with regard to Canada's policy manoeuvres in the magazine industry. While Bhagwati would almost certainly condemn Canada's early attempt to ban US split-run magazines, he has acknowledged that direct subsidies to local producers are a reasonable policy initiative.

Until recently, small countries have accepted the unfairness in trade rules as the price they had to pay for more stable access to the markets in large countries. Now, however, countries from around the world are banding together to confront the issue. Canada is one of the leaders, and was active in passing a resolution at the United Nations body on economic and social affairs (UNESCO) that could lead to a convention on cultural diversity.[19] As awareness grows, the movement toward a more just set of cultural trade rules gathers momentum.

On its own, the WTO's infringement on national culture probably would not cause a great deal of controversy. As an important part of a larger picture, however, cultural sovereignty ought to command the attention of the powerful elite who shape future globalization. For if the dominant countries that control the WTO are content to let basic unfairness be an inherent consequence of globalization, they abdicate their standing as moral actors in the international community. Even the most powerful countries must realize that global peace and prosperity are dependent on an ethical global order.

As Canada considers the ongoing process of globalization, it must weigh carefully the consequences for our national identity. Those who argue that unbridled free trade would bring unfettered benefit to our country are wrong. As they currently stand, the WTO rules make it virtually impossible for small countries such as our own to defend the distinctiveness of our artistic and cultural life. Before signing another trade agreement, Canada should see that those rules are appropriately modified to allow for the protection of cultural diversity.

NOTES

1 "Canada's Cultural Sovereignty Challenge," Media Awareness Network, 22 Sept. 1999.

2 WTO Appellate Body, "Canada—Certain Measures Concerning Periodicals," AB-1997-2, World Trade Organization, Geneva, 1997.

3 Barber, *Jihad vs. McWorld*, p. 93 (n.32).

4 "Pat Schroeder on the State of the US Copyright Industries," International Intellectual Property Association, 7 May 1998. <www.publishers.org/press/iipa.htm>

5 Barber, *Jihad vs. McWorld*, p. 90.

6 "WTO Watch," *Morning NAFTA* (March 1998), <www.clc-ctc.ca/publications/morning nafta/mar98/mornaftamar98-8.html>

7 For all statistics quoted in this paragraph except the first sentence, see Barber, *Jihad vs. McWorld*, pp. 91–92.

8 D. Young, "Iranian Cinema Now," *Variety International Film Guide*, p. 30. Quoted in Barber, *Jihad vs. McWorld*, p. 94.

9 Barber, *Jihad vs. McWorld*, p. 94.

10 "Strike raises Hollywood recession fears," BBC, 2 May 2001. <news.bbc.co.uk/hi/english/business/newsid_1306000/1306723.stm>

11 H. Mackenzie, "US Seen as Cultural Imperialist," *Gazette* 16 March 1999. Global Policy Forum, <www.globalpolicy.org/globaliz/cultural/cultimp.htm>

12 Bhagwati, *Free Trade Today*, pp. 81–82

13 Article 2106, *The North American Free Trade Agreement*.

14 Article 2005, *The Canada-US Free Trade Agreement*.

15 B. Appleton, *Navigating NAFTA* (Scarborough: Carswell Publishing, 1994), p. 191.

16 Government of the United States, *North American Free Trade Agreement Implementation Act*, Section 513. As referenced in Appleton, *Navigating NAFTA*, p.190.

17 General Agreement on Tariffs and Trade, 1947, Article IV (d). <www.wto.org>

18 Mackenzie, "US Seen as Cultural Imperialist."

19 K. Wiwa, *Globe and Mail* online, posted 18 Oct. 2003.

ELEVEN

NAFTA AND THE ENVIRONMENT

Can unbridled free trade undermine our ability to protect the environment? It is a chilling prospect, and there are good reasons to be worried. As industrialization spreads globally, humankind is increasingly capable of altering the entire ecosystem of our planet. Unfortunately, trade agreements have not kept up with the times, and they continue to use outdated principles about the environmental effects of international trade.

The next two chapters will look at how trade has influenced environmental quality around the world. This chapter will focus on NAFTA; the next chapter will look at the WTO and the trade-environment relationship more broadly. Our investigation of NAFTA will touch upon some of the fundamental questions about trade—are Canadians losing their right to protect the environment? Does NAFTA force us to trade away our natural resources, like water and energy? Some of the facts demonstrate clearly that environmentalists are over-reacting. Nonetheless, there is still plenty of room for concern. NAFTA's so-called environmental safeguards have proven ineffective when applied to real-world issues.

CANADA AND THE MMT-ETHYL CASE

In 1998, a story about a gasoline additive called MMT exploded onto the headlines of newspapers and broadcasts. The Canadian government had banned the international and interprovincial trade of MMT out of concern that it was a public health hazard. An American firm named Ethyl

Corporation, however, argued that the trade ban was a violation of Canada's NAFTA obligations. As the sole producer of the MMT used in Canada, Ethyl Corporation was suing the government for $250 million (US) in damages.

This story had all the right sensational elements: here was a dirty, *American* chemical corporation suing the good Canadian government over an honest attempt to protect the health of our citizens. Social activists swung into high gear. Maude Barlow claimed the case was part of "an all-out assault on virtually every public sphere of life, including the democratic underpinning of our legal systems."[1] One group declared that the MMT-*Ethyl* case "represented the low point for the Chrétien government's already pathetic environmental record."[2] Dalton Camp wrote in the *Toronto Star*, "[The crux of the matter is not] whether MMT poisons the air, destroys catalytic converters, is harmful to children, older people, and those suffering from respiratory ailments ... [rather the issue is whether] the Canadian government ... has the sovereign power to pass whatever law it wishes."[3] In the minds of some activists, nothing short of Canadian democracy was at stake in the MMT case—which left little doubt as to how the NAFTA tribunal ought to rule.

Unfortunately, a closer look at this story reveals some disturbing facts about the Canadian government's position. Health Canada had been investigating the effects of MMT ever since it was introduced into Canadian gasoline in 1977. In 1990, Parliament tried, unsuccessfully, to ban MMT as a toxic substance under the Canadian Environmental Act. It was legally unable to do so because it lacked scientific evidence that MMT was a health hazard.[4] In fact, a 1994 Health Canada report stated, "Airborne manganese resulting from the combustion of MMT in gasoline powered vehicles is not entering the Canadian environment in quantities or under conditions that may constitute a health risk."[5] Even after twenty years of research and four separate risk assessments by Health Canada, no one could produce scientific evidence that proved MMT was a health hazard.

Politicians continued to express concern about the public health risks of MMT, but what was the real driving force behind the ban? According to two experts on risk assessment, the government was actually concerned about the automotive industry in Ontario.[6] The auto industry argued that MMT was harmful to a variety of car parts, including the catalytic converters used to reduce environmental emissions. On September 12, 1994, the car manufacturers told Environment Minister Sheila Copps that unless she banned MMT, "they would raise prices by $3000 per vehicle, void parts of their warranties, or close down some Canadian manufacturing units."[7] The auto industry was hoping to bully the federal government into accepting their demands.

The talk about environmental health risks was in fact just a smoke screen around the real MMT battle, which involved two competing corporate interests: the car industry and the gasoline refineries. If an MMT ban was enforced, it would force the gasoline refineries to use a more costly substitute. If the MMT ban was struck down, the auto industry would lose. Apparently bowing to the pressure from the car manufacturers, the federal government banned the international and interprovincial trade of MMT in 1997.

The refineries had been requesting evidence for the car companies' claims for years, but to no avail. A ruling by the US Environmental Protection Agency that the use of MMT in gasoline "will not cause or contribute to a failure of any emission control device"[8] made little difference. The refineries even offered to voluntarily remove MMT if an independent inquiry panel found that the car industry's claims were valid. At every turn, their requests were denied. Frustrated, the refineries turned to the Alberta government to do something. Ever sensitive to the suspected favouritism toward Ontario at the expense of the oil and gas industry of Alberta, the province was swift to act. The government of Alberta took the federal government to court, arguing that the law was inconsistent with Canada's Agreement on Internal Trade. The challenge succeeded, and in July 1998 the federal government repealed the trade ban on MMT.

Thus, the removal of the ban on MMT had nothing to do with NAFTA— it was struck down by a federal-provincial dispute right here in Canada. However, the federal government still had to deal with the lawsuit from the manufacturer of MMT, Ethyl Corporation. Having lost in court already, the Canadian government knew it stood no chance of winning at the NAFTA tribunal. It settled out of court with the Ethyl Corporation for $13 million (US) for legal fees and lost profits.

As frustrating as it is to see the Canadian government pay millions of dollars to an American company, NAFTA is not the real culprit here. In fact, how would Canadians feel if the situation were reversed? Imagine that a small Canadian company, making a product with no known health risks, was struggling to compete in the American market. If the American government simply banned the Canadian firm's products, forcing it out of business, we would be outraged. At the very least, the firm would demand to see some scientific evidence to support the ban. When no such evidence could be produced, Canadians would want to know why they had lost their jobs. If a country can make "environmental" policy without any scientific evidence, there is no limit to the damage that it can do to fairness in international trade.

Some political observers applauded the NAFTA decision. The *Globe and Mail* declared that this was a case of "mad [government] ministers thwarted."[9] The Institute for International Economics insists that the MMT-*Ethyl* case was a triumph, ensuring that "sound science is the touchstone for environmental standards."[10] Indeed, based on the bizarre rationale brought forward for the NAFTA tribunal, the Canadian government deserved to lose this case.

Still, there are good reasons to find this case disturbing. MMT is not yet free from suspicion by health experts. While there is no credible evidence that MMT is a serious health risk in the short term, the long-term effects of MMT exposure are still unknown. Some scientists argue that prolonged exposure to MMT could pose a significant danger of neurological disease, even at very low doses. Given this uncertainty, it is reasonable for governments to take a precautionary approach. Recall from Chapter 8 that the precautionary principle states that we should take extra measures to avoid harm if significant scientific uncertainty exists. If the Canadian government had argued that it was taking precautions due to the uncertainty about the long-term health effects of MMT, it would have stood on much more solid ground to justify its ban. Instead, the government was apparently more interested in the domestic politics of an industrial dispute. Scrambling to cover its true intentions, Ottawa used an unconvincing argument based on MMT's short-term health impact.

The MMT-*Ethyl* case highlights the need for a well-defined precautionary principle in international trade agreements. No one wants to see NAFTA strip Canada of its ability to protect its citizens' health. Adopting the precautionary principle is an important step to ensure that never happens.

NAFTA'S APPROACH TO THE ENVIRONMENT

In many ways, NAFTA is a groundbreaking trade agreement with respect to the environment. Partly because of US political forces and partly because of the circumstances of the deal, NAFTA was the first international agreement to deal with substantive environmental issues.

The dramatic differences in industrial development between Canada and the US, on the one hand, and Mexico, on the other, made the NAFTA negotiations significantly more complex and high-profile than those of previous trade agreements. Activists in Canada and the US were particularly concerned about the labour and environmental standards of Mexico, which were viewed as a threat north of the border. There was fear that major companies from the US and Canada would move south to take advantage of less stringent Mexican regulations. Ross Perot, a US presidential candidate in 1992, famously predicted a "giant sucking sound" as industries and jobs moved across the southern border.

An unrelated but critical event focused attention in the US on international trade and the environment. In 1991, the precursor to the WTO (a GATT panel) ruled that the US *Marine Mammal Protection Act*, designed to protect dolphins and other sea-life, violated America's trade treaty obligations. This case, now known as *Tuna-Dolphin*, will be covered in detail in the next chapter. Although this case was dealt with by the GATT, not NAFTA, concern and anger among US environmentalists were aroused nonetheless. As a result, non-governmental organizations (NGOs) and members of the US Congress swung into action. When President Bush (Sr.) sought to extend his presidential authority to negotiate trade deals (known as *fast-track authority*), Congress imposed environmental objectives on the President.[11]

Also in 1991, Bush was preparing for an election against the Democratic challenger, Bill Clinton. Clinton had a difficult choice to face: should he support NAFTA in the election? Clinton believed that international trade, if managed appropriately, was good for the country and the global economy. However, the Democratic Party was traditionally opposed to free trade deals. In order to increase support for NAFTA, Clinton insisted that the trade deal address environmental and labour issues. When he assumed the presidency in 1992, Clinton negotiated two supplemental agreements to NAFTA focused on the adequate enforcement of domestic environmental and labour regulations.

Thus the North American Agreement on Environmental Cooperation was born. The Agreement establishes a Commission for Environmental Cooperation (CEC), which oversees implementation of the environmental aspects of NAFTA. The CEC may consider and make recommendations on a range of environmental issues. In addition, the Commission may also consider cases where one of the NAFTA countries has an "alleged persistent pattern of failure to effectively enforce its environmental law"[12] that is affecting international trade between the NAFTA parties.

In theory, then, NAFTA has significant built-in environmental safeguards. Indeed, NAFTA did make some advances toward environmental protection. For instance, unlike other trade agreements, "the NAFTA allows a Party [i.e., Canada, the US or Mexico] to impose technical [environmental and health] standards which are more stringent than the international standard."[13] So, unlike WTO rules, NAFTA allows governments to insert an additional layer of stringency into the normal international standards on health and environmental protection. Moreover, while the additional standards are subject to challenge at a NAFTA tribunal, the NAFTA Party that introduces the challenge must establish that the standard is inconsistent with NAFTA. One trade expert notes that "this is a change in the burden of proof that is required under other international trade agreements such as the GATT or the Canada-US Free Trade Agreement."[14] While seemingly small, this change in legal procedures gives countries more flexibility in enacting tough environmental regulations.

The creation of the CEC and the additional rules for environmental protection were landmark decisions. This unprecedented attention paid to environmental issues caused one scholar at the Institute for International Economics to declare NAFTA the "greenest trade agreement ever."[15] However, a close look at NAFTA suggests that there is little cause for celebration.

NAFTA'S LARGELY SYMBOLIC APPROACH

NAFTA may be the "greenest ever," but only because previous trade agreements had virtually no provisions for environmental protection. Barry Appleton, a legal expert on NAFTA, puts it even more bluntly: "the NAFTA is not an agreement which was designed to be 'green' in any other way than to reflect the colour of money. The NAFTA is a mercantile agreement with incidental reference to the environment."[16]

Many of NAFTA's environmental provisions appear to have been created for political purposes rather than out of any serious attempt to add environmental stringency to the agreement. For instance, the Preamble to the agreement contains a statement that the Parties are committed to sustainable development and to strengthening the development of environmental laws. However, Article 102 of NAFTA states the objectives of the treaty, and here there is no mention of either sustainability or strengthening environmental laws. Moreover, Article 102 is far more important than the Preamble. Legally, the Preamble can be used in NAFTA disputes only "as a secondary interpretative vehicle in cases where there is definitional ambiguity."[17] Article 102, however, is an integral part of the treaty, which trumps the Preamble. Thus the politically appealing language of the Preamble is almost entirely without substance.

NAFTA contains other examples of symbolic agreements that carry little real weight. For instance, the NAFTA Parties agreed that they "should not" reduce, or even offer to reduce, environmental regulations as an encouragement for business investment. While this commitment was considered a diplomatic achievement, the wording of the agreement is conditional and not mandatory. As such, it is not a binding agreement and has no legal enforcement power.[18]

The ultimate symbolic agreement, however, was the creation of the Commission on Environmental Cooperation (CEC) itself. Nominally, the CEC's job is to oversee the implementation of NAFTA's environmental components. In truth, however, it is a toothless organization with very little power. Even its ability to write reports is questionable, as it is only at "the direction of a two-thirds vote of the Council, [that] the Secretariat may prepare a report on any environmental matter related to the cooperative functions of the agreement. This report may not deal with questions related to whether a Party has failed to enforce its own environmental laws and regulations."[19] It is tempting to wonder why the CEC would write a report that cannot even answer the basic question of whether governments are enforcing their own laws. In fact, it is possible for the CEC to consider whether environmental laws are being broken, but only after an immensely bureaucratic procedure:

> The Secretariat may also receive submissions from any Non-Governmental Organization or any person alleging the non-enforcement of environmental laws and regulations of a NAFTA Party. The Secretariat has the discretion to determine if the complaint 'merits requesting a response from the Party.' ... After the submission is forwarded, the Party has 30 days to respond. If the Secretariat believes that the Party's response warrants further action, it may inform the Council. The Council may, by a two-thirds vote, order that a factual record be prepared. A draft factual record will be submitted to the

Council when it is completed. Any Party may comment on the accuracy of the draft report within 45 days. These comments, if appropriate, will be incorporated into the final record and then be submitted to the Council. The Council may, by a two-thirds vote, make the final factual record public within 60 days.[20]

Not surprisingly, this procedure has been used rather rarely.

Most troubling of all, NAFTA ensures that any government accused of failing to enforce its environmental laws will always have a defence. NAFTA has a built-in escape clause: a "Party has not failed to 'effectively enforce its environmental law' ... where the action or inaction in question ... results from *bona fide* decisions to allocate resources to enforcement in respect of other environmental matters determined to have higher priorities."[21] In other words, even if the CEC ever managed to report that a NAFTA country was violating its environmental obligations, the accused government could always defend itself by saying that it had other budgetary priorities, and had decided not to spend money on enforcing its own laws. Thus, the environmental conclusions of the CEC are highly unlikely to result in any significant impact.

In sum, the final text of the NAFTA contains virtually no real provisions for environmental protection. Certainly, President Clinton wanted to mollify the "green" lobby before signing NAFTA into law. However, even the most generous observers are forced to conclude that the most the NAFTA was ever intended to do was raise awareness and generate political pressure on environmental issues, not to actually address them by legal means.

Although this chapter focuses on environmental issues, it is worth noting that NAFTA's treatment of labour issues is similar. As mentioned earlier, NAFTA has two supplemental agreements; the second is the North American Agreement on Labour Cooperation. It obliges the NAFTA partners to ensure that their laws provide for "high labour standards consistent with high-quality and productive workplaces and shall continue to strive to improve those standards in that light."[22] However, the Agreement does not contain any commitment to harmonize the standards across borders or even to make the standards compatible.[23] Mexico, for instance, is under no obligation to make its labour standards more stringent in order to match those of the US or Canada. As with NAFTA's environmental provisions, the Agreement on Labour Cooperation is largely symbolic.

While NAFTA is short on environmental protection, it is not entirely silent on trade issues that have environmental implications. Cross-border environmental impacts and obligations were a key topic of discussion during the NAFTA debate, and they continue to be a hot topic today.

THE ENVIRONMENTAL IMPACT OF NAFTA: THE CASE OF THE MEXICAN MAQUILADORAS

Does NAFTA cause environmental degradation? Or does the trade deal actually help the environment by strengthening regulatory cooperation and improving industrial efficiency? The answer is a little of both, and the mixture depends on the industry and the region in question. Environmental activists frequently accuse NAFTA of causing colossal environmental damage in the US-Mexican border region. In reality, however, the region's environmental woes began long before NAFTA was signed.

In 1965, Mexico began providing tax incentives and special arrangements to attract foreign producers to invest in special regions called *maquiladoras* just south of the US border. These incentives were successful in creating an industrial boom in the region. Today, the maquiladora industry provides jobs to more than one million workers and produces 46 per cent of Mexico's total exports.[24] However, the maquiladora boom comes at a considerable cost to the Mexican communities, which NAFTA has done little to alleviate. The Institute for International Economics reports, "The maquiladora program ... was not accompanied by infrastructure for handling wastes and residues. Deplorable environmental conditions are the consequence."[25]

Since NAFTA entered into force in 1994, some progress has been made. During the NAFTA negotiations, the US and Mexican governments developed an integrated environmental plan for the border region. In 1996, the plan was expanded to become the Border XXI program, and by 2000 it had some success to report. By that year, Mexico was providing 93 per cent of its border population with drinking water, 75 per cent with sewage infrastructure, and 81 per cent with waste-water treatment capacity—up from 88 per cent, 69 per cent, and 34 per cent, respectively, just five years earlier.[26] In addition, new tax arrangements between the US and Mexico provide the maquiladora region with $120 million more in government funding, potentially creating a substantial increase in support for infrastructure and environmental services.

However, the overall environmental benefit of NAFTA for the maquiladora region has been small, at best. Environmental pollution and mismanagement persist in the region. According to the Mexican National Ecology Institute, over 20 per cent of the hazardous waste produced in Mexico in 1997 came from maquiladora industries.[27] In 1999, only 34 per cent of waste water was actually treated in Mexican border cities, and excess waste water often flowed into surface and drinking water. Eighteen per cent of Mexican border towns have no safe drinking water, 30 per cent have no sewage treatment, and 43 per cent have inadequate garbage disposal.[28] Observers agree that environmental conditions continue to be deplorable.

There are ways to improve the situation. The NAFTA negotiations set up an institution called the North American Development Bank (NADBank) to provide financing for environmental infrastructure projects at the US-Mexico border. Unfortunately, the NADBank has not been very active. It has a capital base of $3 billion, yet less than 10 per cent of that total was used in the organization's first seven years to finance environmental objectives. The Institute for International Economics suggests that the NADBank "would have to lend or guarantee about $2.6 billion to achieve the $8 billion investment in infrastructure suggested in 1993 as minimally necessary for the recovery of the border region. With the explosive border growth since 1993, the minimal necessary expenditure in 2000 is probably closer to $20 billion."[29] In other words, the NADBank needs to be financing projects at least ten times faster than it currently is, just to achieve the minimum necessary for environmental recovery, as estimated by the US government.[30] US and Mexican policy makers can and should be working to ensure that this rate is achieved.

Since NAFTA was signed, increased attention has been paid to the maquiladora region's environmental problems. However, the "progress is in no way proportional to the depth of the problem."[31] As North America deepens its economic interdependence, the maquiladora region will continue to serve as a litmus test for environmental cooperation between the NAFTA governments.

Clearly, NAFTA's impact on the US-Mexican border is a subject of considerable concern, but there are also environmental concerns among the countries sharing the northern NAFTA border. NAFTA addresses two issues of particular importance to Canadians: water and energy. We turn to those issues now.

NAFTA AND WATER

Canada has an abundance of fresh water—proportionally, more water than any other country on earth. Twenty per cent of the world's fresh water is in Canada, though it is home to only one-half of one per cent of the global population.[32] As humankind's consumption of water grows, we are rapidly approaching the time when fresh water will be a valuable commodity. Water scarcity is already a fact of life in some parts of the United States, and this trend is predicted to continue. Could Canada ever be required by NAFTA to ship fresh water to the US? While the answer remains unclear, the agreement does not appear favourable to Canada.

"Our water won't be safe unless it's exempted from the NAFTA," writes Wendy Holm of the Canadian Environmental Law Association.[33] "What Canada does ... in the water/trade debate will forever define us as a people and as a nation." Maude Barlow adds, "global trade institutions effectively give transnational corporations unprecedented access to the freshwater resources of signatory countries." Holm, Barlow, and many others argue that NAFTA is a lurking threat to Canadian national sovereignty over its lakes and rivers.

Recognizing the potential for this controversy, the Canadian government specifically dealt with water when it passed the NAFTA *Implementation Act* in Parliament. The Act says, "For greater certainty, nothing in this Act or the Agreement ... applies to water."[34] Thus, under Canadian law, NAFTA does not apply to lake or river water. However, this definition is only a position taken by the Canadian government and is not binding on decisions made by NAFTA tribunals. Indeed, the US government has articulated a rather different view of the issue.

In 1993, the US Trade Representative Mickey Kantor wrote that "when water is traded as a good, all provisions of the agreements governing trade in goods apply."[35] This view is echoed by Clayton Yeutter, chief US negotiator for the Canada-US FTA.[36] According to the US, the NAFTA obligations on surface water will start as soon as the first NAFTA trade on bulk water is completed. At the time of this book's publication, no such trade has yet occurred. Newfoundland did express interest in doing so in

2001, but Canadian activists angrily confronted the province for considering it. According to the US government, a trade deal on fresh water would forever after bind Canada to treat water as a NAFTA-eligible good.

So even the governments that signed NAFTA cannot agree on whether fresh water is covered. What does NAFTA actually say? The Agreement covers the trade of economic goods, which are defined as "domestic products as those are understood in the General Agreement on Tariffs and Trade [GATT] or such goods as the Parties may agree."[37] The GATT system includes water, explicitly stating that this includes "ordinary natural water of all kinds (other than seawater)."[38] On this basis, water will be treated as a good under the NAFTA, even when it is in its natural state in lakes or rivers.[39] The American interpretation appears to be correct.

If NAFTA does apply to natural fresh water, the implications are significant. Already, American companies are considering legal action against the Canadian government for restricting access to Canadian lakes and rivers for the purposes of water exports. In 1998, a Californian company, Sun Belt Inc., filed a lawsuit against the Canadian government for $10.5 billion in damages and lost revenue opportunities. If water-trading rights become firmly established under NAFTA, Canada's ability to restrict water consumption will be seriously eroded.

NAFTA AND ENERGY

Every year, Canada exports over 25 million watts of electrical power,[40] over 500 million barrels of oil,[41] and over 100 billion cubic metres of natural gas[42] to the US. At $48 billion, energy is Canada's single most valuable export industry to the US—more valuable than wheat, more valuable than automobiles.[43] Given Canada's huge supply of energy resources and the enormous demand of the US, it should be no surprise that energy became a hot topic in free-trade negotiations.

Under the terms of NAFTA, Canada is obligated to continue trading energy to the US at market rates. Like the 1988 Canada-US Free Trade Agreement (FTA) before it, NAFTA requires Canada and the US to provide *national treatment* to each other with respect to the import and export of energy products between the two countries. This means that neither government can place restrictions on the price or volume of energy that is traded across the border without also placing the same restrictions on the domestic energy market. This agreement was specifically designed to prevent programs like Canada's National Energy Policy of the 1970s, which allowed the federal government to control Canada's energy sales.

Views on the NAFTA energy clause differ dramatically across Canada. Some, particularly those in energy-producing provinces like Alberta, were pleased to see this guarantee. The old National Energy Policy had restricted access to the US market for Canadian oil and gas producers, costing them millions of dollars in lost sales. The industry was understandably delighted by the guarantee that the Canadian government would never again interfere with their access to the US market. In fact, when changes were being considered to the North American energy market in 2002, the Canadian Association of Petroleum Producers said, "Our message is: don't change [NAFTA] too much."[44]

On the other hand, environmentalists were dismayed by NAFTA's energy clause. Not only does NAFTA enshrine the current trade of fossil fuels and other scarce energy resources, it also severely restricts conservation efforts in the future. NAFTA forbids Canada and the US from imposing a higher price for energy exports than the price charged domestically. Because of this, Canadian energy will always be available to Americans at exactly the same price as it is for Canadians. Moreover, any restriction on the energy supply must be done *proportionally*.[45] That is, if Canada restricts its energy exports to the US, the same restriction must also be applied to the domestic energy supply.

The rule might be "proportional," but the effect is quite disproportional. Suppose Canada wants to reduce its energy exports to the US by 10 per cent. The NAFTA rule compels Canada to reduce its own energy supply by 10 per cent. However, Canadian energy exports are only about one-fifth of the US total energy supply—America is also supplied by other countries and its own reserves. A 10 per cent reduction in Canada's exports would reduce the total US energy supply by just 2 to 3 per cent. In other words, if there is ever a need to conserve energy in Canada, NAFTA requires that the majority of the burden will be borne in the Canadian market, not the US market.

It is worth noting that NAFTA's energy clause applies to Canada and the US, but not Mexico. Mexico's oil reserves are deeply intertwined with its national history, and as a result it has a fiercely independent energy policy. In fact, national control of the oil industry is so deeply rooted in the Mexican national identity that its constitution specifically prohibits foreign ownership in the petroleum industry.[46]

Responding to public concern about Canada's energy obligations under NAFTA, the federal government issued a statement on December 3, 1993: "In the event of a shortage or in order to conserve Canada's exhaustible energy resources, the Government will interpret and apply the NAFTA in a way which maximizes energy security for Canadians. The Government interprets the NAFTA as not requiring any Canadian to export a given level or proportion of any energy resource to another NAFTA country."[47] The Canadian government's interpretation is neither well founded nor endorsed by the other NAFTA Parties. As illustrated above, the NAFTA text explicitly requires proportional exports. Moreover, President Clinton wrote that the US government would accept no change to the proportionality commitment contained in NAFTA.[48] Canada's interpretation is unlikely to be found legally sound if the issue ever arises at a NAFTA dispute panel.

The NAFTA does constrain Canada's national sovereignty over its energy policy. However, the issue should be considered within the proper context. Canada is enormously rich in energy resources. As Canadian industry points out, "The world's largest oil reserve is not lying under Saudi Arabian deserts or under the sea, it is clinging to grains of sand in the Canadian boreal forest of Northern Alberta."[49] About 2 trillion barrels of crude oil are spread across the northern reaches of Alberta, much of which is expected to be recoverable. On its own, the Athabascan oil sands could supply current Canadian oil production for the next 350 years.[50] Moreover, recent Canadian discoveries of arctic natural gas, known as gas hydrates, are astoundingly large. The global endowment of gas hydrates is estimated at an astronomical 279,000,000 trillion cubic feet—more than 55,000 times larger than the entire world's proven conventional gas reserves, and 4,650,000 times greater than the Canadian inventory.[51] Whether it is oil and gas, or hydropower and nuclear fuel, Canada is endowed with vast energy supplies.

This is not to say that Canada can or should continue exploiting its fossil fuels forever. Achieving a sustainable supply of energy should be one of Canada's priorities, as no one wants to drain the world of its energy supplies. However, it is misleading to blame NAFTA for an energy policy that is dependent on fossil fuels. NAFTA regulates only the 10 per cent of Canadian oil production that flows to the US; virtually all of the other 90 per cent is being consumed right here in Canada.[52] If Canada wants to extend the life of its oil reserves, it could limit its NAFTA exports tomorrow and concentrate on domestic initiatives. The real barrier to a more sustainable

Canadian energy policy is not NAFTA; it is the lack of financial incentives and political will to change the domestic fossil-fuel economy.

WHAT CAN BE DONE?

Upon closer examination, several of the environmental issues covered in this chapter are revealed to be less significant than they are sometimes portrayed in the media. In the MMT fuel additive case, little scientific evidence existed to support the alleged environmental health risks. Rather than being an indictment of NAFTA's environmental impact, the MMT case instead highlights the bungling attempts of the Canadian government to manage a dispute within the automotive industry.

NAFTA's provisions on energy supply are also less environmentally significant than they are sometimes depicted. Canada has what is likely the largest fossil-fuel reserve in the world, and NAFTA poses relatively little danger of draining that reserve. Nonetheless, Canada can and should pursue a more sustainable energy supply for its future, and work to ensure that its trade agreements do not compromise its ability to do so.

NAFTA's provisions on water do not appear to have any immediate effect, and it is clear that the Canadian government would like to prevent NAFTA from ever applying to ground water in the future. However, there is a significant risk that the first commercial trade of Canadian ground water would set the legal precedent for NAFTA obligations. Accordingly, Canada should avoid any such trade until an explicit NAFTA exemption is made for ground water.

Other aspects of NAFTA are a more significant cause for concern. The NAFTA Commission on Environmental Cooperation, is a weak, ineffective organization. As a result, NAFTA's environmental components are largely symbolic and provide little real ecological protection. The NAFTA parties should work to strengthen the CEC, to ensure that the economic benefits to trade do not come at the cost of environmental integrity.

The NAFTA may not have caused all of the environmental degradation of the Mexican maquiladora region, but it has scarcely contributed to its recovery. The maquiladora region is in desperate need of money for infrastructure and environmental preservation. The NADBank, which nominally exists for the purpose of facilitating such money, needs to increase its rate of lending and finance guarantees dramatically. The people of Mexico deserve nothing less.

Finally, Canada, the US, and Mexico should adopt a well-defined precautionary principle as a working guide for the NAFTA. In situations where a national government is faced with uncertainty, it ought to have the power to safeguard public health. Where there is a credible possibility of harm, especially if scientific data do not yet exist, international trade agreements (including NAFTA and the WTO) should support a nation's sovereign right to create appropriate environmental and health policies. Until this principle is adopted, trade agreements will continue to be viewed as a threat to legitimate efforts toward environmental protection.

NOTES

1 M. Barlow, "Global Rules Could Paralyze Us," *National Post* 31 Aug. 1999: A18. <http://www.nationalpost.com/commentary.asp?f=990831/67261>

2 M. Creek, "Rio Report Card 1998/99," <www.geocities.com/RainForest/Canopy/2727/rio9899.html> Visited 5 Oct. 2002.

3 D. Camp, *Toronto Star*, July 29, 1998. Quoted in D. Schneiderman, "MMT Promises: How the Ethyl Corporation beat the Federal ban," *Parkland Post* 3.1(Winter 1999). <http://www.ualberta.ca/~parkland/post/OldPost/Vol3_No1/Schneiderman-ethyl.html>

4 G. Hufbauer, *et al.*, *NAFTA and the Environment: Seven Years Later* (Washington, DC: Institute for International Economics, 2000), p. 12.

5 Health Canada, "Risk Assessment for the Combustion Products of MMT in Gasoline," 1994.

6 S. Hill and W. Leiss, chapter 4 in *In the Chamber of Risks: Understanding Risk Controversies*, ed. W. Leiss (Montreal: McGill-Queen's University Press, 2001).

7 D. Westwell, "Additive fuels Big Three drive," *Globe and Mail* 29 Oct. 1994: A6. Quoted in Hill and Leiss, chapter 4 in *In the Chamber of Risks*.

8 US *Federal Register*, 17 Aug. 1994 (59 FR 42227). Quoted in Hill and Leiss, chapter 4 in *In the Chamber of Risks*.

9 Quoted in Schneiderman, "MMT Promises."

10 Hufbauer, *et al.*, *NAFTA and the Environment: Seven Years Later*, p. 12.

11 Appleton, *Navigating NAFTA*, p. 192.

12 Appleton, *Navigating NAFTA*, p. 178.

13 Appleton, *Navigating NAFTA*, p. 194.

14 Appleton, *Navigating NAFTA*, p. 196.

15 Hufbauer, *et al.*, *NAFTA and the Environment: Seven Years Later*.

16 Appleton, *Navigating NAFTA*, p. 192.

17 Appleton, *Navigating NAFTA*, p. 193.

18 Appleton, *Navigating NAFTA*, p. 195.

19 Appleton, *Navigating NAFTA*, p. 176.

20 Appleton, *Navigating NAFTA*, pp. 177–78.

21 NAAEC [North American Agreement on Environmental Cooperation] article 45. Quoted in Appleton,*Navigating NAFTA*, p. 198.

22 NAALC [North American Agreement on Labor Cooperation] article 2. Quoted in Appleton,*Navigating NAFTA*, p. 180.

23 Appleton, *Navigating NAFTA*, p. 181.

24 Hufbauer, *et al.*, *NAFTA and the Environment: Seven Years Later*, p. 41.

25 Quoted in Hufbauer, *et al.*, *NAFTA and the Environment: Seven Years Later*, p. 41.

26 Hufbauer, *et al.*, *NAFTA and the Environment: Seven Years Later*, p. 42.

27 Hufbauer, *et al.*, *NAFTA and the Environment: Seven Years Later*, p. 41.

28 According to the US General Accounting Office, 1999. Quoted in Hufbauer, *et al.*, *NAFTA and the Environment: Seven Years Later*, p. 42.

29 Hufbauer, et al., *et al.*, *NAFTA and the Environment: Seven Years Later*, pp. 44–45.

30 The 1992 NAFTA report by the Office of the US Trade Representative estimated $8 billion in infrastructure needs. Quoted in Hufbauer, *et al.*, *NAFTA and the Environment: Seven Years Later*, p. 44.

31 Hufbauer, *et al.*, *NAFTA and the Environment: Seven Years Later*, p. 46.

32 "Freshwater Website: Quickfacts," Environment Canada, <www.ec.gc.ca/water/en/e_quickfacts.htm> Visited 11 Feb. 2004.

33 W. Holm, "The Taking of Canada's Water—the Final Chapter," (Ottawa: CCPA, 2001).

34 *NAFTA Implementation Act* of 1993, Section 7. Note that "water" in this section of the *Act* means natural fresh water from lakes and rivers, and does not include packaged or bottled water. Quoted in Appleton, *Navigating NAFTA*, p. 202.

35 Letter from the US Trade Representative, 28 Oct. 1993. Quoted in Appleton, *Navigating NAFTA*, p. 202.

36 Holm, "The Taking of Canada's Water."

37 NAFTA article 201.

38 Harmonized Commodity Description and Coding System, GATT. Quoted in Appleton, *Navigating NAFTA*, p. 200.

39 Legal coverage of water is strengthened by NAFTA's Chapter 11, which covers investment rights. According to Appleton, "NAFTA's investor rights will apply to all measures that limit water investments." For further analysis, see *Navigating NAFTA*, pp. 201–05.

40 National Energy Board, "Electricity Exports and Imports," Dec. 2003. < http://www.neb-one.gc.ca/Statistics/ElectricityExportsImports/index_e.htm.>

41 National Energy Board, "Total Crude Oil Exports, Annual," 2003. <http://www.neb-one.gc.ca/Statistics/CrudeOil_PetroleumProducts/index_e.htm.>

42 National Energy Board, Natural Gas Table 5, "Exports—By Export Point," Dec. 2003. <http://www.neb-one.gc.ca/Statistics/NaturalGasExports/index_e.htm.>

43 Government of Canada, Ministry of Natural Resources, "Statistics and Facts on Energy" (Ottawa: 2004), <www.nrcan.gc.ca/statistics/energy/default.html> Visited 22 Feb. 2004.

44 G. Park, "Talks continue to establish a 'true' North American energy market," *Petroleum News* 2 June 2002. www.petroleumnews.com/pnarch/020601-04.html Visited 11 Feb. 2004.

45 NAFTA Article 605 (the "proportionality clause") allows energy-supply restrictions under the following conditions : "(a) proportional access of the good must be made available to the other Party on the basis of the average supply over the last 36-month period; (b) a Party may not impose a higher price for exports than the price charged domestically by way of taxes, royalties or minimum price regulation; (c) the restriction does not require the disruption of normal channels of supply of that good." Quoted in Appleton, *Navigating NAFTA*, p. 41.

46 Article 27, paragraph 4, of the Mexican Constitution, 1917.

47 Government of Canada, *Statement of Government Action*. Quoted in Appleton, *Navigating NAFTA*, p. 42.

48 Letter from President Clinton to Representative E. Markey (D-Mass.), 13 Nov 1993. Quoted in Appleton, *Navigating NAFTA*, p. 42.

49 "Canada has world's largest oil reserves," Alexander's Gas and Oil Connections 15 Jan 2002. <www.gasandoil.com/goc/news/ntn20664.htm> Visited 12 Feb. 2004.

50 Assuming 300 billion barrels of recoverable oil. Current crude oil production = 851 million barrels per year. See National Energy Board, Crude Oil Production Table 1, 2003. <http://www.neb-one.gc.ca/Statistics/CrudeOil_PetroleumProducts/index_e.htm.>

51 "Experiment reveals enormous untapped gas supply," Edmonton Journal 11 Dec. 2003: G1.

52 According to figures from the National Energy Board. Canadian crude oil exports to the US = 81 million barrels per year; total Canadian crude oil production = 370,000 m3/day = 851 million barrels per year. See National Energy Board, Crude Oil Production Tables 1 and 3, 2003. <http://www.neb-one.gc.ca/Statistics/CrudeOil_PetroleumProducts/index_e.htm.>

TWELVE

The WTO and the Environment

The previous chapter's look at NAFTA illustrates that international trade can have a mixed impact on environment protection. This chapter will take a second look at trade and the environment, this time focusing on the WTO and the trade/environment relationship more broadly.

In doing so, we will turn to the two most important environmental trade cases: the *Tuna-Dolphin* and *Shrimp-Turtle* disputes. These cases provide insight into the way the World Trade Organization affects a country's ability to pursue environmental laws. Fortunately, the ultimate outcome of these cases was a victory for the environmentalists. Unfortunately, the World Trade Organization has not kept up with the times, and continues to use several outdated principles to guide its decisions about the environmental effects of international trade. There are several steps policy makers could take to safeguard our environment; these will be discussed in this chapter. First, however, we will look at how trade has influenced environmental quality around the world.

THE RACE TO THE BOTTOM

Free trade renders the borders between countries increasingly irrelevant to multinational corporations. While global trade has been rising for hundreds of years, recently it has dramatically changed the face of business in virtually every industry. General Electric, for instance, was once almost exclusively focused on its home American market; now it looks outside of the US for more than 40 per cent of its total sales.[1] As globalization increases the interconnectedness of our world, there is a danger that companies will flock to whichever nation offers the lowest environmental standards. Governments are competing against each other to entice investment and job-creation in their territories, so they are tempted to progressively weaken their environmental laws. Environmentalists call this vicious cycle *the race to the bottom.*

This idea has caught the public's attention. According to the federal government, 58 per cent of Canadians "worry increased international trade is likely to result in countries lowering their environmental standards to be more competitive." Only 20 per cent disagree with that statement.[2] Without question, it is a worrisome possibility. But is it really happening?

The evidence of the race to the bottom is mixed. Academic observers agree that there is a limited number of heavily polluting industries in which the race to the bottom is evident. For companies that work in chemical processing, mining, pulp and paper production, and steel manufacturing, the cost of environmental regulation heavily influences profits. Studies show that these types of companies *are* moving to countries that have weak environmental laws. A World Bank study reports, "Pollution-intensive output as a percentage of total manufacturing has fallen consistently in the OECD [rich countries] and risen steadily in the developing world. Moreover, the periods of rapid increase in net exports of pollution-intensive products from developing countries coincided with periods of rapid increase in the cost of pollution abatement in the OECD economies."[3] In other words, as globalization increases, so does the tendency for poor countries to specialize in heavily polluting industries.

Worse still, some developing countries are so desperate for foreign investment that they are willing to lower their environmental laws or make special exceptions for these foreign companies. The intense pressure to produce economic growth can lead politicians to make a short-sighted sacrifice of environmental sustainability in exchange for up-front cash. This is especially poignant when a dictator is in charge—dictators have a tendency to be more interested in short-term profits than in the health of their citizens or the protection of the environment. To the extent that globalization is enabling dirty companies to move overseas, rich countries bear partial responsibility for exporting their pollution into poor countries.

So far, the worst fears of environmentalists seem confirmed. However, even the author of the report quoted above suggests that the picture is not

188

nearly so bleak. David Wheeler is a World Bank economist and a leading expert on the issue of "race to the bottom." Overall, the evidence he has collected suggests that the race is not happening. He argues that "numerous studies have suggested that pollution control costs are not major determinants of relocation."[4] For instance, Dr. Wheeler studied local air pollution in China, Mexico, Brazil, and the US over the last decade. If countries were truly racing to the bottom, then "after decades of increasing capital mobility and economic liberalization ... pollution should be increasing everywhere. It should be rising in poor countries because they are pollution havens, and in high-income economies because they are relaxing standards to remain cost-competitive." Instead, "the evidence clearly contradicts the [race to the bottom] model's central prediction: The most dangerous form of air pollution has actually declined in major cities of all four countries during the era of globalization."[5] Even more encouragingly, foreign investment has dramatically increased even as air pollution fell. Apparently, environmental protection might actually *attract* foreign investors.

The evidence against the "race to the bottom" hypothesis is substantial. One study looked at the amount of toxic waste produced in Latin America and found that the more closed a country is to free trade, the more likely it is to develop heavily polluting industries.[6] Another scholar studied the impact of Scandinavian pulp-and-paper manufacturers in Southeast Asia. He found that these movements have played a critical role in *improving* environmental outcomes in developing countries for this industry.[7] Still another trade scholar concludes, "'pollution havens' were more likely to exist in protected economies than open ones."[8] Apparently, international trade is actually *helping* the environment. Indeed, economist John Wilson concludes that the world may be characterized by a race to the top, not to the bottom.[9]

Trade can help the environment in two ways. First, countries that are open to trade are far more likely to import advanced technology from rich countries. The advanced technology is usually significantly better for the environment than more archaic manufacturing methods. Second, heavily polluting companies are often also the least efficient companies—their waste comes from a poorly functioning business. Free trade exposes these dirty, inefficient companies to the rigours of international competition, which forces them to either adapt quickly or go out of business. As businesses clean up inefficiencies, they also tend to reduce their waste.

In light of what is known about the race to the bottom, economist Jagdish Bhagwati makes an interesting suggestion. He argues that "since there is little evidence of multinationals ... choosing to exploit lower environmental and labor standards, we should simply extend our key standards ... to our firms abroad, on a *mandatory* basis: do in Rome as Americans do, not as Romans do. It would assuage the fears of the environmentalists and of those seeking dignity and safety for workers abroad, without imposing serious constrains that these firms do not already impose on themselves."[10] One can hope that this sensible proposal is taken seriously by lawmakers.

The interaction between trade and the environment cannot easily be perceived at first glance. On the one hand, trade helps the spread of industrialization, which in turn has a negative impact on the environment. On the other hand, international trade appears to be making overall industrial activity cleaner, not dirtier. In this sense, trade seems to be acting as a mitigating influence on humankind's environmental impact.

This role should not be underestimated. Further industrialization is essential in the effort to reduce global poverty, and that industrialization will have environmental consequences. Managed free trade is a valuable tool in making the process of industrialization less damaging for our natural environment. If we are going to pursue the often-conflicting goals of economic development and environmental sustainability, we are going to need all the tools we can get to make the difficult tradeoffs between these goals more manageable.

As each country looks to address the balance between trade and the environment, its options are limited or expanded by the decisions made at international trade organizations. For Canada, recent landmark decisions by the WTO and NAFTA dispute panels will shape our country's ability to protect the environment. We turn now to look at the history of two pivotal cases in international trade law, so that we can better understand how the WTO can be improved for the future.

THE *TUNA-DOLPHIN* CASE

The "race to the bottom" is doubtful; the evidence in the *MMT-Ethyl* case is even worse. Is it time to stop listening to environmentalists? Absolutely not. Social activists have good reason to be concerned about the World Trade Organization and its ability to impede environmental protection. Internationally, the two most notorious clashes between trade and the environment are WTO disputes, *Tuna-Dolphin* and *Shrimp-Turtle*. Both of them revolve around a country's ability to take *unilateral action*. (In international relations, *unilateral* just refers to a country's ability to do something on its own, without the consent of other countries.)

Easily the most controversial case in the history of international trade law, *Tuna-Dolphin* is the granddaddy of all trade and environment disputes. In 1972, the US Congress passed the Marine Mammal Protection Act (MMPA), which sought to protect dolphins and a wide range of other ocean wildlife.[11] The law established the goal of reducing the number of dolphins killed or maimed to "insignificant levels." At first, the American fishing industry bore the brunt of the regulations, but over time the law came to increasingly affect foreign fishing boats. In 1991, Mexico challenged this law under the panel dispute process under the General Agreement on Tariffs and Trade (GATT).[12]

In the 1970s, the MMPA encouraged American fishermen to find ways of catching tuna without harming dolphins. Fishing techniques improved so much that the number of dolphins killed by American fishermen dropped dramatically. By 1980, the American fishing industry had reduced the number of dolphins killed in the eastern Pacific region by 95 per cent, compared to just eight years before.[13] Unfortunately, improvements in fishing technology were not the only reason for the decline in dolphin deaths. American fishermen were finding it so expensive to comply with the environmental laws that many of them moved their business outside of the country. In the eastern Pacific region where much of the tuna is caught for the American market, the proportion of US-registered fishing vessels declined from more than 90 per cent in the early 1960s to just 32 per cent in 1988.[14] By contrast, the number of Mexican fishing boats in the region tripled from 1976 to 1985. Even though the number of dolphins killed by Americans was declining, the total number of dolphin deaths remained alarmingly high. By 1988, environmentalists convinced the US government to take tougher measures against foreign fishing boats.

Americans eat half of all the tuna consumed in the world. Consequently, access to the American market is crucial for foreign fishing fleets, and the American government wields considerable power over global fishing practices. Many countries, including Canada, Korea, Bermuda, and Nicaragua, simply adopted procedures that would allow their fishing industry to comply with US regulations. Mexico, however, was considerably more reluctant. The tuna industry had become an important source of revenue for the local economy, and Mexico resented the US's moves to impose its regulations on other countries. Rather than enforce the letter of the law, in 1988 the US persuaded Mexico to change its tuna-fishing regulations to help reduce dolphin deaths.

Environmentalists were not satisfied. The tuna industry was still killing tens of thousands of dolphins in the eastern Pacific. In 1990, the California-based Earth Island Institute sued the Department of Commerce, demanding tougher enforcement of the Marine Mammal Protection Act. The lawsuit was successful: a US District Court ordered the Secretary of Commerce to place a ban on tuna imports from Mexico, Venezuela, and the Pacific islands of Vanuatu because their methods of catching tuna violated the MMPA. The decision affected $30-million worth of tuna imports each year.[15]

Mexico challenged the import ban at the GATT council in February 1991. Its challenge was supported by a long list of countries, including Canada, Australia, and Japan. Mexico argued that international trade rules forbid the US from banning its tuna imports on the basis of how the tuna was caught. In the language of the GATT, the US was making a judgment on Mexico's "process and production methods," which is illegal under international trade rules.

The *Tuna-Dolphin* case was the first time that international trade rules would decide the legality of an environmental law that was designed to protect a global resource. Previous trade/environment cases were always about regional issues, but *Tuna-Dolphin* was about saving an entire species of dolphins. No country has jurisdiction over an entire species of life forms;* they are properly considered the common heritage of our entire planet. *Tuna-Dolphin* was a first in this sense—international trade rules now had to deal with the protection of global resources.

---

* At least, no one has jurisdiction over *natural* life forms. Genetically modified organisms, such as the "Harvard Mouse," raise all kinds of questions about the jurisdiction over a species. However, genetically modified (or cloned) creatures are peripheral to the discussion at hand.

The US acknowledged that its import ban conflicted with the normal set of GATT trade rules, but it argued that GATT Article XX allowed the US an exception in this case. Article XX is a list of exceptions for specific policy purposes, and subsections (b) and (g) are designed to allow countries to pursue legitimate environmental policies. The US argued that the MMPA's import restrictions fell under these exceptions, because they served the sole purpose of protecting dolphin lives and that "no alternative measures were reasonably available to the United States to protect dolphin health and lives outside of American jurisdiction."[16] The Mexican government responded that the Article XX exception applied only to the protection of animals within the territory of the nation that wished to protect them. If the US wanted to protect dolphins outside of American waters, that was fine; but the US government would have to negotiate an agreement with other countries. The US could not, Mexico argued, use trade rules unilaterally to punish countries that had different environmental laws.

In part, Mexico's environmental laws (or lack thereof) were undeniably a reflection of their financial stake in the dolphin industry. However, Mexico did have a point: dolphins were not an endangered species. Thanks to changing international practices in tuna fishing, the total number of dolphins being killed in the region in 1991 was only a fraction of the number killed two decades before. Article XX only permits trade restrictions that are "necessary" to protect animal health and life; from the Mexican perspective, the US ban was not "necessary." Thus began a very long (and on-going) argument about what the term "necessary" actually means in trade law.

In the short term, Mexico won the debate. The GATT panel ruled in August 1991 that the American law violated the terms of international trade rules. The ruling stated that trade law does not permit a nation to restrict imports on the basis of another country's "process and production methods." Instead, imported goods can be restricted only on the basis of characteristics of the finished product (in this case, tuna). If the US wanted to protect dolphins, it would have to convince Mexico to sign an environmental treaty. The US law to protect dolphins had to be removed.

Understandably, the public was outraged. Ralph Nader's group, Public Citizen, called the GATT panel decision a "breathtaking attack on the progress made in the last 10 years."[17] Lori Wallach, the organization's attorney, argued, "This case is the smoking gun. We have seen GATT actually declaring that a US environmental law must go. These [trade] agreements must be modified to allow for legitimate consumer and environmental protections."[18] Even the US Congress was irate. Sixty-four senators and nearly a hundred representatives wrote to President Bush (Sr.) to oppose the GATT panel decision. They demanded that the GATT be changed to make it compatible with American environmental laws.[19]

Mexico's victory quickly became meaningless. The uproar around the *Tuna-Dolphin* case was damaging the credibility of free trade in the US, at the very moment that Mexico was desperately trying to conclude the NAFTA negotiations. As a result, in 1992, Mexico suddenly took dramatic steps to protect animal wildlife, particularly dolphins. In addition, Mexico refused to enforce the trade-panel decision against the US. It refused to do so in spite of political pressure from the other 35 members of the GATT council (including Canada), who wanted to see the Americans punished for their unilateral trade ban.

Environmentalists and anti-globalists often miss this important piece of the story. The *Tuna-Dolphin* ruling was *never actually enforced* on the US. Indeed, the American import ban on Mexican tuna was maintained even after US officials admitted that "there is no longer a viable environmental argument" for continuing it. By this time, the Mexican tuna industry in the eastern Pacific was reduced to fifty boats. Total dolphin deaths in 1993 were less than one per cent of what they had been just two decades before.[20]

The Trade/Environment Dilemma

The *Tuna-Dolphin* case strikes at the heart of the trade/environment dilemma. On the one hand, the US should be allowed to pursue a legitimate environmental policy. It was clear from the beginning that America's motive was purely to save the lives of dolphins. The US was not using the Marine Mammal Protection Act as a disguised form of discrimination against foreign producers. In fact, not one American producer favoured the import ban on tuna—they neither requested nor desired government protection from Mexican fishermen. All sides agreed that the US government was acting with good intentions, and that the law was effective in saving dolphin lives. Given this, it is astonishing that the GATT panel essentially decided to trump American's sovereign right to decide its own environmental policy.

On the other hand, most countries felt that the US approach to this issue was arrogant and unilateral. In any country, environmental goals must be balanced with other priorities, such as economic growth or job creation. Everyone agrees that the US is allowed to find the right balance of these trade-offs within its own national boundaries. In the *Tuna-Dolphin* case, however, the US was effectively making a decision about that balance *for other countries*. The US import ban forced other countries to adapt to the American standards or be shut out of the all-important US tuna market.

In Mexico and Venezuela, the principal countries involved in the *Tuna-Dolphin* case, environmental protection comes at the expense of jobs and income for the very poor. For instance, the US tuna ban devastated the Venezuelan fishing industry. Venezuela's tuna fleet shrank by two-thirds after the US imposed the ban.[21] The GATT panel sought to protect Mexico and Venezuela from the harsh effects of American unilateral action. In doing so, it was arguably trying to make the world of international trade fairer for poor countries. Admittedly, the *Tuna-Dolphin* case sat in the middle of this difficult dilemma. Nonetheless, the GATT panel's decision failed to see how this particular dispute sat within a broader context. The panel should have looked to other examples of international law to see if there was a suitable analogy to the *Tuna-Dolphin* case. Not surprisingly, there is.

The issue under consideration in *Tuna-Dolphin* is whether one country has the right to block imports if it has legitimate objections to the way those imports are made. The clearest example of this situation is illustrated by the GATT trade rules on products made by prison labour in a foreign nation. The rules are clear: it is perfectly legal for one country to impose a ban on products made by prison labour. This rule is in place for a simple reason: if one country puts its prisoners in forced labour camps, international trade rules should not require any other country to be a part of it. (Keep in mind that the original GATT treaty was written not long after the horrors of Nazi Germany.)

In much the same way, the GATT panel should have allowed the US to ban certain imports, as long as it was clear that the US was doing so for legitimate (environmental) objectives. If Mexico or Venezuela feels that killing dolphins is essential to their fishing industry, fine, but the US should not be obligated to have any part in it. Mexicans can eat tuna that is dolphin-safe or dolphin-unsafe; that is not part of the American policy. Requiring dolphin-safe tuna for *American* consumers, however, *is* a legitimate part of American policy.

The panel's bureaucratic perspective led it to grossly overestimate the danger that countries would use environmental laws to distort free trade.

According to the panel, "If the United States can dictate conservation measures to Mexico as a condition of Mexico's access to the US market, the GATT will be eviscerated."[22] This is hardly true. The pursuit of legitimate environmental objectives such as in *Tuna-Dolphin* is relatively rare. Governments are notoriously slow to act against environmental dangers, even enormously important ones like global warming. On the few occasions in which a country is acting genuinely to protect global resources, the GATT Council (now the WTO) should support enthusiastically a nation's sovereign right to do so. Instead, the GATT panel stepped well outside of its authority. The panel believed that the US was not properly consulting with other countries, and ruled that if the American government wanted to protect dolphins, it would have to do so through an international treaty.

Environmental treaties are infamously hard to complete; by the time such an agreement was reached, all of the dolphins could be dead. Worse still, without the threat of trade sanctions, the US would lose its best tool to pressure reluctant countries to come to any reasonable deal. As the American government pointed out, "At stake [in the *Tuna-Dolphin* case] is the ability of a nation to take measures to protect global resources."[23] Free trade rules should not prevent the US, or any other nation, from protecting the environment.

Moreover, the GATT panel chose a poor moment to punish the US for acting unilaterally. Admittedly, American unilateralism is annoying to virtually every other country in the world. However, an American trade scholar points out that in this case, "the United States *had* been attempting to seek an international agreement to protect mammals threatened by commercial fishing since the mid-1970s. Indeed, only a week before it requested the GATT panel, Mexico had refused to endorse a new intergovernmental agreement to cut dolphin mortality—a fact which the GATT panel ignored."[24] Not only had the panel overstepped its authority, it had done so without checking its facts.

THE *SHRIMP-TURTLE* CASE

In 1995, the GATT Council was dissolved and replaced with the World Trade Organization. Having learned from the controversy surrounding the *Tuna-Dolphin* case, the WTO was wary of its next confrontation with environmental issues. It did not have long to wait: in 1997, a group of countries challenged a US law that banned their shrimp exports to the US.

As in to the *Tuna-Dolphin* case, the American government had designed an import ban to protect incidental animal deaths due to fishing techniques. In this case, the global shrimp industry was killing a rare and endangered species of sea turtle. In 1987, the US required all American shrimp vessels to use the appropriately named "Turtle Excluder Devices." By 1991, the US law banned the importation of all shrimp that were not certified turtle-safe. Countries could apply for an exception to this ban by showing either that they caught shrimp in geographic areas where there were no sea turtles, or that they adopted the turtle-safe technology. Unfortunately, this technology was expensive, and many developing countries felt the US had no right to impose this extra cost upon their fishing industry. In 1997, Malaysia, Pakistan, Thailand, and India challenged the US law, and the WTO ruled in their favour. Once again, the US appeared to be unable to pursue its environmental objectives because of international trade rules.

Activists were outraged. "The WTO is putting US environmental laws on the chopping block," said Josh Knox of the Sea Turtle Restoration Project. "Not only are sea turtles needlessly dying, but so is the Endangered Species Act and democracy."[25] Alan Oxley, an Australian environmental advocate, declared that the case "set an appalling precedent."[26] "Environmental protection has been consistently trumped by preference for less-restrictive global trade regulation when the two regimes have come into conflict in international courts,"[27] wrote another activist. Anti-globalists continue to point to the *Shrimp-Turtle* case as evidence that international trade cannot be reconciled with environmental objectives.

Nothing could be further from the truth. The WTO did not rule against the US because American policy sought to protect the environment. Instead, it was chastising the US for pushing its policies rigidly onto other countries—just as the WTO should do. The WTO is *supposed* to protect small countries from excessive American power.

The *Shrimp-Turtle* panel ruled that the US law was unjustifiable because it requires "*all other exporting [WTO] Members*, if they wish to exercise their GATT rights, to adopt *essentially the same* policy"[28] as the US. The report stated, "it is not acceptable, in international trade relations, for one WTO Member to use an economic embargo to *require* other Members to adopt essentially the same comprehensive regulatory program ... *without* taking into consideration different conditions which may occur in the territories

of those other Members."[29] In effect, the WTO argued that while it was perfectly acceptable for the US law to protect the environment, it was not acceptable for the US to force its own way of doing that onto every other country.

Unlike the *Tuna-Dolphin* case, the WTO did not insist that the only way
to protect animal wildlife was through environmental treaties. In *Shrimp-
Turtle*, the WTO was prepared to accept that the US was pursuing environmental objectives. The trouble was that the US had not even bothered
to *try* to accommodate the needs of other countries. Since the shrimp
industry is of no small importance to countries like Malaysia and Thailand,
this was understandably viewed as arrogant and unreasonable.

Moreover, the United States had negotiated with some countries (those
in the Caribbean, for instance) but arbitrarily excluded others—including the ones that were now prosecuting the WTO lawsuit. All of the countries with which the US did not negotiate had only four months to
implement the required turtle-safe technology.[30] In the view of the WTO,
"Far greater efforts to transfer that technology successfully were made to
certain exporting countries ... than to other exporting countries, including the appellees."[31] Also, the US did not meet "minimum [GATT] standards for transparency and procedural fairness in the administration of
trade regulations."[32]

Faced with this ruling, the US went back to the drawing board to
make its environmental policy fair to developing countries, particularly
in Southeast Asia. The US participated in (and financially supported)
four separate rounds of negotiations to make its law more flexible, without compromising on the safety of the sea turtles. The US now allows any
country to be excluded from the shrimp import ban, as long as they have
a program to protect sea turtles that is "comparably effective" to the
American version.

The real story, often ignored, is the environmental victory in the WTO's
follow-up case, *Shrimp-Turtle II*. In October 2001, the WTO reversed its
earlier decision and ruled that America's environmental law was now
compliant with international trade agreements. The WTO announced that
its earlier ruling was to prevent the US from applying a "'a single, rigid
and unbending requirement' [on other countries] to adopt *essentially the
same* policies and enforcement practices as those applied to, and enforced
on, domestic shrimp trawlers in the United States."[33] In other words, the
US could not blindly force its policies onto other countries. However, the
US is perfectly entitled to require that environmental regulations of "com-

parable effectiveness" apply to all fishermen that sell in the US, whether they are American or not.

Shrimp-Turtle II was a triumph for the US and its environmental laws. The WTO proved that international trade rules do not necessarily have to be an impediment to environmental objectives. Environmental groups should be applauding this decision. Unfortunately, many of them have become ideologically committed to opposing the WTO. They are unwilling to acknowledge that, in this case at least, the WTO did the right thing.

The reaction of Ralph Nader's group, Public Citizen, is typical of the NGOs. Even after *Shrimp-Turtle II*, it argued that "every public health or environmental law challenged under the WTO has been ruled by trade bureaucrats to constitute an illegal barrier to trade."[34] Other groups continue to complain about the *Tuna-Dolphin* case. On its web site, Friends of the Earth maintains that the *Tuna-Dolphin* case is "a clear indication of how the trade rules will be interpreted in environmental cases."[35] This is despite the fact that *Tuna-Dolphin* was never enforced, and despite the fact that *Shrimp-Turtle II* now replaces that case as the preeminent trade/environment legal precedent.

Given the mistake made in *Tuna-Dolphin*, environmentalists have good reason to be wary of international trade agreements. Unless we scrutinize the WTO and hold it publicly accountable, it cannot be trusted to balance trade agreements against other international priorities, such as environmental protection. Nonetheless, environmentalists need to offer an intelligent critique of the way international organizations work. Without this, their position will only hurt their credibility.

THE WTO AND COUNTRIES' ABILITY TO HELP THE ENVIRONMENT

Admittedly, the reaction among environmentalist groups to *Shrimp-Turtles II* has been poor. The victory for American environmental laws has gone almost completely unnoticed in the popular press, and ignored by activist groups. Nonetheless, based on the total package of the WTO cases on *Tuna-Dolphin* and *Shrimp-Turtle*, environmentalists do have a deeper argument to make. The WTO is taking a very active—and not terribly wise—role in curbing a nation's ability to take unilateral actions to protect the environment.

Apparently aware that this case would have dramatic effects on international environmental policy, the GATT judges wrote that its *Tuna-Dolphin* decision was "not intended to discourage nations from harmonizing their environmental policies or cooperate to solve global environmental problems."[36] Unfortunately, saying so doesn't make it so. Although it was never enforced, *Tuna-Dolphin* represents a powerful example of what international trade law could do. Trade scholars call this the *regulatory chill*—when the mere threat of a WTO lawsuit makes it difficult for countries to pursue environmental protection. For example, "green countries," such as Sweden and Denmark, now face an uphill battle when working to protect the international environment. Countries that are less interested in environmental goals can threaten to challenge any environmental agreement at the WTO dispute panel, which may or may not decide to uphold it. This constant threat means that the WTO is making global cooperation on environmental issues considerably more difficult.

Moreover, the WTO is preventing countries from using one of the most effective tools for environmental protection: trade sanctions. Sanctions are instrumental in persuading reluctant countries to preserve wildlife and protect the environment. However, the WTO makes most trade sanctions illegal, even when they are being applied for legitimate environmental ends. No country has been more effective at using trade sanctions for environmental objectives than the United States. For example, the 1979 Packwood-Magnuson Amendment authorized the US President to "impose an embargo on all fish from any country that fails to live up to the International Whaling Convention [IWC]."[37] The threat of such an embargo persuaded Spain, Peru, Korea, Taiwan and Chile to bring their whaling practices into conformity with the IWC. Moreover, the threat also achieved a partial victory with an egregious violator of the Whaling Convention: Japan. In the early 1980s, the US persuaded Japan to remove its objection to the IWC moratorium on commercial whaling.

The same law that caused the *Shrimp-Turtle* dispute also provides a second example of the value of trade threats. Before the US turned its attention to Southeast Asia, it focused on the small country of Suriname. In May 1991, the US Department of State banned shrimp from Suriname until that country complied with a sea turtle protection program. Suriname did so only a few months later, and the ban was lifted.[38] The same pattern was repeated with French Guyana shortly thereafter. This kind of "constructive bullying" is vital to the process of international diplomacy, especially in the pursuit of legitimate social and environmental goals.

In its often aggressive pursuit of unbridled free trade, the WTO is too eager to obstruct this type of political activity. The WTO has to find a balance to manage trade. Admittedly, no one wants to see countries put up trade barriers without good reason. It has happened: reportedly, Japan once argued that only skis made by Japanese manufacturers were right for the particular characteristics of Japanese snow![39] Even so, it is clear that the WTO is overstepping its authority in cases like *Tuna-Dolphin*.

For too long, free-trade advocates have ideologically opposed the use of trade mechanisms to achieve environmental objectives. This approach fails to recognize that trade policy can and should play an important role in environmental conservation. One trade scholar writes, "Economic theory might suggest that trade restrictions are a blunt means to the policy end of biological conservation or hazardous waste source reduction. But politically, the leverage provided by the trade bans has been a critical element in moving upstream to deal with domestic practices."[40] Economists usually object to government action that regulates free trade, because they feel that trade policy is always a "second-best" solution to a social problem. Other policies could be more economically efficient and direct at solving the problem. What economists are reluctant to acknowledge, however, is that democratic politics is rife with "second-best" solutions.

In fact, real-world policies are almost never the most economically efficient ones; they are invariably a compromise between interested parties. There is no compelling reason why trade policy should be any different. To do so would unjustifiably elevate unbridled free trade above all other competing priorities. Trade policy, like every other kind of policy, should be balanced to meet the needs of our society. This is especially true when trade intersects with our need to protect the global environment. Ecological protection is too important to get lost in the shuffle on some trade bureaucrat's desk.

WHAT CAN BE DONE?

Environmentalists have a saying: "We don't inherit the Earth from our parents; we borrow it from our children." In an age when our world faces so many threats, this message has never been more urgent. The evidence on global climate change is now disturbingly clear in many parts of the Earth, and nowhere more so than Canada's North. Moreover, whole species of plants and animals are disappearing from the globe at an alarming rate. Likewise, tropical rainforests almost seem to be evaporating.

Even as economic standards of living rise, our global environment faces new threats. If we are to meet these challenges, international trade needs to support environmental legislation, not impede it. Specifically, there are five things that the World Trade Organization should do to help countries create proactive environmental policies.

First, the WTO needs to adjust its rules to allow countries to take a balanced approach to trade and the environment. Currently, the WTO requires countries to take the "least trade restrictive" policies available. In other words, the WTO rules forbid a country from enforcing an environmental law that impacts international trade, unless it is the *most* economically efficient one. This standard is simply unrealistic: in democratic countries, politics demands compromises. The WTO must learn to defer to national governments, as only the latter have legitimate jurisdiction over social policy.

Second, the WTO needs to be more responsive to environmental problems that cross international boundaries. As we saw in *Tuna-Dolphin*, international trade tribunals continue to rely on an outdated principle of protecting national "process and production methods." That principle has only limited validity today: the WTO should not apply it when one country's production methods have global environmental effects. This was the case in the *Tuna-Dolphin* dispute. Mexico's fishing practices were destroying a resource over which no single nation has jurisdiction—Pacific dolphins. International trade rules have no business obstructing laws that seek to safeguard our planet's wildlife and natural resources.

Third, the WTO can do more to embrace the system of existing international environmental treaties. Conflicting duties to the WTO, on the one hand, and treaties like CITES (the Convention on the International Trade in Endangered Species) on the other hand, force countries into impossible situations under international law. A simple clause in the WTO's agreement would suffice to remedy this: "Nothing in these rules shall be interpreted as overruling legitimate actions taken in accordance with multilateral environmental agreements." Already, a number of scholars are urging the WTO to adopt rules along these lines.[41]

Fourth, the WTO should explicitly authorize the use of eco-labelling. Well-designed labels can give consumers the environmental information they need to make educated choices in the market place. Unfortunately, trade rules often forbid this kind of labelling. For example, Austria was forced to withdraw legislation that required labels on wood products from tropical rainforests, because some nations argued this was unfair discrimination. Consumers have a right to make informed decisions about the products they buy, but regrettably, the WTO is reluctant to take a firm stance on the issue. Worse still, as we saw in Chapter 8, even the Canadian government is unwilling to advocate for eco-labelling. Both the WTO and Canada need to re-examine their policies on this matter.

Finally, and perhaps most importantly, the WTO ought to allow countries to impose "environmental tariffs" on products that are manufactured in ways that hurt the *global* environment. This is not meant to allow one country to interfere with another's policies on *local* environmental issues. However, environmental tariffs should be allowed if one country has such heavily polluting industrial methods that its environmental effects are contributing to a global problem.

For instance, the Canadian government presently seeks to reduce the greenhouse gases that are causing global climate change. If another country, Nigeria for example, has extremely dirty manufacturing methods for a particular kind of product, Canada should be allowed to impose an environmental tariff upon imports of those products. The environmental tariff would be equivalent to the cost of environmental compliance in Canada for the same product. This would create a level playing field for environmental regulation on the international level. At the same time, it would encourage Nigerian producers to adopt cleaner technology and produce fewer greenhouse gases. This kind of environmental tariff could be instrumental in addressing the serious problem of global climate change.

These five steps could go a long way to helping the WTO improve its image in the environmental community. The WTO needs to re-assess its approach to the challenging intersection of trade and the environment. So far, it has leaned too heavily on its trade expertise. By recognizing the need for a balance between free trade and other social objectives, the WTO could put the international trade system in a much more legitimate and sustainable position.

NOTES

1   Jeff Immelt, CEO and Chairman, General Electric, "A Global Company," Speech to customers, Philadelphia, 27 Feb. 2002.

2   DFAIT, "International Trade."

3   M. Mani and D. Wheeler, "In Search of Pollution Havens? Dirty Industry in the World Economy, 1960–1995," *Journal of Environment and Development* 7(1998): 215–47.

4   D. Wheeler, "Racing to the Bottom? Foreign Investment and Air Pollution in Developing Countries," *Journal of Environment and Development* 10.3(2001): 225–45.

5   D. Wheeler, "Racing to the Bottom?"

6   N. Birdsall and D. Wheeler, "Trade Policy and Industrial Pollution in Latin America: Where are the Pollution Havens?" in P. Low, *International Trade and the Environment*. Quoted in Vogel, *Trading Up*, p. 123.

7   D. Sonnenfeld, "Vikings and Tigers: Finland, Sweden and adoption of environmental technologies in Southeast Asia's pulp and paper industries," *Journal of World-Systems Research* 5.1(Spring 1999): 26–47.

8   Vogel, *Trading Up*, p. 123.

9   Quoted in J. Bhagwati and R. Hudec, *Fair Trade and Harmonization*, vol. 1 (Cambridge, MA: MIT Press, 1996).

10   Bhagwati, *Free Trade Today*, p. 60.

11   Unless otherwise noted, the research in this section was derived from Vogel, *Trading Up*, Chapter 3, "Greening the GATT." The author gratefully acknowledges Dr. Vogel's assistance with this chapter.

12   GATT Council, 1991.

13   Vogel, *Trading Up*, p. 104.

14   Vogel, *Trading Up*, p. 105.

15   Vogel, *Trading Up*, p. 108.

16   R. Houseman and D. Zaelke, "The Collision of the Environment and Trade: The GATT Tuna/Dolphin Decision," *Environmental Law Reporter* (April 1992): 10271. Quoted in Vogel, *Trading Up*, p. 110.

17   Vogel, *Trading Up*, p. 114.

18   Vogel, *Trading Up*, p. 114.

19   Vogel, *Trading Up*, p. 115.

20   Vogel, *Trading Up*, p. 117.

21   Vogel, *Trading Up*, p. 111.

22   GATT panel ruling, quoted in J. Trachtman, "GATT Dispute Settlement Panel," *American Journal of International Law* 86.1(1992): 151. Vogel, *Trading Up*, p. 112.

23   Vogel, *Trading Up*, p. 124.

24 Vogel, *Trading Up*, p. 120.

25 Sea Turtle Restoration Project, "Sea Turtle Banner Unfurled Inside WTO meeting," 3 Dec. 1999. <www.seaturtles.org/press_release2.cfm?pressID=39 >

26 Alan Oxley, "Implications of the Decisions in the WTO Shrimp Turtle Dispute," Feb. 2002. <www.tradestrategies.com.au/pdfs/aoshrimpturtlefinal.doc>

27 D. McKillop, "Trade and Environment: International Dispute Resolution," *Journal of the Pace Center for Environmental Legal Studies* 4.2(2001): 1, 4–5, 13-19, 22.

28 WTO Dispute Panel Ruling, "United States—Import Prohibitions of Certain Shrimp and Shrimp Products" [WTO Shrimp-Turtle], Appellate Body Case 1998–4, Final Report, Paragraph 161. Emphasis in the original.

29 WTO Shrimp-Turtle, paragraph 164. Emphasis in the original.

30 WTO Shrimp-Turtle, paragraph 172.

31 WTO Shrimp-Turtle, paragraph 175.

32 WTO Shrimp-Turtle, paragraph 183.

33 WTO "United States—Import Prohibition of Certain Shrimp and Shrimp Products" [WTO Shrimp-Turtle II], Appellate Body Case 2001-4, Final Report, 22 Oct. 2001, Paragraph 140. Emphasis in the original.

34 Public Citizen, "MAI Shell Game—The World Trade Organization," <www.citizen.org/trade/issues/mai/Investor/articles.cfm?ID=1040> Visited 5 Oct. 2002.

35 Friends of the Earth website, "Citizens' Guide to Tuna-Dolphin Dispute," <http://www.foei.org/trade/activistguide/tunaban.htm> Visited 30 Sept. 2002.

36 Vogel, *Trading Up*, p. 113.

37 Vogel, *Trading Up*, p. 126.

38 Vogel, *Trading Up*, p. 128.

39 National Wildlife Federation, "Turtles, Trade and NWF," *International Wildlife*, Nov. 1999. <www.nwf.org/internationalwildlife/1998/WTO.html>

40 K. Conca, "The WTO and Global Environmental Governance," *Review of International Political Economy* 7.3(2000): 484–94.

41 For example, see M. Weinstein and S. Charnovitz, "The Greening of the WTO," *Foreign Affairs* 80.6(2001): 147–156.

THIRTEEN

CONCLUSION

Globalization is not just a catchy word or a political fad. Rather, it reflects an underlying shift in the character of our world. Air travel shrinks distances, making it possible for a person to travel the entire span of the globe before the sun sets twice. Just as quickly, products and consumer goods cross international borders. Information and money move even faster. Like no other time in history, vast sums of money sweep around the globe at an almost unlimited speed. As recently as 1980, international bank lending was a mere $324 billion (US); just eleven years later, it had leapt 2000 per cent to $7.5 trillion.[1] Stock markets are globalized: cross-border transactions in private equities shot from $120 billion in 1980 to $1.4 trillion in 1990.[2] Today it is even higher.

The international flow of money represents a tidal wave of power: it can bring in new riches to poor and desperate countries, or it can savage the hopes of an otherwise stable nation. In our grandparents' generation, it was still possible for leaders in some countries to isolate themselves from the world. Today, even the most powerful countries cannot afford to stand as islands, unresponsive to global change. The increasing interconnectedness of our globe means that seemingly minor forces, acting on the other side of the planet, can intimately affect our lives.

No wonder globalization is attracting attention, both from proponents and from critics. Benjamin Barber, author of *Jihad vs. McWorld*, argues that free trade is ruining the social fabric of our society. He points to the NAFTA, in particular, as a disruptive element in North America. "NAFTA— McWorld's global strategy in its North American guise—serves American business as well as world markets and is unquestionably a policy geared to the future: but it does not and cannot serve American or global public interests such as full employment, the dignity of work, social safety nets, and pension protection."[3] Barber is joined by a widespread and diverse group of social activists in condemning the current direction of globalization.

On the other side, advocates of unbridled free trade argue that the greatest danger posed by globalization is not that it will continue, but that it might be stopped. After the massive protests against the Seattle meeting of the World Trade Organization in December of 1999, *The Economist* was quick to condemn the anti-globalists. The protestors "claim that [the meeting] marked the high point of globalisation in general and freer trade in particular. On this view, globalisation will now at least be halted, but preferably even be forced into reverse. The battle to prevent this from happening needs now to begin."[4] According to some, the defence of free trade can never be too strong.[5]

The thesis of this book is that both of these positions are too polemical. Benjamin Barber's picture of globalization is far too bleak: the leaders of the international trade system are neither evil nor incompetent. However, this does not excuse the willingness of some free-trade proponents to turn a blind eye to the actual history of international trade and economic development. An unyielding loyalty to free-market ideology ignores important problems that are cropping up in the global economic order.

FROM THE DINNER TABLE TO THE GLOBAL ENVIRONMENT

Globalization, more so than any other political force, affects our lives in a myriad of ways. In Part I, we saw how international trade has led to economic growth in Canada and around the world. Almost magically, the benefits of free trade are additive: one country's gain does not need to be another country's loss. Comparative advantage and a judicious use of economic specialization can boost productivity and bring new wealth to the world. Unfortunately, we also saw how specialization can expose a country to enormous risks and cripple its opportunity to develop into the future. The economics behind international trade does not tell as simple a story as free-trade advocates would like. Many developing countries, such as Argentina and Zambia, have lived through the worst of what unbridled free trade can bring.

Globalization has brought enormous inequality to our world. This inequality means that the social reality of North America and Western Europe is increasingly remote to the daily lives of those in the developing world. Worse still, the *rate* at which global incomes diverge is also increasing. Unless there is a dramatic change in our economic paradigm, the prospects for the poor grow dimmer each year.

Not only are the large, rich economies pulling away from the developing world, but they are also manipulating trade rules to make life difficult for small countries. The American tobacco industry successfully used international trade law to pry open the cigarette market in Thailand. Pharmaceutical corporations fought bitterly against South Africa's program to make AIDS drugs affordable to regular citizens. And the long-standing battle over softwood lumber between Canada and the US demonstrates how large countries can flout the so-called "rule of law" in international trade.

In Part II, we looked at the social dimensions of international trade. We looked at Canada's dual role in the "brain drain," and how the existing trade rules can make brain drain worse. We saw how the economics of cultural products puts Canadian artists at a huge disadvantage, demonstrating the growing necessity for international trade rules that support cultural sovereignty. We observed the tremendous uncertainty surrounding genetically modified food, and how it typifies the need for a precautionary approach at the WTO. The WTO's environmental record, especially on the *Tuna-Dolphin* case, only deepens this need. While it is slowly improving, the WTO still has a long way to go before it could be considered "green."

Throughout, we have looked at the arguments of both the proponents and the critics of globalization. Now, more than ever, it is important for both sides to inform their views with the history of international trade. Anti-globalist activists, however well intentioned, are hurting their own credibility when they advance arguments that are unsupported by the facts. It is time for unions to put down their placards and to recognize that free trade, if managed properly, can bring jobs to Canadians. It is time to recognize that trade does not have to mean a "race to the bottom" in social and environmental standards. It is even time to recognize that international trade could be a boon for us all—including the global poor.

Notwithstanding the great promise of globalization, we must also acknowledge its faults. One often hears free-trade advocates tout the "Asian Tigers" as exemplars of what unbridled free trade can accomplish.[6] Rarely do they acknowledge that the Tigers grew their economies by pursuing government policies that were decidedly anti-free trade. The international elites of the World Bank and the IMF are too quick to push free-market policies, blinded by the belief that what works in large, advanced economies will also work anywhere else in the world. Canada's experience illustrates that standard economic theories are often inappropriate to small economies. The experience in developing economies, especially Argentina and Russia, is even worse.

A NEW FRAMEWORK FOR FREE TRADE

In Chapter 3, UBC economist John Helliwell reminded us that good government is about far more than the usual array of economic indicators. His message was that "a balanced evaluation of policies requires a much wider and richer canvas—one that takes full account of the sources of well-being."[7] In 1987, when the Canada-US Free Trade Agreement was being hotly debated, virtually all of the attention was focused on jobs and economic growth. Today, Canadians' views on free trade are noticeably more sophisticated. It is time we updated our conceptual framework.

I propose that we think of a four-point compass to guide our thinking on trade (see Figure 13.1). By reminding ourselves that we have to consider not just one or two but all four points of the compass, Canada will have a better chance of avoiding the pitfalls of unbridled free trade.

On the vertical axis, we have a balance between Economic Growth and Social Justice. Traditional economic concerns, of course, will still be a critical factor in our thinking on a proposed free trade agreement. Does it grow our economy? Does it provide jobs for Canadians? Does it hurt the poor? Does it help particular regions of our country? These questions will continue to shape our thinking, just as they should.

Our focus on economics, however, should not prevent a broader perspective on the social impact of international trade. If we ratify a new trade agreement, how will it affect our national culture? Does it hurt our environment? Does it encourage a ceaselessly consumer society? Does it promote the dignity of work? Without the answers to these questions, no amount of traditional economics is sufficient to inform our decision.

On the horizontal axis, consider the balance between Canada's global impact, and globalization's impact on Canada. On the one hand, we have seen how trade agreements can create an uneven playing field for small coun-

FIGURE 13a :: A new framework for trade

tries like Canada. Neither excessive corporate power nor overzealous trade bureaucrats should be allowed to weaken our national sovereignty. Democracy means that the power to shape Canadian public life ultimately lies with Canadians. As international economics grows increasingly complex and powerful, we must ensure that trade does not undermine our democratic tradition.

On the other hand, we ought to be concerned about how our participation in the world economy reflects Canadian values. Obviously, we have limited powers as a small country. We cannot think that Canada alone can shape the foundations of international relations. Nevertheless, our position does not excuse us from the obligation to guide international conduct along moral principles. Despite our relatively small role in global affairs, Canada has a history of remarkably effective diplomacy. Canada can and should work to ensure that the rules of international trade echo our national sense of fairness.

Thus, international trade demands attention along four important dimensions. Admittedly, four dimensions is a lot. Perhaps it is too much to hope that Canadians will be able to consider four dimensions of any public issue, even an important one such as trade. Perhaps the public is so simple that they cannot see free trade as a complex issue. I do not share that view. I have considerably more optimism about the Canadian electorate than that. I believe that Canadians can, and will, see free trade from an increasingly sophisticated perspective as our country becomes more immersed in the world economy.

In the mid-1990s, Canadians were instrumental in rejecting the Multilateral Agreement on Investment (MAI). Social activists, led by the Council of Canadians, launched an onslaught of public pressure against the MAI.[8] Public awareness mounted in Canada and quickly spread to activist groups in the United States and Europe. As citizens raised more and more questions about the deal dubbed as "the Charter of Rights and Freedoms for Corporations,"[9] the MAI negotiations crawled to a halt. At least in this instance, Canadians were capable of seeing a complex economic issue in social and democratic terms that defied the expectations of most national politicians. As international trade grows increasingly important to the Canadian economy, there is every reason to expect that public awareness on free trade will rise.

AN AGENDA FOR CHANGE

As discussed in Chapter 5, the anti-globalist movement may now be at an inflection point. Canadians are quite right to have grave concerns about the current direction of globalization and international economic integration. Sometimes, as in the MAI issue, protest and vociferous opposition is the best way—perhaps the only way—to call attention to the need for socially responsible trade policy. Nonetheless, it is not clear that the continued agenda of protest and opposition will suffice in the future.

My own experience, on both sides of the protest barricades, suggests that those who are concerned about the current direction of globalization need a change in tactics. Virtually all Canadians *want* international trade, at least in some form. This suggests that where Canadians have concerns about free trade, they would prefer to see constructive, alternative approaches to our trade policy, rather than the complete reversal of it.

Our collective challenge is to open up new channels for democratic accountability. We should look to new models of policy interaction, like the one taken by *Canada25*. This enthusiastic, innovative group of young

Canadians has consistently engaged policy makers to shape Canada into a more dynamic, attractive place to live and work. As a result, *Canada25* has the ear of policy makers in a way that is virtually unthinkable to most anti-globalist protestors. The key? Consistently take a positive, constructive approach to participative democracy. Those with concerns about globalization could learn a lot from *Canada25*'s example.

In 1900, Canada was a country steeped in the traditions and power of the British Empire. The next hundred years proved to be the most tumultuous century in history, and at every point Canada was immersed in international affairs. Our people saw two world wars, experienced the struggles of economic depression, and enjoyed the prosperity of a post-war baby boom. We joined in the battle against communism and we battled among ourselves for a Canadian constitution. Today, at the dawn of a new century, Canada remains one of the most promising and prosperous places on earth.

As we face the new challenges of the twenty-first century, Canada will continue to be deeply engaged in the international arena. Globalized economic trade will shape the Canadian economy, and we must be prepared to look at the issues from a deeper and more insightful perspective than ever before. Never before has international trade meant so much for our country. Let us choose wisely.

NOTES

1 A. Kouziman and A. Hayne, eds., *Essays in Economic Globalization, Transnational Policies and Vulnerability*, 1999. p. 79.

2 Kouziman, Op cit., p. 79.

3 B. Barber, *Jihad vs. McWorld*, p. 95.

4 "The Real Losers," *The Economist*, London, UK. Dec. 11, 1999: 15.

5 "Champions of trade; Economics focus." *The Economist*, London, UK. Feb. 9, 2002: 80.

6 See, for instance, "The Real Losers."

7 J. Helliwell, *Globalization and Well-Being*, UBC Press (Vancouver: 2002) p. 53.

8 See, for instance, "Council of Canadians Chair Campaigns for Withdrawal from MAI Negotiations," Press Release, Council of Canadians, Jan. 23, 1998.

9 "The New Multilateral Agreement on Investment gives the corporations so much power, Parliament won't matter," <http://www.web.net/coc/maiad.html>. Supported by: Sierra Club of Canada, Canadian Labour Congress, Citizens Concerned About Free Trade, the Canadian Conference of the Arts, and the Council of Canadians.

APPENDIX

SUMMARY OF RECOMMENDATIONS

CHAPTER 2: Free Trade and the Promise of Prosperity

Embrace the Promise of International Trade: Canada should see free trade as a way to develop our economy and stimulate our industries for long-term, sustainable growth.

CHAPTER 3: The Dangers of Market Fundamentalism

Moving Beyond the Numbers: Rather than judging Canada's progress solely by indicators such as GDP, we need to make progress in the underlying fundamentals of our standard of living.

Avoid "Cookie-Cutter" Policy Solutions: Free-market policies are not always the answer.

CHAPTER 4: Learning and the Risks of Specialization

Look to the Future: Consider free trade in light of the balance between the short-term benefits and Canada's long-term development. Let us be wary of a trade agreement that encourages over-specialization.

CHAPTER 5: The Dangers of Protestor Mentality

Change the Tactics: Those concerned about the path of globalization need to find new ways of influencing the policy process. Activists should do more to engage national governments and elected officials, rather than merely the major international organizations. Policy makers can do more to engage in a dialogue about power structures and globalization. Our collective challenge is to open up new channels for democratic accountability.

Stay Constructive: Focus on concerns about globalization that are supported by the facts, and persist in the search for constructive answers. Acting individually, or in groups like *Canada25*, we can influence the policy process by engaging policy makers and generating innovative policy solutions.

CHAPTER 6: Free Trade and the Rise of Inequality

Level the Playing Field for Developing Countries: Canada should push hard to even the playing field in international trade rules, especially in the areas of textiles and agriculture.

Live Up to Our Moral Obligations: Growing inequality due to unbridled free-trade policies can inform policy debates in other areas. When it comes time for other international commitments, such as environmental treaties, the rich countries ought to recall our obligations. Industry in the developed countries is responsible for most of the pollution in our skies, the damage to the ozone layer, and the havoc in the planet's climate. The cost of addressing these problems ought to fall to those who have benefited most from the global order.

CHAPTER 7: Trade Rules, the New Weapons of Corporate Warfare

Apply Copyright Rules with Fairness: Push for greater flexibility in the international agreement on patent rights (TRIPs). The WTO must recognize that any law genuinely aimed at the public good, such as access to affordable pharmaceuticals, should trump the desire for more corporate profits.

Give Legal and Technical Aid at the WTO: Canada and other rich nations ought to provide funding for legal aid at the WTO for developing countries.

SUMMARY OF RECOMMENDATIONS

To date, Canada has donated a paltry $1.3 million for trade-related technical assistance to developing countries. Moreover, money is not enough; developing countries need experienced analysts and technical training to prepare them for the next round of trade negotiations. An international effort to provide reasonable resources for developing countries would give the WTO greater legitimacy and give globalization a brighter future.

Protect National Sovereignty: Canada should continue to be wary of any provisions to extend the rights of foreign investors. Even now, the WTO wants to expand the current agreement on international investment (TRIMs) to make its rules disturbingly similar to the NAFTA's Chapter 11. Canadians should oppose this agreement with the same passion that defeated the MAI. The WTO ought to delay the negotiation of such agreements until everyone is better able to understand the powers it gives to foreign investors to interfere with public policy.

CHAPTER 8: Morality, Genetically Modified Food, and Free Trade

Create Democratic Dialogue on GMOs: Canada should demand that the WTO explicitly recognize the debate over GMOs as an issue of national policy, one that will not be decided behind closed doors by trade bureaucrats. The WTO ought to defer to national policy, including the right to label GMO foods.

Be "Precautious": Explicitly adopt the precautionary principle into GMO rules.

CHAPTER 9: Free Trade and the Brain Drain

Defend our Right to Regulate: Canada must refuse to compromise our right to regulate the labour requirements for foreign investments. All countries, especially developing ones, ought to be able to negotiate with foreign-owned companies to ensure that when they invest, they create high-quality opportunities for local people.

Recruit and Retain Canadian Talent: Consider tax incentives to encourage Canadian émigrés to return home.

CHAPTER 10: Free Trade and the Arts

Level the Playing Field for Artists: Make an exception to free-trade rules for mass-market cultural products. This could be done by extending GATT Article IV (which focuses on the film industry) to cover all cultural goods, including magazines, books, television, radio, and film. The loophole in Article IV (d) should be closed.

Support National Culture: Explicitly allow, under WTO rules, national policies that support local cultural products.

CHAPTER 11: NAFTA and the Environment

Don't Trade Water: Canada should avoid any commercial trade on ground water (i.e., lakes and rivers) until an explicit NAFTA exemption is made for such water.

Strengthen the CEC: The NAFTA parties should work to strengthen the NAFTA's Commission on Environmental Cooperation, to ensure that the economic benefits to trade do not come at the cost of environmental integrity.

Increase NADBank funding: The North American Development Bank nominally exists for the purpose of providing funds for infrastructure and environmental projects. The NADBank needs to dramatically increase its rate of lending and finance guarantees for such projects.

Be "Precautious": Explicitly adopt the precautionary principle into NAFTA (and WTO) rules.

CHAPTER 12: The WTO and the Environment

Allow a Balance in Trade Policy: Abandon the WTO 's "least trade-restrictive" test on national environmental policies. The WTO must allow governments to balance free trade with competing priorities, such as environmental objectives.

Update the Policy for Environmental Externalities: Abandon the WTO's "process and production methods" principle. The WTO should not apply it when a country's production methods have global environmental effects. This was the case in the *Tuna-Dolphin* dispute. Mexico's fishing practices were destroying a resource over which no single nation has jurisdiction.

Place Trade in a Sustainable Context: The WTO must do more to embrace the system of multilateral environmental agreements (MEAs). A simple clause in the WTO's agreement would suffice to remedy this: "Nothing in these rules shall be interpreted as overruling legitimate actions taken in accordance with multilateral environmental agreements."

Label for Consumer Choice: Explicitly authorize the use of eco-labelling under WTO rules. Well-designed labels can give consumers the environmental information they need to make educated choices in the market place. In addition, the Canadian government must reconsider its stance on eco-labelling.

Level the Playing Field for Greens: Modify WTO rules to allow countries impose "environmental tariffs" on products made in ways that hurt the global environment. This is not meant to allow environmental tariffs that restrict one country's *localized* pollution, over which another country has no legitimate jurisdiction. However, environmental tariffs *should* be allowed if one country has such heavily polluting industrial methods that its environmental effects are contributing to a global problem.

CHAPTER 13: Conclusion

Move beyond the paradigm: Consider free trade from a four-point perspective: Economic Growth, Social Justice, Canadian Democracy, and Global Impact. Free trade can be considered a success only when it improves the standard of living, on balance, between all four of these points.

BIBLIOGRAPHY

Aaronson, S. *Taking to the Streets.* Ann Arbor: University of Michigan Press, 2001.

Abbott, F. Professor of Law, University of California, Berkeley. Personal communication. April 2001.

Abbott, F. "The TRIPS-Legality of Measures Taken to Address Public Health Crises: Responding to USTR-State-Industry Positions that Undermine the WTO." Presented at the "Conference in Honour of Robert Hudec." Sept. 2000.

ABC News. "EU calls for UN weapons inspectors to return to Iraq." 21 Sept. 2002. <http://abc.net.au/news/2002/08/item20020831082646_1.htm>

Alexander's Gas and Oil Connections. "Canada has world's largest oil reserves." 15 Jan. 2002. <http://www.gasandoil.com/goc/news/ntn20664.htm>

Ali, A., and S. Saccoccio. "Softwood lumber." CBC News—In Depth Backgrounder. 8 Dec. 2003. <http://www.cbc.ca/news/indepth/background/softwood_lumber.html>

American Consumers for Affordable Homes. "A Brief History of the US-Canada Softwood Lumber Dispute." <http://www.acah.org/history.htm.>

Appleton, B. *Navigating NAFTA.* Toronto: Carswell Publishing, 1994.

Arrighi, G., and J. Drangel. "The stratification of the world-economy: an exploration of the semiperipheral zone." *Review* 10.1(1986): 9–74.

Axworthy, L. *Navigating a New World*. Toronto: Alfred A. Knopf Canada, 2003.

Barber, B. *Jihad vs. McWorld*. New York: Random House, Inc., 1995.

Barlow, M. "Washington to Canada: Fill 'er Up." *Globe and Mail* 26 Sept. 2000. <http://www.commondreams.org/views/092600-101.htm>

Barlow, M. "Global Rules Could Paralyze Us." *National Post* 31 Aug. 1999: A18.

——. *Parcel of Rogues*. Toronto: Key Porter Books, 1991.

Barlow, M., and T. Clarke. "Who owns water?" *The Nation* 275.7 (2 Sept. 2002): 11.

BBC. "Strike raises Hollywood recession fears." 2 May 2001. <news.bbc.co.uk/hi/english/business/newsid_ 1306000/1306723.stm>

BBC News. "US blocks cheap drugs agreement." 21 Dec. 2002. <http://news.bbc.co.uk/2/hi/health/2596751.stm>

Berglas, E. "The Case for Unilateral Tariff Reductions: Foreign Tariffs Rediscovered." *American Economic Review* 73.5(1983): 1141–42.

Bhagwati, J. *Free Trade Today*. Princeton: Princeton University Press, 2002.

——. "Trading for Development: Poor Countries *Caveat Emptor.*" *The Economist*. June 2002. <http://www.columbia.edu/~jb38/paper2001/ Economist%20June%2010%20Revised%20Final.pdf>

——. *The Feuds Over Free Trade*. Singapore: Institute of Southeast Asian Studies, 1997.

——. *Free Trade, 'Fairness' and the New Protectionism*. London: Institute of Economic Affairs, 1995.

Bhagwati, J., and R. Hudec. *Fair Trade and Harmonization* vol. 1. Cambridge, MA: MIT Press, 1996.

Bhagwati, J., and V. Ramaswami. "Domestic Distortions, Tariffs, and the Theory of Optimal Subsidy." *Journal of Political Economy* 71 (1963): 44–50.

Birdsall, N., and D. Wheeler. "Trade Policy and Industrial Pollution in Latin America: Where are the Pollution Havens?" In P. Low. *International Trade and the Environment.* Washington, DC: World Bank, 1992.

Bordt, M. "The Measurement of International Migration to Canada." In *International Mobility of the Highly Skilled.* Paris: OECD, 1999.

Bryan, L., *et al. Race for the World.* Boston: Harvard Business School Press, 1999.

Burgess, J. "Cigarette Sales Overseas Light a Fire under US Tobacco's Tail," *Washington Post National Weekly Edition* 24 Dec. 1990: 21.

Bush, George W. Presidential address. New York. 11 Sept. 2002.

Cable News Network. "AIDS drug case adjourned." 18 April 2001. <http://www.cnn.com/2001/WORLD/africa/04/18/safrica.drugs.02/>

Cameron, M., and B. Tomlin. *The Making of NAFTA.* Ithaca: Cornell University Press, 2000.

Canada. Department of External Affairs. "The Canada-US Free Trade Agreement." Ottawa: 1998.

Canada. Department of Finance. "Fiscal Reference Tables." Ottawa: 2002. <http://www.fin.gc.ca/toce/2002/frt_e.html>

Canada. Department of Foreign Affairs and International Trade. "International Trade—The View of Canadians." 23 May 2002.

Canada. Department of Foreign Affairs and International Trade. "Canada contributes $1.3 million in trade-related assistance to developing countries." 10 March 2002.

Canada. Department of Foreign Affairs and International Trade. <http://www.dfait-maeci.gc.ca/tna-nac/text-e.asp>

Canada. Department of Foreign Affairs and International Trade. "2001 —WTO Consultations: Trade and Environment—Information Paper." <www.dfait-maeci.gc.ca/tna-nac/env-info-e.asp> 25 Sept. 2001.

Canada. Department of Natural Resources. "Statistics and Facts on Energy." Ottawa: 2004. <http://www.nrcan.gc.ca/statistics/energy/default.html>

Canada. Environment Canada. "Freshwater Website: Quick facts." <http://www.ec.gc.ca/water/en/e_quickfacts.htm>

Canada. Health Canada. "Risk Assessment for the Combustion Products of MMT in Gasoline." Ottawa: 1994.

Canada. National Energy Board. "Crude Oil Production Tables." Ottawa: 2003. <http://www.neb-one.gc.ca/Statistics/CrudeOil_PetroleumProducts/index_e.htm>

Canada. National Energy Board. "Natural Gas Tables." Ottawa: 2003. <http://www.neb-one.gc.ca/Statistics/NaturalGasExports/index_e.htm>

Canada. National Energy Board. "Electricity Exports and Imports." Ottawa: 2003. <http://www.neb-one.gc.ca/Statistics/ElectricityExportsImports/index_e.htm>

Canada. Statistics Canada. "Unemployment statistics." Ottawa: 2002.

Canada. Transport Canada, "Transportation and Trade." <http://www.tc.gc.ca/pol/en/anre2000/tc0008be.htm>

Canada's Forest Network. <www.forest.ca>

Canadian Centre for Policy Alternatives. *Paying the Price*. Ottawa: 1991.

Canadian Labour Congress. "Nothing for Workers." *Morning NAFTA*. June 1998. <www.clc-ctc.ca/publications/morningnafta/june98/june98-3.html>

Canadian Labour Congress. "No Success Story." *Morning NAFTA*. June 1998. <www.clc-ctc.ca/publications/morningnafta/june98/june98-1.html>

Canadian Labour Congress. "Canada, Inc." *Morning NAFTA*. March 1998. <www.clc-ctc.ca/publications/morningnafta/mar98/mornaftamar98-2.html>

Canadian Labour Congress. "Jobs still going." *Morning NAFTA*. March 1998. <www.clc-ctc.ca/publications/morningnafta/mar98/mornaftamar98-10.html>

Canadian Labour Congress. "WTO Watch." *Morning NAFTA*. March 1998. <www.clc-ctc.ca/publications/morningnafta/mar98/mornaftamar98-8.html>

Canadian Press. "National poll and cross-country protest demonstrate consumers won't be fooled by GE foods." Press Release. 31 March 2000. <http://www.biotech-info.net/canadian_poll.html>

Canadian Press. "Conflict, unfair trade blamed for global poverty." *Globe and Mail* 25 Nov. 2003. <http://www.globeandmail.com/servlet/story/RTGAM.20031125.whunger1125/BNStory/International/>

Chase, S. "US, lumber industry agree to terms for ending softwood dispute." *Globe and Mail* 6 Dec. 2003. <http://www.globeandmail.com/servlet/story/RTGAM.20031206.wsoftwood1206/BNStory/National/>

Christensen, J. "AIDS in Africa: Dying by the numbers." Cable News Network. <http://www.cnn.com/SPECIALS/2000/aids/stories/overview/>

Chui, T., and M. Devereaux. "Canada's newest workers." *Perspectives*. Ottawa: Statistics Canada, Spring 1995: 17–23.

Clarkson, S. "Disjunctions: Free Trade and the Paradox of Canadian Development." In Drache and Gertler, eds. *The Era of Global Competition*. Montreal and Kingston: McGill-Queen's University Press, 1991.

Cobb, C., *et al.* "If the GDP is Up, Why is America Down?" *The Atlantic* Oct. 1995. <http://www.theatlantic.com/politics/ecbig/gdp.htm>

Cohen, M. "Exports, Unemployment and Regional Inequality: Economic Policy and Trade Theory." In Drache and Gertler, eds. *The Era of Global Competition*. Montreal and Kingston: McGill-Queen's University Press, 1991.

Coleman, W. *Financial Services, Globalization and Domestic Policy Change*. London: Macmillan Press, 1996.

Conca, K. "The WTO and Global Environmental Governance. " *Review of International Political Economy* 7.3 (2000): 484–94.

CorpWatch, "World: Rich and Poor Clash Over Farm Aid."
<http://www.corpwatch.org/news/PND.jsp?articleid=8450>

Council of Canadians. "Council of Canadians Chair Campaigns for
Withdrawal from MAI Negotiations." Press Release. 23 Jan. 1998.
<http://www.web.net/~coc/release20.html>

Creek, M. "Rio Report Card 1998/99." <http://www.geocities.com/
RainForest/Canopy/2727/rio9899.html>

DeVoretz, D.J. "The Brain Drain is Real and It Costs Us." *Policy
Options* Sept. 1999: 18–24.

Dollar, D., and A. Kraay. "Trade, Growth and Poverty." Working
Paper. Washington, DC: World Bank, June 2001.

Drache, D., and M. Gertler, eds. *The New Era of Global Competition.*
Montreal and Kingston: McGill-Queen's University Press, 1991.

Drache, D., and S. Ostry. "From Doha to Kananaskis: The Future of the
World Trading System and the Crisis of Governance." Conference
Proceedings. Toronto: University of Toronto, 1–3 March 2002.

The Economist. "Fast Track to Doha." 3 Aug. 2002: 12.

The Economist. "A Decline without Parallel." 2 March 2002: 26–28.

The Economist. "Champions of Trade." 9 Feb. 2002: 80.

The Economist. "Going Global; Globalisation and Prosperity." 8 Dec.
2001: 87.

The Economist. "Another Blow to Mercosur." 4 May 2001: 32-33.

The Economist. "Economist GM poll—57% of US citizens less likely to
buy GM foods." 15 Jan. 2000.

The Economist. "The Real Losers." 11 Dec. 1999: 15.

The Economist. "White Man's Shame." 25 Sept. 1999: 89.

The Economist. "A survey of Canada: Where the Grass is Greener." 24
July 1999: S7–9.

The Economist. "Clouds over Argentina." 4 July 1998: 29–30.

The Economist. "Argentina's Economy: Nearly Time to Tango." 18 April 1992: 17–19.

The Economist. "Country Profile: Canada." <http://www.economist.com/countries/Canada/profile.cfm?folder=Profile-Economic%20Structure>

Edmonton Journal. "Experiment reveals enormous untapped gas supply." 11 Dec. 2003: G1.

Edwards, S., and D. Lederman. "The Political Economy of Unilateral Trade Liberalization: The case of Chile." Cambridge: National Bureau of Economic Research, 1998.

Eiseman, K. "Food labelling: Free trade, consumer choice, and accountability." In Weiss and Jackson, eds. *Reconciling Environment and Trade.* New York: Transnational Publishers, 2001.

European Commission. "Eurobarometer 55.2: Europeans, science and technology." Dec. 2001. <http://europa.eu.int/comm/research/press/2001/pr0612en-report.pdf>

Farrell, D., *et al.* "The truth about foreign direct investment in emerging markets." *McKinsey Quarterly* 1(2004).

Frank, R. *Luxury Fever.* Princeton: Princeton University Press, 2000.

Frankel, J. "Integrating Transportation and Geography into Trade Analysis." In W. Coyle and N. Ballenger, eds. *Technological Changes in the Transportation Sector: Effects on US Food and Agricultural Trade.* Washington, DC: US Department of Agriculture, 2000.

Frankel, J., and D. Romer. "Trade and Growth: An Empirical Investigation." NBER Working Paper 5476. National Bureau of Economic Research, Inc., 1996.

Friedland, J. "Green Chile: Across Latin America, New Environmentalists Extend Their Reach." *Wall Street Journal* 26 March 1997: A1.

Friedman, T. *The Lexus and The Olive Tree.* Vancouver: Douglas & McIntyre, 1999.

Friends of the Earth. "Citizens' Guide to Tuna-Dolphin Dispute." <http://www.foei.org/trade/activistguide/tunaban.htm>.

Galbraith, J.K. *The Affluent Society.* Boston: Houghton Mifflin Company, 1998.

Gambrill, D. "Court allows patent for Harvard Mouse." *Law Times.* Vancouver: Canada Law Book, 2002. <http://www.canadalawbook.ca/headlines/headline52_arc.html>

GATT Council. *Thai Cigarettes Case.* Geneva: World Trade Organization, Nov. 1990.

Gehlhar, M. "Incorporating Transportation Costs into International Trade Models: Theory and Application." US Department of Agriculture, 2001.

General Agreement on Tariffs and Trade (GATT). 1947.

Ghosh, B., and R. Ghosh. *Economics of Brain Migration.* New Delhi: Deep and Deep Publications, 1982.

Global Exchange. <http://www.globalexchange.org/wbimf/Shultz.html>

Globe and Mail. "Poll shows huge support for GMO labelling." 3 Dec. 2003. <http://www.globeandmail.com/servlet/story/RTGAM. 20031203.wfood1203/BNStory/National/>

Globerman, S., and M. Walker. *Assessing NAFTA: A Trinational Analysis.* Vancouver: The Fraser Institute, 1993.

Grandmont, J., and D. McFadden. "A Technical Note on Classical Gains from Trade." *Journal of International Economics* 2 (1972): 109–125.

Greider, W. "The Right and US Trade Law: Invalidating the 20th Century." *The Nation* 15 Oct. 2001. <http://www.thenation.com/doc.mhtml?i=20011015&s=greider>

Gu, W., and M.S. Ho. "A Comparison of Industrial Productivity Growth in Canada and the United States." Ottawa and Cambridge, MA: Industry Canada and Harvard University, 2001.

Harrison, G., *et al.* "Trade Liberalization, Poverty and Efficient Equity." Working paper. Washington, DC: World Bank, 2001.

Hart, M. *Fifty Years of Canadian Tradecraft: Canada at the GATT, 1947–1997.* Ottawa: Centre for Trade Policy and Law, 1998.

Helliwell, J. *Globalization and Well-Being.* Vancouver: UBC Press, 2002.

——. *Balanced Growth: The Scope for National Policies in a Global Economy*. Kingston: Queen's University, 1999.

——. *Are Nations Growing Together or Falling Apart?* Saskatoon: University of Saskatchewan, 1991.

Holm, W. "The Taking of Canada's Water—the Final Chapter." Ottawa: Canadian Centre for Policy Alternatives, 2001.

Holmes, J. "The Globalization of Production and the Future of Canada's Mature Industries: The Case of the Automotive Industry." In Drache and Gertler, eds. *The Era of Global Competition*. Montreal and Kingston: McGill-Queen's University Press, 1991.

Homer-Dixon, T. *The Ingenuity Gap*. Toronto: Vintage Canada, 2001.

Hoogvelt, A. *Globalisation and the Postcolonial World*. Hong Kong: Macmillian Press, 1997.

Houseman, R., and D. Zaelke. "The Collision of the Environment and Trade: The GATT Tuna/Dolphin Decision." *Environmental Law Reporter*. April 1992.

HRH The Prince of Wales. "Questions about Genetically Modified Organisms." *Daily Mail* 1 June 1999.

Hufbauer, G., *et al. NAFTA and the Environment: Seven Years Later*. Washington, DC: Institute for International Economics, 2000.

Human Rights Watch. *Unfair Advantage*. 2002.

Immelt, J. (CEO and Chairman, General Electric). "A Global Company." Speech to customers, Philadelphia. 27 Feb. 2002.

International Food Information Council. "Americans Remain Positive on Food Biotechnology." Oct. 1999. <http://www.biotech-info.net/IFIC_survey.html>

International Intellectual Property Association. "Pat Schroeder on the State of the US Copyright Industries." 7 May 1998. <http://www.publishers.org/press/iipa.htm>

Irwin, D. *Free Trade Under Fire*. Princeton: Princeton University Press, 2002.

——. *Against the Tide*. Princeton: Princeton University Press, 1996

James, J. "Hundred Million Dollar Program for Public-Private AIDS Research and Outreach in Africa." *AIDS Treatment News* 319. 21 May 1999. <http://www.aids.org/atn/a-319-04.html>

Jeter, J. "The Dumping Ground." *Washington Post* 22 April 2002. <http://www.globalpolicy.org/globaliz/econ/2002/0422ground.htm>

Jones, R., and Kennan, P., eds. *Handbook of International Economics, Vol. 1*. Amsterdam: Elsevier Science Publishers, 1984.

Khor, M. *Rethinking Globalization*. London: Zed Books, 2001.

Kirton, J., and V. MacLaren, eds. *Linking Trade, Environment and Social Cohesion*. Cornwall, UK: Ashgate Publishers, 2002.

Klein, N. *No Logo*. Toronto: Vintage Canada, 2000.

Krugman, P. *The Great Unravelling*. New York: Norton, 2003.

——. *The Return of Depression Economics*. New York: Norton, 1999.

——. "The Myth of Asia's Miracle: A Cautionary Fable." *Foreign Affairs* Nov. 1994.

Kouzmin, A., and A. Hayne. *Essays in Economic Globalization, Transnational Policies and Vulnerability*. Netherlands: IOS Press, 1999.

Kristoff, S. (Assistant US Trade Representative for Asia and the Pacific Region). *Tobacco Control and Marketing: Hearings on US Tobacco Export and Marketing Practices on May 17, 1990 Before the Subcommittee on Health and the Environment of the House Committee on Energy and Commerce*. No. 101–171: 112. Washington, DC: 101st Congress, House of Representatives, 1990.

Laxer, J. *Leap of Faith*. Edmonton: Hurtig Publishers, 1986.

Leiss, W., ed. *In the Chamber of Risks: Understanding Risk Controversies*. Kingston and Montreal: McGill-Queen's University Press, 2001.

Lippert, O. "Poverty, Not Patents, is the Problem in Africa." Paid advertisement (Pfizer). *The Economist* 12 Oct. 2002.

Lipsey, R., D. Schwanen, and R. Wonnacott. *The NAFTA: What's In, What's Out, What's Next*. Toronto: C.D. Howe Institute, 1994.

Losey, J.E., L.S. Raynor, and M.E. Carter. "Transgenic pollen harms Monarch larvae." *Nature* 399(1999): 214.

Lubitz, R. "Export-led Growth in Industrial Economies." *Kyklos* 26.2 (1973): 307–321.

Mackenzie, H. "US seen as cultural imperialist." *Gazette* 16 March 1999. <http://www.globalpolicy.org/globaliz/cultural/cultimp.htm>

Magnusson, P. "Uncle Sam Shouldn't be a Travelling Salesman for Tobacco." *Business Week* 9 Oct. 1989: 61.

Mani, M., and D. Wheeler. "In Search of Pollution Havens? Dirty Industry in the World Economy, 1960–1995." *Journal of Environment and Development* 7.3(1998): 215–247.

Maskus, K.E., and J.S. Wilson, eds. *Quantifying the Impact of Technical Barriers to Trade*. Ann Arbor: University of Michigan Press, 2001.

McCall, C., and S. Clarkson. *Trudeau and Our Times: The Heroic Delusion*. Toronto: McClelland and Stewart Inc., 1994.

McKibbin, W. "Regional and Multiregional Trade Liberalization: The Effects on Trade, Investment and Welfare." Washington, DC: The Brookings Institution, 1997.

McKillop, D. "Trade and Environment: International Dispute Resolution." *Journal of the Pace Center for Environmental Legal Studies,* 4.2(2001): 1, 4–5, 13–19, 22.

McMahon, F. "Anti-globalists have it wrong." *Saint John Telegraph-Journal* and the *New Brunswick Telegraph-Journal* 28 May 2001.

———. "The Debate over Free Trade." *Saint John Telegraph-Journal* and *New Brunswick Telegraph-Journal* 15 Feb. 2001.

McQuaig, L. *The Cult of Impotence*. Toronto: Penguin Books, 1998.

Medd, A. "We're young and we're ready. So listen up." *Globe and Mail* 27 June 2003: A17.

Media Awareness Network. "Canada's Cultural Sovereignty Challenge." 22 Sept. 1999.

THE PROMISE AND PERIL OF INTERNATIONAL TRADE

Mejia, A. "World Physician Migration." In A.B. Zahlan, ed. *The Arab Brain Drain.* Seminar proceedings, 4–8 Feb. 1980. London: Ithaca Press, 1980.

Moore, O. "Super Crops Lead to Super Weeds." *Globe and Mail* 8 Aug. 2002. <http://www.globeandmail.com/servlet/ArticleNews/front/RTGAM/20020808/wmodi0808/Front/homeBN/breakingnews>

Moran, T. *Beyond Sweatshops.* Washington, DC: Brookings Institution Press, 2002.

Murray, B. "GMO-Free Zone." *Supermarket News* 14 May 2001. <www.biotech-info.net/GMO_free.html>

Nader, R., *et al. The Case Against Free Trade.* San Francisco: Earth Island Press, 1993.

National Institutes of Health. "HIV/AIDS Statistics." Washington, DC: Sept. 2002. <http://www.niaid.nih.gov/factsheets/aidsstat.htm>

National Wildlife Federation. "Turtles, Trade and NWF." *International Wildlife* Nov. 1999. <http://www.nwf.org/internationalwildlife/1998/WTO.html>

"The New Multilateral Agreement on Investment gives the corporations so much power, Parliament won't matter." <http://www.web.net/coc/maiad.html>

New York Times. "Medical Association Assails US Policy on Tobacco Exports." 21 June 1990: A5.

North American Free Trade Agreement, Chapter 11. 1994.

Organization for Economic Cooperation and Development. *Economic Outlook 2002.* Statistical Annex Tables. Paris: OECD, 2002.

——. "Agricultural Policies in the OECD Countries: Monitoring and Evaluation 2002." 6 June 2002.

——. "Agricultural Policies in the OECD Countries: A Positive Reform Agenda." 26 Oct. 2002.

——. Development Assistance Committee. "Disbursements and Commitments of Official and Private Flows (Table 1)." *International Development Statistics.* Paris: OECD, 2002.

Orme, W. *Understanding NAFTA*. Austin: University of Texas Press, 1996.

Osberg, L., and A. Sharpe. "Trends in Economic Well-Being in Canada in the 1990s." In K. Banting, *et al.*, eds. *Review of Economic Performance and Social Progress*, vol. 1 (2001).

Oxley, A. "Implications of the Decisions in the WTO Shrimp Turtle Dispute." Feb 2002. <www.tradestrategies.com.au/pdfs/aoshrimpturtlefinal.doc>

——. *The Challenge of Free Trade*. New York: St. Martin's Press, 1990.

Park, G. "Talks continue to establish a 'true' North American energy market." *Petroleum News* 2 June 2002.

Pogge, T. Paper delivered for the Charles T. Travers Conference on International Ethics. Berkeley: University of California, 2001.

Public Citizen. "MAI Shell Game—The World Trade Organization." <http://www.citizen.org/trade/issues/mai/Investor/articles.cfm?ID=1040>

Ricardo, D. *On the Principles of Political Economy and Taxation*. 1817.

Robert, M. *Negotiating NAFTA*. Toronto: University of Toronto Press, 2000.

Rodrik, D. "Comments on 'Trade, Growth and Poverty,' by D. Dollar and A. Kraay." Cambridge, MA: Harvard University, 2001. <http://ksghome.harvard.edu/~.drodrik.academic.ksg/Rodrik%20on%20Dollar-Kraay.PDF>

Rosenberg, T. "The Free-Trade Fix." *New York Times* 18 Aug. 2002.

Ruggie, J. "At home abroad, abroad at home: International Liberalization and Domestic Stability in the New World Economy." San Domenico di Fiesole, Italy: Jean Monnet Chair Papers, 1995.

Rumack, L. "Naomi Klein." *Now* 26 Sept. 2002. <http://www.nowtoronto.com/issues/2002-09-26/cover_story.php>

Rusell, R. *The Choice: A Fable of Free Trade and Protectionism*. Toronto: Prentice-Hall Canada, Inc., 1994.

Salgado, R. "Productivity Growth in Canada and the United States." *Finance and Development* Dec. 1997. <http://www.imf.org/external/pubs/ft/fandd/1997/12/pdf/salgado.pdf>

Salvatore, D., *et al.*, eds. *Small Countries in a Global Economy.* New York: Palgrave, 2001.

Samuelson, P. "The Gains from International Trade Once Again." *Economic Journal* 72 (1962): 820–829.

Saunders, J. "Wheat dispute goes against the grain." *Globe and Mail* 8 Sept. 2003: B1.

Sauvé, P., and D. Schwanen. *Investment Rules for the Global Economy.* Toronto: C.D. Howe Institute, 1996.

Schmeisser, P. "Pushing Cigarettes Overseas." *New York Times Magazine* 10 July 1988: 20.

Schneiderman, D. "MMT Promises: How the Ethyl Corporation beat the Federal ban." *Parkland Post* 3.1(1999). <http://www.ualberta.ca/~parkland/post/OldPost/Vol3_No1/Schneiderman-ethyl.html>

Sea Turtle Restoration Project. "Sea Turtle Banner Unfurled Inside WTO meeting." 3 Dec. 1999. <http://www.seaturtles.org/press_release2.cfm?pressID=39>

Secure The Future. <http://www.securethefuture.com/aidsin/data/aidsin.htm>

Sen, A. "Beyond the Crisis: Development Strategies in Asia." Second Asia and Pacific Lecture. Singapore: 12 July 1999.

Shillington, R. "Canada's 'Brain Drain' a trickle not a flood." *Analyze This* 7 June 2000. <www.straightgoods.com/Analyze/0018.asp>

Smith, A. *The Wealth of Nations.* 1776.

Sonnenfeld, D. "Vikings and Tigers: Finland, Sweden and adoption of environmental technologies in Southeast Asia's pulp and paper industries." *Journal of World-Systems Research* 5.1(1999): 26–47.

Soros, G. *The Crisis of Global Capitalism: Open Society Endangered.* New York: Public Affairs, 1998.

Specter, M. "The Pharmageddon Riddle." *The New Yorker* 10 April 2000: 58–71.

Stiglitz, J. "Democratizing the International Monetary Fund and the World Bank: Governance and Accountability." *Governance* 16.1(2003): 111–139.

——. *Globalization and its Discontents.* New York: Norton, 2002.

——. "From Miracle to Crisis to Recovery: Lessons from Four Decades of East Asian Experience." In J. Stiglitz and S. Yusuf, eds. *Rethinking the East Asian Miracle.* Washington, DC, and New York: World Bank and Oxford University Press, 2001.

Stubbs, R., and G. Underhill, eds. *Political Economy and the Changing Global Order.* Toronto: Oxford University Press, 2000.

Sukhatme, S.P. *The Real Brain Drain.* Bombay: Orient Longman, 1994.

Teeple, G. *Globalization and the Decline of Social Reform.* Toronto: Garamond Press, 1995.

Time. "What do People Want? Polls on Genetically Engineered Food." Jan. 1999. In M. Guru and J. Horne. "Food Labelling." Kerr Center for Sustainable Agriculture. <http://www.kerrcenter.com/publications/FOODLABEL.pdf>

Trachtman, J. "GATT Dispute Settlement Panel." *American Journal of International Law* 86.1(1992).

UNAIDS. "Report on the Global HIV/AIDS Epidemic 2002." Barcelona: United Nations, 2002.

United Nations. "Nigeria: Abacha's son freed, to return over $1 billion." *IRINNews* 24 Sept. 2002. <http://www.africahome.com/annews/categories/culture/EpFkAZuFuVHhjFlege.shtml>

United Nations. *Statistical Yearbook 1994.* New York: 1994.

United Nations. *Charter of the United Nations.* San Francisco: 1945.

United Nations Commission on Trade and Development. *Trade and Development Report 1999.* Geneva: United Nations, 1999.

United Nations Development Programme. *Human Development Report, 1999.* New York: United Nations, 1999.

United Nations International Children's Emergency Fund. *Mortality of Children Under Five—World Estimates and projections 1950–2025.* New York: United Nations, 1988.

United States Trade Representative. "US Response to EU Beef Import Ban." *USTR Fact Sheet*: July 1997.

Van Den Bulcke, D., and A. Verbeke, eds. *Globalization and the Small Open Economy.* Cheltenham, UK: Edward Elgar Publishing, 2001.

Victor, D., and C.F. Runge. "Farming the Genetic Frontier." *Foreign Affairs* 81.3(2002): 107–121.

Vogel, D. *Trading Up.* Cambridge, MA: Harvard University Press, 1995.

Warrian, P. "The Social Costs of Moving to 'Lean Production': A Canadian View of NAFTA." In Kouzmin and Hayne, eds. *Essays in Economic Globalization, Transnational Policies and Vulnerability.* International Institute of Administrative Sciences. IOS Press, 1999.

Watson, W. *Globalization and the Meaning of Canadian Life.* Toronto: University of Toronto Press, 1998.

Weinstein, M., and S. Charnovitz. "The Greening of the WTO." *Foreign Affairs* 80.6 (2001): 147–156.

Weintraub, S. NAFTA: *What comes Next?* Washington, DC: Center for Strategic and International Studies, 1994.

Weiss, E.B. and J. Jackson, eds. *Reconciling Environment and Trade.* New York: Transnational Publishers, 2001.

Westwell, D. "Additive fuels Big Three drive." *Globe and Mail* 29 Oct. 1994: A6. In W. Leiss, ed. *In the Chamber of Risks: Understanding Risk Controversies.* Kingston and Montreal: McGill-Queen's University Press, 2001.

Wheeler, D. "Racing to the Bottom? Foreign Investment and Air Pollution in Developing Countries." *Journal of Environment and Development* 10.3(2001): 225–245.

Williamson, J. "The Washington Consensus." In *The Progress of Policy Reform in Latin America.* Washington, DC: Institute for International Economics, 1990.

——. "What Should the Bank Think about the Washington Consensus." Background Paper to the *World Development Report 2000*. July 1999.

Wiwa, K. *Globe and Mail*. Online column (without title). 18 Oct. 2003.

World Bank. <www.worldbank.org>

World Bank. *World Development Report 2001*. Washington, DC: World Bank, 2001.

World Bank. *World Development Indicators 2001*. Washington, DC: World Bank, 2001.

World Bank. "Meeting the Challenge for Rural Energy and Development." Washington, DC: World Bank, 2001.

World Bank. *The East Asian Miracle: Economic Growth and Public Policy*. New York: Oxford University Press, 1993.

World Health Organization. *The World Health Report 1999*. Geneva: World Health Organization, 1999.

World Trade Organization. <www.wto.org>

World Trade Organization. <http://www.wto.org/english/thewto_e/whatis_e/10ben_e/10b06_e.htm>

World Trade Organization. *Sanitary and Phytosanitary Measures* (SPS), Article 3.

World Trade Organization. "WTO Services and Agriculture negotiations: meetings set for February and March." Press Release. 7 Feb. 2000.

World Trade Organization. Appellate Body. "United States—Import Prohibition of Certain Shrimp and Shrimp Products." (*"Shrimp-Turtles II"*) AB-2001-4, Final Report. Geneva: World Trade Organization, 2001.

World Trade Organization. Appellate Body. "United States—Import Prohibitions of Certain Shrimp and Shrimp Products." (*"Shrimp-Turtles I"*) AB-1998-4, Final Report. Geneva: World Trade Organization, 1998.

World Trade Organization. Appellate Body. "Canada—Certain Measures Concerning Periodicals." AB-1997-2. Geneva: World Trade Organization, 1997

World Trade Organization. Appellate Body. "EC Measures Concerning Meat and Meat Products (Hormones)." AB-1997-4. Geneva: World Trade Organization, 1997.

Young, D. "Iranian Cinema Now." *Variety International Film Guide*. In B. Barber. *Jihad vs. McWorld*. New York: Random House, 1995.

Zimmerman, R., and P. Pesta. "Drug Industry, AIDS Community Is Jolted by Cipla AIDS-Drug Offer." *Wall Street Journal* 8 Feb. 2001. <http://www.aegis.com/news/wsj/2001/WJ010207.html>

INDEX